China's Wired!

Your guide to the Internet in China

by Lawrence Jeffery

with a preface by E. Mervyn Davies

China's Wired!

A Euromoney Publication

Copyright © 2000 Stonecutter Communications Inc. and Standard Chartered Bank.

Exclusive publishing rights held by Euromoney Publications (Jersey) Ltd.

Published by
Asia Law & Practice
Euromoney Publications (Jersey) Ltd.
5/F Printing House
6 Duddell Street
Central
Hong Kong

Telephone: +852 2523 3399
Facsimile: +852 2543 7616
E-mail: enquiries@alphk.com
Internet: www.asialaw.com
　　　　　www.euromoneyplc.com

Editor: J. Roger Decavele
Production Manager: Simon P. Kay
Marketing Manager: Bibi O. Y. Tam
Associate Publisher: James L. Burden
Managing Director: Patrick M. Dransfield

Produced by
Stonecutter Communications Inc.
Copyright Clearance Center
1235 Bay Street, Suite 400
Toronto, Ontario M5R 3K4

Telephone: +1 416 966 9391
　　　　　 +1 416 699 3036
Facsimile: +1 416 699 1165
E-mail: btytus@chinanewsletter.com
Internet: www.flyingarmchair.com (the China's Wired! resource site)

For author interviews or publicity information please contact Stonecutter Communications Inc. at the above address.

Managing Editor: Bob Tytus
Editor: Walter Stewart
Illustrations: A. E. Munn
Design: Kaleidoscope
Art Direction: Stephen Hunter

For sales enquiries and general information on China's Wired! please call the relevant Euromoney Customer Service hotline:

Asia +852 2842 6906/6910
Europe +44 20 7779 8999
North America +1 800 437 9997

ISBN: 962-936-086-1

Printed in Hong Kong

法
ASIA LAW
& PRACTICE
A EUROMONEY COMPANY

Standard Chartered
渣打銀行

China's Wired!

acknowledgements

The author would like to thank Mike DeNoma for identifying the need for this book, Mervyn Davies for giving it shape and breadth, and Lance Browne for authenticity. The author would also like to thank Simon Murray for introducing him to Mike DeNoma, and for his many insights on business in the Far East.

A Euromoney Publication in association with Standard Chartered and Stonecutter Communications Inc.

About the author

Portrait by John Reeves

Lawrence Jeffery's interest in China springs from his family's connections to the Far East. His maternal grandfather, W.J.H. Twilley, was a silk and linen merchant with Mackenzie & Company in Shanghai in the 1920s and 30s. His mother was born in that city. The family lived in the old French Concession at 143 Route Amiral Courbet—the family home is pictured, bottom right, as it appeared in 1930. Above it is the home as the author found it in February 2000, under a new address, 271 Fumin Lu.

Jeffery was born in Vancouver, B.C., and completed his Honours BA in Art History at York University in Toronto. After graduation, he travelled extensively throughout Europe, the Mediterranean and the former U.S.S.R.

Jeffery has written for film, television, radio and theatre, in addition to his books. His non-fiction work includes *Chinese Canadians, Voices from the Community* and *Hong Kong, Portraits of Power*, with photographs by Lord Snowdon—co-authored with Evelyn Huang. He is also a co-founder and the Editor of China Business Monthly www.chinanewsletter.com.

When not researching and travelling, he lives in Toronto.

Table of contents

preface

This book is about the Internet and e-commerce in China. The Internet – unlike any other medium we have known – is a conscious medium. It can interact with the viewer on a personal level. Television and radio can only speak; the Internet asks a question, listens to the answer, and then responds. It interacts.

The growth of the Internet over the last five years has been remarkable. It now affects the lives of an ever-growing number of people and can reach those who until recently had little access to the wealth of information available on the Net.

China is rapidly catching up and getting wired. The younger generation in China has embraced the Internet. They see it as one of their greatest hopes for the future. The Chinese government has recognized the critical role this new technology can play in China's economic development as a way to remain competitive in a global economy. They realize that the Internet could provide the communications network which China lacks at a fraction of the cost of traditional information infrastructures, and that government departments would be able to communicate – hence their efficiency and accountability would increase.

China is in the midst of its second industrial revolution in 50 years. Innovations brought about by the emerging hi-tech companies will forever change the way many industries – including my own, the banking industry – operate in China.

Hong Kong has been a catalyst in this process by providing Web expertise, facilitating access to foreign funding and giving Chinese Internet entrepreneurs some high-profile role-models.

Lawrence Jeffery charts the development of the Internet in China and discusses the practical and positive impact the Internet will have on China's economic development. The author has interviewed many of the key players and takes the reader backstage to reveal what drives the people who are behind some of the big Internet names in China.

This book brings clarity and insight in the fascinating but complex story of the Internet in China. The author unearths a mine of information but doesn't overwhelm. His approach is comprehensive and is sprinkled with anecdotes.

In short, the book enlightens and entertains.

– E. Mervyn Davies,
Group Executive Director,
Standard Chartered PLC

Back to the future

The origins and nature of the Internet boom

"To obtain Gold"

There were over 200,000 people in the streets of Hong Kong on February 22—each and every one hoping to get a piece of Tom.com, Li Ka-Shing's Internet start-up. Most were well-dressed professionals. Many held umbrellas against the light rain. They stood quietly and patiently in orderly queues. Nevertheless, they made sidewalks impassable and brought traffic to a standstill. Police were called. CNN arrived and the story made the front pages of newspapers around the world.

These people, and hundreds of thousands of others, were after a piece of the action—the 'new' economy—the Internet boom. But how many of them truly understood the nature of the social and economic revolution that has brought AOL, Amazon.com, China.com and now Tom.com into their lives? Very few.

Most were betting on the man behind the listing rather than the stock itself. Tom.com is the Internet start-up of Hong Kong's legendary billionaire Li Ka-Shing, or 'superman' as they call him. They may not know what the Internet is, or what digital means, but they recognize the

The domain name for Li Ka-Shing's Internet start-up was purchased in the United States. It was chosen because it was seen to be simple and easy to remember. There is no information available on how much they paid for Tom.com. But the price of some domain names is soaring. In January 2000, Nation Multimedia Group, which publishes Thailand's largest circulation daily business newspaper, paid almost US$7 million for Thailand.com. The company plans to launch a multilingual portal offering airline ticketing, hotel reservations, online shopping and news.

www.tom.com

China's Wired!

Midas touch of K.S. Li. So they buy, and buy in a frenzy.

If K.S. is behind it—it must be right. And if it isn't, he has the resources— and the pride—to make it right. And maybe someday it will be. But on February 22, 2000 Tom.com was little more than a few flickering pages on a Web site barely two months old. They might be hiding their better judgement behind Li Ka-Shing's legend and sense of honour, but they were betting on the Web. One thing was certain on that wet February day; the Internet boom had finally hit the shores of China.

What is the Internet?

The Internet is first and foremost a means of communication. It's a pipe, a highway—a high-speed conduit between separate but connected destinations. Today, those destinations are—by and large—the personal computers on our desks. Tomorrow, they'll include mobile phones, palm pilots and pagers—and many other portable wireless electronic devices whose form and purpose we can't begin to imagine.

 www.pbs.org/internet/

Some people describe the Internet as a by-product of the Cold War. Certainly, it benefited from the billions of dollars the United States Department of Defence poured into scientific research through the 1950s and 60s. Its earliest development grew out of a government agency called the Defense Advanced Research Projects Agency, or DARPA. But it's also a product of a certain way of thinking that values freedom, openness and intellectual exchange. It was an idea whose time had come in a nation with the means and will to deliver it.

The first person to articulate the concept of the Internet was J.C.R. Licklider of MIT. In 1962, he described it as a 'Galactic Network,' an interconnected set of computers anyone could access from any location around the globe.

"OBTAINING GOLD," OR "DOT COM"

Traditionally, the most entrepreneurial – and most successful – Chinese business-people have come from southern China. The Chinese dialect spoken in Guangdong Province (and in Hong Kong) is Cantonese. "dot com" sounds very much like "dut kam", Cantonese for "obtaining gold".

But before his theory could be turned into fact two fundamental technological problems had to be solved. First, they had to figure out how to send data from one computer to the next. Second, they had to find a way to draw the computers into a network so they could 'speak' to each other. The history of the evolution of the Internet is a record of the successive and ever-more effective refinements of these two basic problems.

www.pcg-group.com

In July 1969, Leonard Kleinrock—also of MIT—published the first paper on packet switching. Kleinrock's theoretical solution to data transmission was to package the data in discreet but coded units. These packets would be dropped into the information stream like postcards into a mail box. They might not arrive at the same time, or in the same order, but they would carry enough information to be sorted and reassembled by the receiving computer. Separating the data into discreet packages also made it possible for many messages to travel along the same route simultaneously— much like cars on a multilane superhighway.

Finding a system and a language to connect computers together into a network was equally challenging. But by 1966, Lawrence Roberts, an MIT researcher working at DARPA, outlined a computer networking concept he called ARPAnet. By 1969, both theories had been refined sufficiently to be put into practice and computers at UCLA and at Stanford Research Institute communicated successfully. The first message transmitted over the Internet? Log in.

In the 1970s, a group of MIT graduates connected together a series of university mainframe computers across the country and called it the Information Superhighway. But the most important step in accelerating network research and development was the introduction of the personal

PROFILE

PACIFIC CENTURY CYBERWORKS

Richard Li, Li Ka-Shing's second son, and CEO of Pacific Century CyberWorks, recently paid US$10 million for a 12.5 per cent stake in United States-based DigiScents. DigiScents has developed a 'scent synthesizer' capable of re-creating a few thousand different scents. The scent synthesizer will sell for US$200. The code to activate the synthesizer and enable it to download digitized scents will be delivered over the Internet.

computer (PC) in the late 1970s.

Bob Metcalfe, who had helped build the original ARPA network, developed the 'ethernet network,' a system that could connect hundreds of computers together. When Metcalfe's employer, Xerox PARC, showed little interest in exploiting his discovery, Metcalfe resigned and founded 3com.

3com's ethernet card was an essential ingredient in the success of Sun Microsystem's Work Station, introduced in the early 1980s. The Work Station's power came from networking. A single Work Station was as powerful as the sum of the computers it was attached to. By 1983, 3com's revenues were growing 50-80% per quarter.

FIGURE 1.1

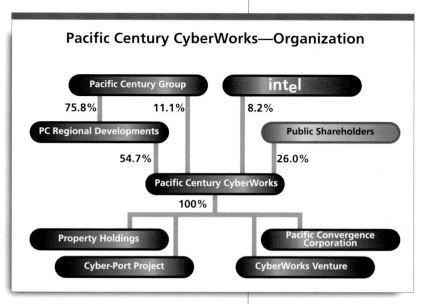

Pacific Century CyberWorks—Organization

The pace of the development of any new technology is directly related to its potential for making money. The closer it gets to the gold, the more resources are committed to making it happen and bringing it to market. The key step in that process is the development of the 'killer application,' the software that turns the hardware into a money machine. E-mail was the Internet's killer application.

E-mail showed everyone the Internet's potential for communicating quickly, cheaply and globally. Suddenly, the computer became a device not only for computation, but also communication. And if you could send words or whole

www.hotmail.com

NOTE

"There are 35,600,000 e-mail accounts in China."

documents over the Internet, why couldn't you also send music, video or even scent?

The principal obstacle to creating a truly open global Internet network was incompatibility between computers and networks. There was no common protocol for access. Communication was only possible if you knew the specific protocols of the computer you were trying to reach.

In 1990, Tim Berners-Lee, an English physicist working at CERN, the European Particle Physics Laboratory in Geneva, developed the World Wide Web, a software protocol that finally allowed many different systems and networks to communicate freely. Essentially, he gave each and every user an address.

But perhaps the most profound aspect of Berners-Lee's innovation was his decision to make it freely available to anyone on the Web. Profit may drive technological innovation, but the very human need to communicate freely and openly is the spiritual foundation upon which the Web has been built.

In 1992, Rick Boucher, a Virginia Congressman, proposed an amendment to the U.S. National Science Foundation Act of 1950. Boucher's amendment freed the development of the Internet from the government and set it loose in the private sector.

And that's when things really started to speed up. By 1994, 25 million people were using the Web. By the end of the decade it was 100 million. In another five years it'll be a billion.

What is e-commerce?

I was asked that question by a 23-year-old university graduate in Beijing. Initially, I was confused. Not because I didn't know the answer but because I knew she did. She was, after all, developing her own e-commerce business.

So why was she asking the question? Because she wanted to know if she and her friends had got it right. They were all working on some kind of e-commerce innovation that they hoped would make them millions. They understood that the basic platform was the Internet, but could it support their ideas?

I said that e-commerce was anything that transpired over the Web that resulted in the exchange of services, products or money. That was dismissed as too broad a definition. They wanted an example—preferably some opportunity that I'd stumbled across during my travels in China.

One of the group had relatives in the United States. I asked him if he ever sent them letters or

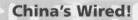

photographs. He did, as did other members of his family. I said he could probably start a nice little business using e-mail and a scanner. Undercut the Post Office's price, and sell them on the speed of delivery.

None of them had seen that as an opportunity, but all of them felt it was viable once they'd heard it. What they were searching for was an understanding of the limits of e-commerce. They only really knew what they'd seen. They had a hard time understanding that I didn't think it had any 'limits,' in fact I said I thought it was going to transform our lives so much that it would make choice and possibility even broader.

It seems a week doesn't go by any more without news of yet another skyrocketing Initial Public Offering (IPO). But the biggest e-commerce story of the last six months was probably the announcement of the merger of the media giant Time Warner with e-commerce portal America On Line (AOL). Early reports claimed Time Warner had bought control of AOL. How could it be any other way? But it was AOL that bought control of Time Warner and they paid for it with stock—and stock valued at a price many feel bears no relationship to reality. It's reality that's changed, not business.

What makes the Internet and e-commerce so hot? And how can such values be assigned to companies like Amazon.com when they have yet to show a profit, or even operate without losses? And why are so many young people in China trying to launch e-commerce start-ups?

This economic revolution is unlike any other in that the price of entry is simply a good idea and the discipline and energy to execute it. And if your idea's good, if it works, it'll be **scalable**[1]—services and revenues can be increased with little cost and less time. The new economy's factories,

1 If a company's business model is highly scalable, it means that the company's capacity to deliver products and/or services can be increased at a rapid rate without straining core management, staff or technology.

railroads and highways are all virtual.

Everything about this e-commerce revolution is changing quickly and dramatically. Internet years are dog years—one equals seven. What makes sense today will be irrelevant tomorrow.

Presently in China, as elsewhere, the poster-children of e-commerce are the most popular and highest-profile Web sites. And by and large, the Web sites that receive the most attention or hits are portals: Sina.com, Yahoo.com, China.com etc.

A portal is a gateway, a point of entry. People are drawn to portals because of the variety and quality of the connections they may offer. Most of a portal's revenue comes from advertising or commissions from goods or services sold through their site by others.

There are fewer and fewer pure portals. Most are beginning to add some kind of product or service—in large part because advertising revenue doesn't cover the cost of operations.

The second most talked about e-commerce is business to consumer, or B2C. One of the most famous B2C sites is Amazon.com, whose founder Jeff Bezos was named Time Magazine's 1999 man of the year. They're not making money yet, but boy are they selling a lot of books!

B2B, or business to business, is on everybody's lips these days. Generally, these sorts of Web sites remain focused on narrow economic verticals: food, plastics, electronics, etc. The Web site tries to create a community of producers and processors, or manufacturers and retailers. A hog farmer might post the number of hogs he has for slaughter and the price he wants for them. Processors can purchase at that price or bid lower. Additionally, processors might post a need they have for a specific amount of a product and how

 Business to Business B2B

 Business to Consumer B2C

 Consumer to Consumer C2C

 Employee to Corporation E2C

www.yahoo.com

NOTE

"Yahoo means:
Yet
Another
Hierarchical
Officious
Oracle."

much they're prepared to pay for it. B2B cuts out the middle man, flattens the playing field and offers both parties more choice.

C2C is a new one—at least on the scale the Internet permits. These sites allow consumers to post goods for sale or exchange. The host charges a commission on all transactions. It's the barter system on a global scale, the Web as a huge garage sale.

E2C or employee to corporation is a relatively new configuration. The host is a job-posting site. Employees post their resumés, and a description of the location and the kind of job they're after. Corporations post job openings. Zhaopin.com in Beijing would be an E2C site. Zhaopin would also qualify as a B2C—and perhaps even a hybrid B2B—site as it's attached to a traditional head-hunting company. They also sell advertising on their site. The point is that all the names given to Web-based businesses are only attempts at categorizing something that is extremely fluid and evolving rapidly.

There are also many hidden e-commerce or Web-based businesses. A company that designs software for inventory control is involved in e-commerce as is a software company that develops Web-based applications to sweep accounts or track multiple debtors. Bar coding is an e-commerce application. It's almost impossible to find any commerce that is not being facilitated by some kind of Web-based software application. It's everywhere—at least in North America. In China, it has only just begun.

Not long after I left Beijing I came across an article in the Asian Wall Street Journal about a Shanghai post office that offered e-mail services. For US$2, the post office would scan a customer's letter and e-mail it anywhere in the world. And if you were online and wanted to send an e-mail to someone who wasn't wired, you could e-mail it to the post office, which would then print it, put it in an envelope, and post it. In China, good ideas and commercial opportunities don't remain unexploited very long.

How is the Internet changing business and society in China?

One of the key dates in China's Internet history will surely be May 7 1999. That was the day that NATO planes bombed China's embassy in Belgrade. The first news source to break the story inside China was Sina.com. It was both a brave gamble and a commercial stroke of genius. Beijing could have closed down the site; as it was, it made Sina.com China's most popular Web site.

Recently, Beijing has been trying to find a way to exercise more control over the content of Web sites. Some of this is as a result of concern over pornography, some as a result of perceived threats to national security. But some must also be coming from the collision of old and new media. China's traditional news sources, Xinhua News, China Daily, Shanghai Daily, CCTV etc., are slow-moving, bureaucratic organizations employing thousands. Not only were they scooped by the upstart, they had their weaknesses held up for all to see.

Now that the Internet boom is really heating up, the traditional media are suffering a second indignity, losing many of their best and brightest writers and editors to e-commerce start-ups. How it will end is impossible to say.

Recently however, Sina.com has begun showing slightly more sensitivity to the old guard. In January, a mentally ill farmer blew himself up in Tiananmen Square. Sina.com had the story within an hour but waited for Beijing TV to post the story before releasing it themselves. They're either being more respectful, or they're concerned about getting approval from the China Securities Regulatory Commission

FIGURE 1.2

$$$ **Cost of Domain Names in millions**

= US$1million

Business.com

Altavista.com

Wine.com

Wallstreet.com

beijinghouses.com

AOL-China.com

Yahoo-China.com

(CSRC) to list on the National Association of Securities Dealers Automated Quotations (Nasdaq).

In January of this year the China Internet Network Information Center (CNNIC) released its semi-annual report on the development of the Internet in China. The CNNIC only began carrying out these surveys in 1997. The surveys are compiled in conjunction with China's four major Internet networks. The report claims that approximately 8,900,000 people used the Internet in 1999, a four-fold increase over 1998. The report also notes that there are some 35,600,000 e-mail accounts in China. I would have thought that the number of e-mail accounts would be closer to the number of users.

A few years ago, a friend of mine was selling software to universities and government ministries in China. He told me that the number of users was ten or twenty times the number posted. In his travels he'd often been asked if he knew of a software program that would protect the privacy of the multiple users of one e-mail account. Many offices had only one computer and one e-mail account. Ten or twenty people had to share not only the machine but the same e-mail address.

It's almost impossible to know the true extent of Internet use in China. It's certainly higher than the estimates. One thing is certain, the younger generation, particularly single-child families in urban areas, are almost universally online.

China's Internet army comes from single-child families

There are approximately 70 million single-child families in China—the result of the single-child policy introduced in the late 70s to help control population growth. Today, the first wave of these children is entering adulthood and the workforce. This is China's Internet army. It's the first computer generation to come of age, and the generation

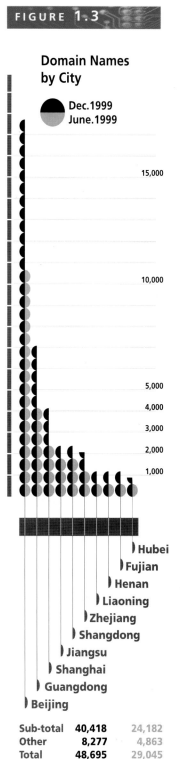

FIGURE 1.3

Domain Names by City

● Dec.1999
● June.1999

15,000

10,000

5,000
4,000
3,000
2,000
1,000

) Hubei
) Fujian
) Henan
) Liaoning
) Zhejiang
) Shangdong
) Jiangsu
) Shanghai
) Guangdong
) Beijing

	Dec.1999	June.1999
Sub-total	40,418	24,182
Other	8,277	4,863
Total	48,695	29,045

that will be at the vanguard of China's Internet and e-commerce development.

www.cnnic.net

Almost all of the young people I talked to in China had computers at home and used the Internet. By and large their parents had bought them the computer. And if they didn't have a computer at home they used one at work and surfed the Net at a local cybercafé. My enquiries confirmed the CNNIC survey that claims that most surf the Net for information. (The CNNIC survey claims that 57.97% surf the Net primarily for gathering information.) This can be general news, entertainment or education.

Message time arrives in China

One hotel employee in Beijing told me his parents had recently bought him a new computer that cost RMB16,000—a huge sum of money in China where the average monthly wage in urban areas hovers around RMB700. He told me he spent at least two hours on the Internet every day. He'd wake up at 4 a.m. when the connection was faster and the rates cheaper. I asked him why his parents had bought him such an expensive computer. Most of his peers had computers that cost RMB2,000-3,000. He said it's because it's 'message time.' It took me a few seconds to interpret 'message time' as meaning the Information Age. But the more I thought about it the more I preferred his description. A message is sent, it moves, it's dynamic and connects people and communities—just like the Internet.

The older generation is equally intrigued by technology, but for different reasons. An administrator in Beijing told me his father was indifferent to the Internet until his brother-in-law made a 50 per cent profit in one year trading stocks online. His father is a cook in a Beijing hotel and his brother-in-law is a labourer. Internet use and access in China is not necessarily related to income level.

The Internet is even having a profound effect on foreign business in China. A number of the large consulting companies have been forced to close offices or scale back operations due to staff defections. For once it's not the competition that's hurting them but the lure of share options and IPOs.

Many of China's brightest students travel overseas to complete their studies. More often than not they stay. Some stay for the lifestyle, some because they perceive few opportunities for their new skills back home. The Internet has changed that decades-old dynamic. For the first time in a very long while, China has a link to a field where overseas students are particularly skilled. In fact, they have a huge advantage, as many have watched the Internet boom develop first-hand.

What does the Internet mean for China's economic development?

A few of China's hot start-ups were created by Chinese who have never studied overseas. The majority, however are headed by Chinese with degrees from Harvard or Stanford or some similarly illustrious Ivy League school. They have the best of both worlds and a huge advantage in China's Internet boom.

In February I bought a Kodak disposable camera in a large camera store on the Nanjing Road in downtown Shanghai. It was the middle of Spring Festival and the place was packed.

The camera I wanted, or thought I wanted, was in a glass case behind a counter watched over by two uniformed women. I pointed to the camera I was interested in. One of the women reached under the counter for the keys to the cabinet, opened the cabinet and handed me the camera. I looked at it for a few seconds, nodded my head in approval and reached into my pocket for some cash. The woman quickly took the camera out of my hands and placed it back under lock and key in the glass cabinet. She then reached under the counter and pulled out a thick receipt book.

After filling out countless lines and boxes she tore out three copies – leaving a master receipt behind. She stamped all four copies with her **chop**[1] and then handed me two copies and pointed for me to line up at a desk across the room.

I handed my money and the two copies to a woman at that counter. She stamped both copies with her chop and

Nanjing Road, Shanghai

1 *A chop is a stone engraved with a person's name. It's usually about three inches long and one half inch square. The owner stamps the chop on an ink pad before stamping the document receipt.*

returned one copy with my change. I then returned to the first counter and handed the remaining copy to the first woman. She took out the original receipt and stamped it. She opened the cabinet and handed me the camera along with the original receipt.

What will e-commerce and the Internet do for China's economic development. Are you kidding?

There are many supermarkets and shops in China that have such things as bar code readers and electronic cash registers. But there are many more like this one with antiquated, inefficient, time-consuming cash and accounting systems.

One of the greatest impediments to China's economic modernization has always been the lack of sufficient traditional infrastructure: roads, highways, railways, airports and telephone lines. Though China has protected its telecommunications industry from foreign domination, it has encouraged foreign companies such as Motorola, Nokia and Ericsson to sell billions of dollars worth of mobile phones. These foreign companies have also made huge investments in China. Motorola has over twenty branch offices, two wholly-owned companies, ten co-operative projects, six joint ventures, fourteen research and development centers and over 10,000 employees. Presently, China's mobile phone network can accommodate 250-300 million users and has approximately 35 million mobile phone subscribers. Today, China is the world's third-largest mobile phone market after the United States and Japan.

There's no question that China would not be where it is today if it had been obliged to lay the millions of miles of telephone cable a growing economy needs. The mobile phone—new technology—allowed China to leapfrog over a potentially crippling infrastructure problem.

Bricks and mortar becomes bricks and clicks

In the past, most industries—and nations—relied on their own internal systems of organizational procedures, structural procedures, business procedures, controls and communication. It was an insular world with insular systems. The Internet is taking over more and more of what were internal processes. It is laying down an extremely rich, open and ubiquitous network infrastructure that is replacing more and more of our organizational or purely functional procedures. The Internet becomes the accounting department, the marketing strategy, the sales staff—even the delivery truck.

The more dependent traditional businesses become on the Internet, the more they are transformed. This creates tensions in more highly developed nations where markets are often dominated by large, well-established conglomerates. Do we go digital, or wait and see? It's increasingly apparent that they have no choice. Bricks and mortar must become bricks and clicks if any business hopes to survive.

The theory of business is the law of survival.

The Internet has a greater opportunity to create a business infrastructure—and way of thinking—in China because it's not competing against well-established business conglomerates, networks and notions. The only business philosophy that exists is the law of survival.

One of the most significant implications of China's membership in the World Trade Organization (WTO) is the lifting of the restrictions China had imposed on foreign ownership in such sectors as retail, wholesale and distribution. these include restrictions on leasing, freight forwarding, warehousing and packaging—sectors that will benefit tremendously from e-commerce and the Internet.

Restrictions on foreign investment in Internet Service Providers and Internet Content Providers have been raised to 49%. Eventually, foreign investment will be allowed to rise to 50 per cent.

The proliferation of the mobile phone solved some of China's basic communication problems. It also allowed the government to devote precious resources to other sectors. The Internet is cheaper, faster and will penetrate many more sectors in a more profound way. It will revolutionize China's primitive distribution systems, wholesale markets, retail and service sectors. Broadband wireless technology, and new mobile phone technology, will only accelerate the modernization process.

Things are never quite what they seem—or what other people tell you they are. One of the research projects for this book was to try and find as many publications as I could in China about the Internet and e-commerce. I wanted to know what was being written and how broad the

TOP TEN WEB SITES IN CHINA:

1. Sina.com
2. 163.com
3. Sohu.com
4. 163.net
5. Yahoo.com
6. 263.net
7. Yahoo.com.cn
8. China.com
9. 21cn.com
10. East.net.cn

coverage was. Well, it's everywhere and covers all the subjects everyone anywhere wants to know. But I wondered if there wasn't one magazine, journal or newspaper that was better than all the rest. The best information, with the most insightful writing and the broadest perspective.

I asked a young journalist in Beijing if the publication she wrote for was the best. It came out of Beijing—China's Internet capital—had many articles on a broad range of subjects and was jammed with advertising. She thought for a minute and then shook her head. I asked which publication—in her opinion—was the best. She said she couldn't speak for other publications but she was pretty sure hers wasn't the best. I pressed her for an explanation. Where was it weak—writing, research? She was quiet for a moment and then explained that the circulation department was disorganized and weak. What does the circulation department have to do with the quality of a newspaper?

FIGURE 1.4

Internet user growth in China

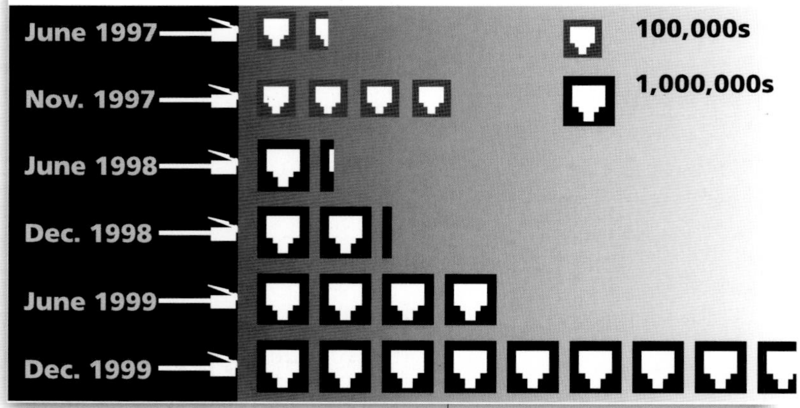

		100,000s
June 1997		1,000,000s
Nov. 1997		
June 1998		
Dec. 1998		
June 1999		
Dec. 1999		

I'm telling this anecdote to highlight the very divergent perspectives we brought to the same issue. I wanted to know which one had the best writing—the best content, the best read, the best bang for your buck. She didn't see the newspaper as a separate product but as part of a single inseparable organism. In her eyes—in China—the newspaper was always a sum of its parts.

A few days later, I asked this same woman if she'd read the

Different strokes

book that had been written by a former Microsoft executive in Beijing. It had received a lot of press in the West. We were told the book was a bestseller and had sold several hundred thousand copies—in large part because it was an attack against Microsoft and its management. She'd read it but said its success had nothing to do with an attack against Microsoft. Why would that be interesting? She said people bought it because it was written by a Chinese woman who had risen up the ranks. She was a success. People wanted to know how she did it.

One of the greatest moral tests life puts us through is to learn to accept differences in others. If it's different it's not necessarily right or wrong, it's just different.

The 1960s were a time of great social upheaval in the United States. Many were looking to Eastern cultures to help restore some spiritual values to their lives. A social prophet of the time claimed a new culture was emerging. He said that Western culture has always developed toward the west—into the wind and against nature's forces—carving highways through the countryside and drilling railroads through mountaintops. Eastern culture searches for harmony with nature —flowing eastward with the wind, and down rivers to the sea. He claimed that the two cultures had finally come together on the western coast of North America.

California was a pretty crazy place in the 1960s. There was Timothy Leary, Haight Ashbury, The Grateful Dead and Jerry Brown. Ronald Reagan was governor. There was also UCLA and Stanford and the birth of the Internet.

This book is about the Internet and e-commerce in China. Much of it discusses the practical and positive impact the Internet will have on China's economic development. But

 www.deadradio.com

the Internet—unlike any other medium we have known—is a conscious medium. It can interact with the viewer on a personal level. Television and radio can only speak; the Internet asks a question, listens to the answer, and then responds. It interacts. The Internet can serve millions at once but speak to every one of them as individuals in a voice that reflects the viewer's needs. At least that's what it's capable of. If it can bring that to China, it will realize the prophet's notion of a seamless integration of East and West.

go to...

For additional information and updates to charts and graphs, visit: **www.flyingarmchair.com** *the* China s Wired! *resource site.*

China
The Last Battleground
of Commerce

China's economic development: 1978-2000

I met Richard Boucher, Hong Kong's former U.S. Consul General, at a Hong Kong Government dinner in the spring of 1998—20 years after China's market reforms had begun and a few months before President Bill Clinton's trip to China.

www.info.gov.hk

Richard Boucher's career in China had begun in Guangdong province in the late 1970s. He was there when the reforms were first put in place. He told me that no one was quite sure what to make of Deng's ideas. The end of the **Cultural Revolution**[1] in 1976, the death of Mao, the rise and fall of the **Gang of Four**[2] and the tensions surrounding Mao's succession had left people anxious and apprehensive. Would the market reforms last, or would the political winds shift yet again and swing the pendulum back violently in the opposite direction?

Everyone was overly cautious—especially about displaying open enthusiasm, or criticism. Nevertheless, the reforms were working and more and more consumer goods were entering the market. Boucher said someone would pedal by on a bicycle with the front basket overflowing with socks, T-shirts or underclothes. They'd stop if someone showed interest in the product. Soon, a crowd would have gathered, thrusting money in the cyclist's face and grabbing for the socks. It didn't matter if they were different colours or sizes as long as there were two of them. As soon as the basket was

[1] *The Cultural Revolution was an attempt to create a new China by wiping out all traces of the past. To get rid of old ideas and replace them with new.*

[2] *Gang of Four —Jiang Qing, 3rd wife of Mao and leader of the Gang of Four was tried in 1980 and received a life sentence. Jiang Qing died in prison.*

empty the guy would hop back on his bike and disappear.

But it wasn't the consumer feeding frenzy that convinced Boucher that the reforms were here to stay—to him that seemed a perfectly normal reaction to the circumstances. After all, they had gone for so long with so little.

The moral of a woman's pink sweater

At the time everybody still wore traditional Mao suits. They were generally ill- fitting and only came in two colours: dark grey and navy blue. Boucher said that one day he saw the edge of a pink sweater peeking above the collar of a dark grey Mao jacket worn by a young woman in her twenties. That's when he knew the reforms were here to stay.

Deng Xiaoping was one of the great survivors of 20th century politics. He was also largely responsible for the policies that have led to China's economic rebirth.

www.smprc.gov.cn

Deng suffered two near-fatal falls from grace during his long political career. During the Cultural Revolution (1966-1976) he was denounced, demoted and sent to the countryside. Though in his sixties at the time, he was too capable, too experienced and too well connected to be counted out for good. Deng was soon brought back to Beijing and in January 1976, he was made vice chairman of the party and a member of the Standing Committee of the Politburo. Later that month, the National Congress made Deng First Vice Premier, third in line behind Chou Enlai and Mao. In 1976, the Gang of Four briefly assumed power and dismissed Deng yet again. But in October of 1976, a month after Mao's death, the Gang of Four was arrested and the real fight for succession began. It took Deng another two years before he could consolidate his power enough to assume the role of paramount leader.

Once in power, Deng introduced his 'open door' policy. He argued for more foreign investment and greater trade with the West. He was particularly interested in high technology, and

PROFILE

JIANG ZEMIN

General Secretary, Central Committee of the Communist Party of China (CCCPC), and State President of the National People's Congress (NPC)

Jiang Zemin studied electrical engineering at a Chinese university before being sent to Moscow in 1955 to study heavy industry. He has climbed the ranks as a politician, not a warrior.

In 1985, Jiang was made Mayor of Shanghai. The political fallout of Tiananmen brought him to Beijing in 1989. And in 1993 he was elected President of the People's Republic of China and chairman of the Central Military Commission.

Jiang is married, with two grown sons, a granddaughter and a grandson. His children live and work in Shanghai, but join Jiang and his wife for winter and summer vacations. Jiang likes to swim, read, play musical instruments, and occasionally dances a waltz or foxtrot with his wife.

www.gov.cn

what it could do for China's modernization. He understood that China was only going to be able to feed its people and take its place on the world stage if it had a strong and modern economy. It was a huge gamble, as it reversed China's traditional indifference to—or suspicion of— exchange with the West.

Deng also introduced two key reforms that continue to shape China's economic development: the one-child policy, and market reforms. The one-child policy was an attempt to control China's population growth and was focused primarily on those in urban centres. But the most profound effect of this policy is the generation of children it has created that is now coming of age and entering the work force. These children, today numbering approximately 70 million, have grown up bearing the expectations and attention of two parents and four grandparents. On average, fully 50 per cent of their parents' income is spent on the child's well-being— schooling, toys, clothes and computers. It's a generation that has known only peace and increasing prosperity. It's also a generation with extremely high consumer expectations.

The one-child policy has been effective in slowing China's population growth, if not bringing it to a standstill. There are, however, problems. As the culture prefers male children to continue the family line, there are now more men than women for them to marry. Nevertheless, the policy remains in effect.

Deng's market reforms began in the countryside. Under the old system, farmers were obliged to fulfill government quotas. They were told what to plant and how much they were expected to produce. The old quotas remained more or less in effect but farmers were allowed to plant other crops as well. If the government didn't want or need the other crops, they could sell them for whatever the market would bear.

FIGURE 2.1

Population growth in China

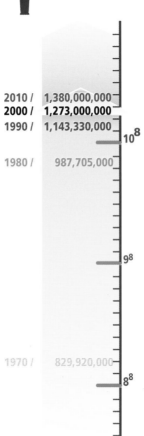

2010 /	1,380,000,000
2000 /	1,273,000,000
1990 /	1,143,330,000
	10^8
1980 /	987,705,000
	9^8
1970 /	829,920,000
	8^8

Deng turned the 'command' economy on its head. Traditionally, Beijing decided everything from the top down. Beijing decided the pillar industries and the resources the pillar industries required. By initiating economic reforms in farmers' fields, Deng allowed the new market system to grow up through the old system at its own pace.

Local markets soon appeared where farmers sold their excess produce. New produce began to appear in response to market demand. Distribution routes began to make their way to urban centres. Slowly, new produce, and the reforms that had made it possible, began to work their way up the **system**.[1]

1 *Shanghai Agricultural Web Site was launched in March 2000. It offers information on agricultural products, e-commerce market deals, weather forecasting and farming technologies, as well as wholesale and retail prices of agricultural products. It had over 5,000 hits in its test week.*

Birth of the Chinese consumer

The forces that have shaped China's economic rebirth emerged in a breathtakingly short period of time. China has truly pulled itself—sometimes kicking and screaming—into the 21st century. It's often extremely difficult for people to adapt to such fundamental changes to their way of life. As a result, China's consumers have characteristics unlike any other consumer population in the world.

In the early days, when Boucher first saw a pink sweater, people remained highly skeptical that the reforms would actually last. And because there had been so little available in the way of consumer goods for so long, anything that appeared was quickly snapped up and hoarded.

Consumers had grown accustomed to 'one size fits all' and 'any colour you want as long as it's black.' Most early consumer goods were highly practical items. Produce, clothes and household utensils. But supplies were limited and shipments erratic. If a shop received a shipment of frying pans, it wasn't unusual for one customer to buy five. After all, you never knew when another shipment might come along.

Many visitors to China returned with stories of ever more remarkable examples of this kind of frantic spending, a kind of 'shop til you drop' mentality. There was a women's clothing shop in Shanghai that became quite famous for its sales technique. In the morning, each salesgirl would be assigned a rack of dresses to sell. They were all the same colour but came in three sizes: small, medium and large. The salesgirl would slip into one of the dresses and then wheel the rack out onto the sidewalk and start selling. As soon as her rack was empty, she'd wheel it to the back of the shop, take another, slip into a new dress and start all over again.

www.china.org.cn

This kind of consumer spending lasted until the mid 1980s when it became clear to most that the reforms, and consumer goods, were here to stay. This was also the point where the variety and quantity of consumer goods available began to surpass immediate demand. The Chinese consumer began to be more selective and began to develop more sophisticated buying criteria.

Soon, sales began to be driven by such issues as quality and reputation. Japanese cameras and electronics sold because they were perceived to be the best quality. Chanel perfume, French Cognac and Rolex watches became the goods of choice for the new rich.

The look was right, the spelling was wrong

There were many weird and wonderful manifestations of this status hungry and 'label crazy' period in China. You'd often see men wearing suits with labels stitched on their sleeves so everyone would know the garments were from Armani or Hugo Boss. Men would wear their ties outside their sweaters so you could see that the neck-joy was Hermes and silk. You also started to see 'Addidocs,' 'Nile' and 'Rebot' running shoes. Pirates got the look right but the spelling wrong. The most amusing story I heard from this period was of the shirt factory in Guangdong Province that made a killing selling business shirts with the left sleeve two inches shorter than the right sleeve—perfect for keeping your new Rolex in the open, for everyone to see.

In 1992, Deng Xiaoping toured Guangdong Province and called for an acceleration of the reforms and an even greater opening up to the West. Foreign and domestic goods flooded the market. And Chinese consumers began to add more subtle and esoteric criteria to their buying habits. They wanted quality, but were not prepared to pay for a name alone. In the early days, Japanese electronics had dominated the market; by the mid 90s, Chinese brands held the top four places in a list of the top ten best-selling television brands in China.

Today, China's consumers are by and large a very sophisticated bunch. They're beyond shopping solely for necessities, or hoarding for shortages. They prefer locally manufactured goods if and only if they're cheaper than the imports and just as reliable.

www.zj.cninfo.net

The shelves in the supermarkets in China's largest cities are laden with brand-name goods found anywhere in the world. Department stores and shopping malls sell everything from duvets to expensive silk suits by Ermenegildo Zegna.

Manufacturers often send the newest models of electronic goods to North American and European markets first, releasing the product in other parts of the world six to nine months later. This has never worked in China. In fact, Chinese consumers will often only buy the most current electronic goods or camera equipment if it's released in China first. They're extremely sophisticated consumers and are well aware of what's available in other markets. They want it before anyone else and they want it now.

www.giftme.com

In spite of a growing similarity to consumers anywhere else in the world, the Chinese **consumer**[1] retains a certain uniqueness. Though food, shelter and consumer goods appear abundant, there remains a certain hunger. Sometimes it seems they're too hungry and consume for the sake of consumption.

They eat a kilo at a time

A number of years ago a friend of mine started a food services business in Shanghai. His company supplied two meals a day to employees at Fortune 500 companies. Sanitary concerns and cost made it impractical for the companies to set up their own kitchens. To his, and his investor's, surprise, he found that local Chinese were eating an average of one kilogram of food at a sitting—75 per cent of recommended daily caloric intake. He had a number of theories as to why they ate so much. First, it was perceived as a benefit and they were going to get as much of it as they could. Second, it was very good food, so why not?

Apparently, some companies had tried other methods with

FIGURE 2.2	
CONSUMER PRICE INDEX — CHINA	
2000	0.1%
1999	1.4%
1998	-0.8%
1997	2.8%
1996	8.3%

[1] *GiftMe.com is an Internet-based personal shopping service, which offers personalized services and a wide variety of goods. They are opening their latest called GiftMe.com in Shenzhen, China.*

little success. One company had offered meal tickets but at the end of the month those who'd missed a day's work often presented two or three tickets and asked to be served the meals they'd missed there and then. Companies that offered cash instead of food had to change their policy because their employees pocketed the money and went hungry. I joked that buffet-style restaurants would find it a difficult environment to operate in. He told me there was one buffet in Shanghai, but you could only go up once and you were penalized if you left anything on your plate. Customers would pile the food on their plates, make a crown of carrot sticks, and pile it higher still.

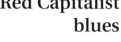
www.china-embassy.org

I don't think this has to do with memories of privation. Nor do the 57.97% of Internet users who go online in search of information do so because there is a general dearth of information. It's something more profound. It's as if the mechanism that was set in motion in 1978 unleashed a pent-up hunger for everything, a psychology suggesting that no amount is ever going to be enough.

About a year ago, I asked a young and very ambitious entrepreneur in Shanghai how much money he needed to be satisfied. He shrugged his shoulders. What if someone gave you a cheque for $10 million, would that be enough? He shook his head. I asked him what he would do with the ten million. He said he'd buy more companies and make more money.

Red Capitalist blues

There is a wonderful private club in Beijing called the Red Capitalists' Club. The restaurant and bar fill

TEN GOLDEN RULES:

1. Go to China with an open mind.

2. Take the long view.

3. It's going to take longer than you think - be patient.

4. Build relationships. Cultivate contacts with everyone.

5. Keep your sense of humour.

6. Never say no! Be prepared for your counterpart to be ambiguous.

7. Learn about the culture & language.

8. Letters of intent are merely the beginning of negotiations.

9. Select your joint venture partners carefully. Remember to give face.

10. Be prepared for the intense competition and rapid change in this marketplace.

the rooms of a beautifully restored traditional courtyard dwelling hundreds of years old. The name comes from a group of Deng's colleagues who were assigned the task of building some of China's greatest conglomerates. In the menu there is a picture recreating the scene.

Deng assigns one the task of building Everbright, a company to handle China's import and export trade. To another, Rong Yiren, Deng assigns the task of building a company called China International Trust and Investment Company (CITIC), to handle China's international trade and investment. Beside the image are Deng's words to his colleagues. He advises them to enter into contracts only if they are fair, and arrangements only if they are just. Wise words, and judging from the success of Everbright and CITIC, words taken to heart. They also made the families of both founders extremely wealthy— hence the term 'Red Capitalists.'

Among the cleverest of Deng's innovations were the Special Economic Zones, or SEZs, he allowed to spring up throughout the country. Essentially, they were insulated commercial accelerators—isolated zones where commerce and commercial exchange could thrive without 'polluting' the rest of the country—at least not until the rest of the country was ready. Parts of Pudong in Shanghai, and Shenzhen north of Hong Kong are two of the better-known and more successful of these zones.

www.focus.com.cn

The Shanghai stock exchange was reopened in 1986. When the Shenzhen stock market opened in July 1991, more than a million and a half Chinese lined up to play the market. By 1994, the combined total trading volume of the A shares on both markets reached US$95 billion. Both markets trade both A and B class of shares. The A shares can only be purchased or sold by local Chinese; B shares can be traded internationally by Chinese in Shenzhen and Shanghai.

PROFILE

ZHU RONGJI

Zhu Rongji's appointment as Premier in March 1999 coincided with China's Third Wave of economic development and opening to the West.

He is unusual among China's leaders in that he has no independent power base within the Communist party or the People's Liberation Army. Zhu is largely responsible for bringing China's inflation down from 25% in 1994, to less than 3% today.

Zhu seems a straight-shooting, no-nonsense sort of man. He is also rare among China's leadership in that he has earned the praise of the United States.

Deng's trip to the South in 1992 was essential to overcome the dark clouds of Tian'anmen and keep the economy growing. The problem was that it probably worked too well. In the two years that followed his trip, over 100,000 foreign companies entered into joint ventures with Chinese companies. In 1993, foreign investment in China surpassed US$20 billion. In 1994, the amount of foreign investment almost doubled.

Tourism grew at a phenomenal rate, bringing badly-needed foreign currency. In 1980, 5.7 million foreign tourists entered China. By 1995, this number rose to 46.4 million.

Telecommunications traffic volume was growing at 50 per cent annually. By the end of 1994, there were more than 600,000 pagers in Beijing and 117 paging stations. Nokia, the Finnish mobile phone manufacturer, entered the China market in 1994. By 1996, Nokia had pushed past Panasonic to dominate the market. Sales were increasing an average 20% per month.

The widespread installation of residential telephone lines only began in 1992. In the early days, installation cost a prohibitive RMB5,000. (Today, the price of installation has fallen to RMB300.)

www.net.cn

Sales for PCs were also growing at a phenomenal 50 per cent annually. Legend and Great Wall Corporation are the two largest domestic PC manufacturers. But they face stiff competition from international giants like IBM, Compaq, HP and Acer. IBM in particular had tremendous early success. In 1993, IBM sold 5,000 units, in 1994 sales soared to 45,145 units and by 1995 reached a phenomenal 87,131 units. All the groundwork and hardware necessary for China's coming Internet boom.

But it couldn't last forever. By 1993, inflation reached 25 per cent. Unemployment and slowing foreign investment began to affect economic growth. A relaxation of residence requirements had created a floating population of largely rural unemployed. Tens of millions were drawn to the cities in search of better-paying jobs, or jobs of any kind. The closing of inefficient State Owned Enterprises increased unemployment and social instability. The notion of a job for life disappeared forever. The disparities between rich and poor and urban and rural life grew. China's interior, to the West, fell far behind the rich coastal regions. It seemed for a while that the whole thing might fall apart.

And Deng's health was failing. Every month new rumours popped up about his health and well-being. Some said he was well but confused, some said he was in a coma, others claimed that he had died. No one knew how the succession might turn out. Or who it would be. Li Peng, Jiang Zemin or Zhu Rongji? And would the new guard sweep away the old man's reforms?

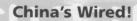

www.chinatradeworld.com

One of Deng's last moves was to put Zhu Rongji at the head of the Central Bank with orders to bring inflation under control. Deng believed Zhu was about the only one of the top leadership who knew anything about economics. Nevertheless, it was a dangerous move. If Zhu failed it would certainly mean the end of his career.

Last hurdles

By 1995, China's economy seemed the least of anyone's concerns. Deng was now into his 90s. His health was failing and no clear successor had emerged. Li Peng, Jiang Zemin and Zhu Rongji were always considered among the top candidates. But none of them was making the kind of political moves or public statements that would suggest he'd won the top spot.

What would happen when the old man died? Would the hard-liners step back in and stomp out Deng's carefully nurtured reforms? Would the military make a move?[1] The PLA has over one million soldiers—the largest standing army in the world—what could stop them? Or would a new generation emerge, a new kind of leader, a technocrat unburdened by memories of the Long March and Cold War politics?

And there were new challenges on the horizon, the hand-over of Hong Kong in 1997, and Macau in 1999. Would they be peaceful transitions or chaos?

Stanley Ho, the Macau casino king, was extremely confident that the hand-over would go well. He told me that it was the dream of every emperor and every leader China has ever had to see the country united. It was a mythic quest. He said that this was why China would make sure there were no slipups during the transfer of power in 1997. And they would be just as careful over Macau in 1999. The ultimate goal was and remains the reunification of China with Taiwan, and that

SIGN OF THE TIMES

Please leave your values at the front desk.

In a Shanghai hotel elevator.

1   *The People's Liberation Army (PLA) includes the Ground Forces, the Navy (Marines and Naval Aviation), the Air Force, the Second Artillery Corps (strategic missile force), and the People's Armed Police.*

www.chinainvestguide.org

would never happen if Hong Kong and Macau went badly. So far, events have shown him to be accurate in his predictions.

Miraculously, Zhu was able to bring inflation down from a high in 1994 of approximately 25%, to a comfortable 8% in 1996 and 3% today. Zhu also managed to hold the exchange rate steady at US$1=RMB8.3, a move designed in part to boost China's exports. At the same time, China's foreign reserves grew dramatically, reaching US$114 billion by March, 1997. Only Japan held higher foreign reserves.

The Internet began to make its presence felt in the years leading up to the hand-over. The first time I saw an e-mail address on a business card was in Hong Kong, in late 1995. By September of 1996, there were approximately 20,000 active Internet accounts in China. The Internet was available in all of the 27 provinces and four provincial-level cities. At the time, Internet use was predicted to grow at 400% per year.

The first private access Internet provider in China opened in Shanghai on October 4, 1996. It was called the Internet Café and offered Web access for RMB50 per hour. (In January 2000, Beijing's Sparkice Cybercafé was charging RMB30 per hour.)

Every five years, China's leadership meets to map out the direction the country will take for the next five years. Traditionally, the government decides the country's pillar industries and the resources that should be allocated to each of these key pillar industries. The old-style command economy in action.

In the early days of Deng's reforms, the government decided that the automotive industry would be a pillar industry of this new economy. They assumed that the first thing consumers would want to buy, once they had the necessities, would be cars. But Chinese consumers were more concerned with

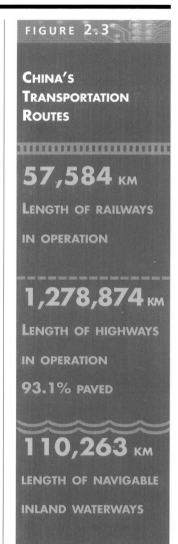

FIGURE 2.3

CHINA'S TRANSPORTATION ROUTES

57,584 KM

LENGTH OF RAILWAYS IN OPERATION

1,278,874 KM

LENGTH OF HIGHWAYS IN OPERATION

93.1% PAVED

110,263 KM

LENGTH OF NAVIGABLE INLAND WATERWAYS

FIGURE 2.4

Vehicle Ownership in China

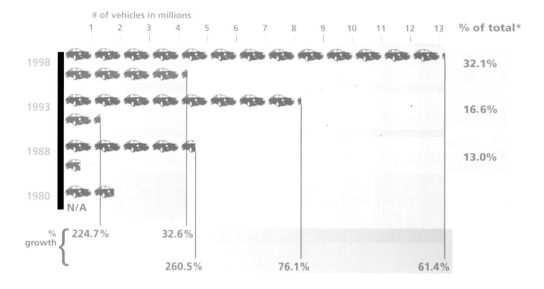

* This represents the number of privately-owned vehicles as a percentage of the total.

improving the quality of their living environments than owning private cars. It was more efficient, and faster, to travel by bicycle in the city. And there were precious few modern highways to connect large urban centres. Housing was the Chinese consumer's first priority, not cars.

For the first time, China's leadership changed its economic policy to suit the needs of the consumer. In 1996, the Ninth Five Year Plan (1996-2000) shifted the allocation of government resources from the automotive industry to the residential construction industry. Economic democracy in action.

Deng Xiaoping died in February 1997, a few months before

the historic hand-over of Hong Kong. And nothing happened, or at least nothing apparent. And in September 1997, the Fifteenth Party Congress confirmed the line-up most had come to accept as China's new leadership, with Jiang Zemin as General Secretary, and Zhu Rongji as Premier.

Jiang Zemin remained an unknown quantity for many in the West. How and why did he become paramount leader? It was obvious that Zhu Rongji's political success was directly related to his economic success. Zhu had brought inflation under control and had begun to address the problem of the inefficient and often bankrupt State Owned Enterprises.

The hand-over of Hong Kong also went without incident. The real crisis occurred on July 2, when the Thai Baht went into a free-fall. It was the beginning of a crisis that continued to threaten both Hong Kong and China through to the turn of the century.

As the 90s drew to a close, Zhu Rongji took on ever more complex and dangerous problems. In the early days, the People's Liberation Army had been encouraged to enter into business. It was a way to make up for the low wages the government could barely afford to pay. But the PLA quickly turned out to be much more entrepreneurial and successful than anyone suspected.

One of the most successful five-star hotels in Beijing, the Palace Hotel, is a joint venture between the Peninsula Group of Hong Kong and the PLA. The PLA has also won huge contracts to lay fibre optic cables

www.peninsula.com

FIGURE 2.5

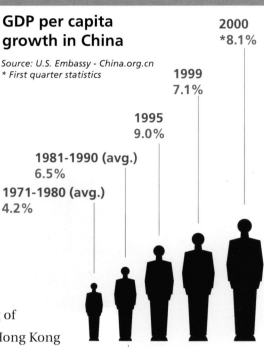

GDP per capita growth in China

Source: U.S. Embassy - China.org.cn
* First quarter statistics

1971-1980 (avg.)
4.2%

1981-1990 (avg.)
6.5%

1995
9.0%

1999
7.1%

2000
*8.1%

across the country. Of course, this isn't what armies or the military is supposed to do. Zhu has ordered the army to divest itself. When or if is anyone's guess.

Zhu has been more successful attacking corruption. The last few years have seen the trials and executions of ever-more-powerful political figures. More successful attacking it, not necessarily solving it.

Fast forward

What's really happening with China's economy today? Is it up or down or stagnant? Does anyone really know for sure?

I visited Beijing, Shanghai and Guangzhou in January and February of this year to do research for this book. Each of these cities has a population in excess of 10 million. Together the three cities represent approximately 60% of China's GDP. The last time I'd been to these cities was only sixteen months before. The changes I saw were dramatic.

Everybody told me that China's economy was slowing, that Shanghai's real estate market had gone bust and that unemployment had reached record levels. All that may be true. But that's not what I saw or felt from the people in the streets.

I'm not an economist, or a businessman or a sociologist. I'm a writer. Writers are observers—at best—honest witnesses. When I want to measure a country's economy I look to what I call common sense fundamentals. What do you read from the faces of the people in the street? Do they look you in the eye, or turn away? Are they suspicious, or confident? Are the restaurants full and the markets busy? Are people spending money or saving it? And is the

FIGURE 2.6

GDP growth in China

Source: U.S. Embassy - China.org.cn
* First quarter statistics

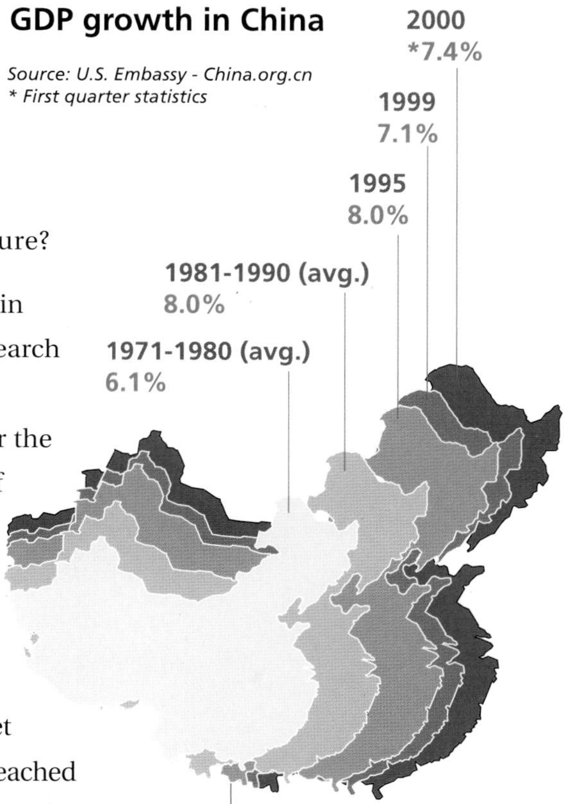

2000
*7.4%

1999
7.1%

1995
8.0%

1981-1990 (avg.)
8.0%

1971-1980 (avg.)
6.1%

exchange rate on the black market up or down?

www.shu.edu.cn

The official exchange rate is US$1=RMB8.3. Usually, the black market exchange offers a rate 15-20% higher. If the spread increases, then that tells me people are getting nervous. All is not well at the grass-roots level. This is a common sense fundamental, not a scientific one.

China's sex museum

You can't walk two blocks up the Nanjing Road in Shanghai without somebody trying to get you to exchange money. This time, to my astonishment, when I shook my head, they said, "Hashish? Good stuff, from the south?" Hashish on the Nanjing Road? There's also a new sex museum on the Nanjing Road. It's a collection of largely historic artifacts tracing the history of sex in China. The exhibition was assembled, and is overseen by, Professor Liu Dalin of Shanghai University. Professor Liu has spent decades assembling his collection. There are some intriguing historic pieces, and some quite graphic contemporary works. It costs RMB30 to tour the exhibition. During my tour, the only other visitors I saw were also foreigners.

I was told by a long-time resident of Shanghai that groups of school children are often brought through the museum. There's nothing wrong with school tours of a sex museum, it's just not what you'd expect to find in the People's Republic of China. I felt very much the same way I'm sure Richard Boucher felt when he saw that pink sweater peeking up out of the collar of the Mao jacket. That a sex museum exists, and that someone is bold enough to try to sell drugs on the Nanjing Road, suggests that China is going through some very profound and fundamental social changes.

And the economy? I spent most of my time talking to people in China who were involved in the Internet. This is still a relatively narrow niche. Most of them were young people between the ages of 25 and 35. I was struck by how excited they all were about the possibilities the Internet and e-commerce offered for them and for China. I was also surprised by their naivete or general ignorance about how you transform an idea into a business. There is business there, without a business culture.

www.surfchina.com

Young people in China have grabbed onto the Internet for the very reason that makes the Internet boom different from any other economic boom or innovation, or revolution. They understand very clearly that all they need is a good idea. This is true as far as it goes. But there are critical steps needed to take any idea from ether to reality.

During the Industrial Revolution, you couldn't make a serious fortune without first having the capital to build a factory and employ labour. Capital was also required to build railways.

All you need today is to devise an Internet-based solution to a business problem and you'll make millions. That is, if you can present that idea succinctly in an executive summary. And you'll need that executive summary to construct the forty-page business plan from which your idea will grow. You'll also need that cracker-jack business plan to get money from investors to turn your idea into reality and deliver it to market where it will reap its greatest rewards.

www.ubuytimeshare.com

The young Chinese entrepreneurs I met do not want for ideas and enthusiasm. What they lack is business culture, the environment and the steps necessary to grow an idea into a business. They all understand the phenomenal scale of the opportunity in front of them. All they lack are some simple tools to make it happen. No doubt they'll soon find the tools, or someone will bring them to them. And then the China boom will go ballistic.

China is committed to Deng's course

There is little doubt in most people's minds that China is committed to the course Deng set in 1978. It doesn't really seem to have much choice. The real question seems to be how the system will continue to evolve. What will China look like in five or ten years time?

In 1987, the government began to experiment with full direct elections for village leaders. A similar from-the-bottom-up step, as in the economic reforms of 1978. Traditionally, the post of village-committee chairman would be held by someone appointed by the regional Communist Party. In the early days, the ballots would carry the name of the incumbent village-committee chairman and one other nominee chosen by the village establishment. Clearly, these were not 'democratic' nor free elections as we in the West understand them to be. But it was a first step.

Suddenly, real elections

In November 1998, the National People's Congress changed

FIGURE 2.7

China's vital stats

Population
# of beds/10,000
# of doctors/10,000

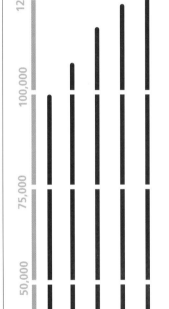

Population/
ten thousand people

125,000
100,000
75,000
50,000
25,000
1 - 25

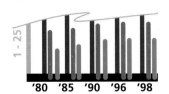

'80 '85 '90 '96 '98

the rules. Villages now hold a sort of primary election where every villager has the opportunity to write down all the candidates he or she feels are qualified for the contested post. Those receiving the most votes in the primary become candidates in the run-off election. Suddenly, the election process became less predictable and more democratic.

There have been some experiments with similar direct elections at the township level but the larger the population, the more awkward and inefficient the process becomes. A logical solution to this would be for separate political parties to choose their representatives to run in the elections. At least that's how we do it.

www.xinhua.org

But China isn't experimenting with direct elections to please the West. China is doing this because it believes this kind of election enhances social stability and raises the quality of leadership. More and more, if that's what they say, that's what they mean. ➡

FIGURE 2.8

go to...

For additional information and updates to charts and graphs, visit: **www.flyingarmchair.com**
the China s Wired! *resource site.*

2000.12:59:59

1999.12:59:59

1998.12:59:59

1997.12:59:59

1996.12:59:59

1996.12:59:59

3

Invasion of the Wired World

From the Cultural Revolution to the Web

www.net.edu.cn

C hina's universities were closed during the Cultural Revolution (1966-1976). Higher learning was a bourgeois sin. Institutions, libraries and research facilities were abandoned. So were the minds of a whole generation of China's best and brightest. Slowly, in the late 1970s, after the death of Mao and the beginning of the economic reforms of Deng, the universities began to re-open. Funding was scarce. China had fallen behind the times. Nevertheless, Deng recognized that technology was the key to China's rebirth.

China lost many of the best and brightest of those early post Cultural Revolution graduates. China trained them well, but had few jobs requiring their skills. Many left to build careers and lives in the West. For the young scientists who stayed behind there was little funding for research. They could read about the astonishing developments at UCLA and Stanford, but had little hope of participating in them. Their Internet revolution could only begin once they were plugged in.

The Internet in China first came to life in a university

DENG XIAOPING

Deng Xiaoping (1904-1997), Chinese Communist leader who governed China from 1976 to 1997. He was born in Sichuan Province and by the age of sixteen, had travelled to France and Russia to study.

Deng participated in the Long March and began his own long climb up the ladder of success in the Communist Party. In 1956, he was appointed Secretary General of the party. Deng managed to survive two purges and several reversals of fortune as the Communist Party went through such tumultuous periods as the Great Leap Forward, the Cultural Revolution and the reign of the Gang of Four.

It was not until three years after the death of Mao that he was finally able to secure the position of undisputed leader.

By that time, Deng had begun a series of economic reforms and set-up the Special Economic Zones, that jump-started China's economic rebirth.

research laboratory in Beijing. A few scientists and research assistants huddled around two terminals connected by cables a few feet long. One computer was plugged into the Internet; the other was not. The equipment was foreign and the language of the first message that zipped between the computers was English. The message only travelled a few feet but bridged the huge technological and cultural gulf between China and the West.

In 1986, Chinese scientists at the Beijing Computer Application Technology Institute successfully transmitted a message to the German University **network**[1]. The following year, the first **node**[2] connecting China to international e-mail was constructed. Finally, China was plugged in.

The next step was to decide how and where to grow the Internet inside China. In 1990, the NCFC (National Computing & Networking Facilities of China) was founded with a grant from the State Planning Commission and a loan from the World Bank. Overseen by the Chinese Academy of Science, the purpose of the NCFC was to connect three Beijing campus networks CASnet (Chinese Academy of Science Network), PUnet (Peking University Network), and TUnet (Tsinghua University Network). Nestled in between these three campuses is the Zhongguancun area, today referred to as China's Silicon Valley, and the location of the greatest concentration of high technology research, development and manufacturing in **China.**[3]

Once you've created a network you need an organization to manage it. In 1990, CSTNET (China Science & Technology Network) was constructed by the Computer Network Information Centre of the Academy of Science. CSTNET

www.cnc.ac.cn

[1] *Professor Qing Tianbai is credited as the first person to send e-mail from China to Germany in September, 1987*

[2] *Internet node address is the portion of your e-mail address that appears after the @ symbol.*

[3] *There are currently 1,075 universities in China, 390,000 professors and staff members, 94,200 graduate students and 2,184,000 undergraduate students.*

was the first of five internal networks China would construct for the Internet. The network was focused primarily on technological or scientific institutions. By early 1998, CSTNET had over 200 network organizations and 20-30,000 clients. Presently, 22 cities across China are connected to Beijing through CSTNET.

By 1993, China's government had fully embraced the Internet. They recognized the critical role this new instrument could play in China's economic development. The Internet could provide the communications infrastructure China lacked at a fraction of the cost of traditional information infrastructures. Government departments could communicate. Efficiency and accountability would increase.

Some argue that China's government strongly supports the Internet's development because of the increased control it will give the government over China's citizens. They say the Internet in China isn't about what you see on your screen, but what you can't; the real incentive, this argument goes, lies in what the government believes it can do for them. But that assumes that access equals control. I think China's government has taken to the Internet for entirely practical and wholly economic reasons. First, it's the only way to remain competitive in a global economy. And second, it would take twenty years and countless billions to gain such communications capability through traditional means.

Soon after China established the first permanent, direct connection with the international Internet in 1993, the IHEP (Institute of High Energy Physics) leased a 64k bps(i.e 64 thousand bits per second) line from AT&T to connect to

NOTE

The China Academic Network (CANET) in 1988 established the first network cooperating with the outside world via a gateway to Karlsruhe University in Germany.

1987

First link to international e-mail

China's Wired!

the Stanford University Linear Accelerator Center. Finally, scientists at the NSFC (National Science Foundation of China) had their own e-mail accounts.

Also in 1993, and in an effort to accelerate the development of the Internet in China, the State Council created the Joint Committee of National Economic Informatisation. The committee had three primary goals. First, to build an information superhighway that would assist in China's modernization and economic development. Second, to begin developing China's own information technology industry. Finally, to build a communication network that would interconnect all parts of the country, and allow a free-flow of communication across all sectors and levels of government and industry.

The Committee of National Economic Informatisation also oversaw the creation of a series of initiatives involving every aspect of government and the economy. The initiatives fell under the title of the Golden Projects. The first three initiatives of the Golden Projects were Golden Bridge, Golden Card and Golden Gate.

Golden Bridge was first proposed in March 1993 by then Vice-Premier Zhu Rongji. The intention was to create a national network connecting all 30 provinces and provincial level cities. The network itself is composed of both satellite and land line networks and was meant to provide a base upon which other networks could grow.

In June, 1993 President Jiang Zemin called for an acceleration of the development of credit cards and electronic banking in China's largest cities. Fittingly, the initiative was labeled the Golden Card. Its intention was to

NOTE

Moore's Law

Gordon Moore (who co-founded Intel) said in 1964 that the amount of information storable on a given amount of silicon has roughly doubled every year since the technology was invented. This held true until sometime in the late 1970s, when the time span slowed to 18 months.

www.planet-payment.com

set up a credit card verification system and an inter-bank and inter-region clearing system. One of the goals of Golden Card was to see 200 million credit cards in use in China by 2000.

Golden Gate was proposed by then Vice Premier Li Lanqing in June 1993. This is a foreign trade information network linking the Ministry of Foreign Trade and Economic Cooperation and the Customs Bureau.

In those early days, it's probably more accurate to say that these initiatives were establishing an Intranet within China, or a series of Intranets. The goal was internal connectivity, not an opening up. The wired world was seen as a tool to increase government control over the administration of economic development. It was also seen as a tool to pull the farthest reaches of the country closer to the centre.

The early Golden Projects were concerned with developing online capacity for three fundamental areas: communications, finance and trade. A series of other Golden Projects followed—each involving different ministries, aspects of the economy or administration, or industry sectors.

One of the most important of these projects is the Golden Sea Project (Jinhai). The Golden Sea Project connects China's top leadership to the key organs of State control—or at least what they perceive to be the key organs of State control: The State Statistical Bureau, The People's Bank of China, and the State Information Centre.

At this time in China, China Telecom was essentially the sole state telecommunications entity. If you wanted a telephone you had to call China Telecom. But monopolies don't always provide the best service, or the best price. In 1994, two new state telecommunications companies were formed, China Jitong Corporation—which was an amalgamation of 26 state-owned companies, and China Unicom (China United Telecommunications Company). UNINET, or Unicom Net is the network run by China Unicom. China Unicom and China Jitong still pose little threat to the commercial supremacy of China Telecom.

www.cernet.edu.cn

In 1994, the Central Government allocated RMB80 million (US$9.6 million) to begin construction of CERNET (China Education and Research Network). Construction of

1989

The NCFC is founded

China's Wired!

CERNET began at Tsinghua University and was overseen by the State Development Planning Commission and the Ministry of Education. Initially, the goal was to connect ten key universities in China. Geographically, these universities were fairly evenly distributed throughout this vast nation. In central China they included Tsinghua University, Beijing University, Beijing University of Posts & Telecommunications, Shanghai Jiaotong University and Southeastern University in Nanjing. In the south they included South China University of Technology in Guangzhou and Huazhong University of Technology in Wuhan. In the west, they included Xi'an Jiaotong University and Chengdu University of Electronic Science & Technology. And in the north, Northeastern University in Shenyang. CERNET's ultimate goal is to create a network amongst all of China's universities, institutions of higher learning and centres of research and development. Eventually, this network will be connected to similar educational networks around the world.

Today, CERNET's network is composed of a total of 300 universities, research and development institutions, and middle and elementary schools. The network has three overlapping and interconnected tiers: national backbones, regional networks and campus networks. CERNET spans 70

WHAT'S IN AN INITIAL:

Some Acronyms on the Internet

BOF —Birds Of a Feather

BTW —By The Way

Ebonepan —European Backbone service

GOSIP —Government OSI Profile

HIPPI —High Performance Parallel Interface

IMHO —In My Humble Opinion

MAN —Metropolitan Area Network

MIME —Multipurpose Internet Mail Extensions

MUD —Multi-User Dungeon

NAK —Negative Acknowledgement

NSF —National Science Foundation

PING —Packet Internet Groper

SLIP —Serial Line IP

TTFN —Ta-Ta For Now

TTL —Time To Live

WRT —With Respect To

1990

CSTNET Network born

China's Wired!

cities and has over 50,000 clients.

In the spring of 1994, the Institute of High Energy Physics Research of the Academy of Science established China's first Web server and created China's first Web-site. Initially, the site was called Touring China and contained general news and information. It was later renamed China Window. The Academy of Science also began to oversee the registration of domain names with a CN designation.

www.rdc.com.au

China was still miles behind developments in the West, so there was only one thing to do. Concoct a stew of initials. Technocrats love initials, and bureaucrats swoon to see them. The old American crack about Give Me liberty or Give Me Death has been modified in our time to read, Give me an Acronym, or Show Me the Door. No need to depart; over the next few years the place began to put forth acronyms as a Japanese cherry tree puts forth blossoms. You will find them peeping shyly from the thicket of the following paragraphs.

In 1994, a number of networks were connected to the international Internet using Sprint America Inc. A 64k bps (kilobites per second) link via a Sprint International router was connected to the National Foundation of Science network (NFSNET). CSTNET (China Science & Technology Network) was connected via a 64k bps line, and CHINAGBN (China Golden Bridge Network) opened a 128kbps international line. Twice as fast, in other words.

www.chinatelecom.cninfo.net

In September of 1994, China Telecom and the Commercial Department of the United States government signed a contract of international Internet cooperation, which stipulated that China Telecom was to open two 64k bps lines with Sprint America Inc, one through Beijing and the other through Shanghai, which it did. This was the beginning of China Telecom's construction of CHINANET, the nation's largest Internet network.

Also in September 1994, with funding from the Tokyo Institute of Technology, the Beijing University of Chemical Technology established its network (BUCTNET). I'll bet you thought a buctnet was something you need to catch dollars in. In the same month, the Beijing Telecommunication Administration used an MC164kbps satellite line to connect to CAREN (Consortium of Asian Research and Education Network), and JYNCNET (John Von Neumann Center Network). Somebody will some day make a Country and Western song out of all this.

All of this, as I suggested earlier, was more Intranet than Internet. The breakout came in early 1995, when China Telecom hooked Beijing and Shanghai to the international Internet through two Sprint America 64kbps fixed lines. China Telecom also began to offer DDN (Data Delivery Network) and X.25 access. The Academy of Science, at about the same time, established a network including its branches in Hefei, Wuhan and Nanjing. The next step came in April 1995, with the launching of the Nanjing International Internet Network (NJNET).

www.gdcb.gd.cn

By July 1995, the network of the Institute of High Energy Physics had approximately 500 registered e-mail accounts. The National Computing & Network Facilities of China came in second with approximately 300 e-mail accounts, while CERNET had only about one-third of that number. Together, they made a very small spattering of drops in a very large bucket, but the low number of users was explained by the high cost of opening an account. In 1995, it cost RMB 1,100 (US$132) to open an e-mail account. At the time, most of these were held by university researchers, who paid for the accounts with money from their research grants. Holders of e-mail accounts also had to pay RMB 25 (US$3) a month for the server as well as all local or long-distance telephone charges.

Demand was slowly growing, and in response, CERNET switched to a Sprint line that moved at twice the old speed, a 128 kbps line. CERNET also began to carry BBS.tsinghua.edu.cn, the first broad band Internet service in China.

> *A professor is one who talks in someone else's sleep.*
> —*Anonymous*

In 1995, CERNET switched to a heavier Sprint 128kbps line.

As the traffic began to edge upwards, the authorities began to edge in. In 1996, the State Council began to formulate laws governing the Internet and Internet use. The key directive was Order Number 195, which rejoiced in the title, " The Temporal Administration Regulations of Computer Information Networks and the Internet in the P.R.C." Known to friends as plain old 195, or, if close friends, Good ol' 195. This was modified in May of 1997 to make it a little tougher, but the title, thank God, was not changed.

Okay, now we had the technical gizmos in place, and a beginning to a regulatory regime to make sure nobody got away with anything. It was time to let the public into the act. Accordingly, in June, 1996, CHINANET began offering Internet service to the people. They liked it; they couldn't afford it, but they liked it. By 1998, CHINANET had 160,000 clients; by the end of 1999 its client base had risen to 680,000.

A major component in this growth was CHINAGBN (**China Golden Bridge Network**),[1] which began service in September 1996. CHINAGBN is run by China Jitong Telecommunications Company and is connected to the international Internet via a 265kbps line. China Jitong is a state-owned company formerly linked to the Ministry of Electronic Industry. Today, CHINAGBN relies primarily on satellite and microwave transmission and has built more than 70 satellite stations throughout China. The network is connected to the networks of the Academy of Science and the National Information Centre. Presently, CHINAGBN has three international Internet connections, two out of Beijing and one out of Shanghai. The speed of the Beijing

www.gd.com.cn

[1] *CHINAGBN has established 10 backbone nodes in the cities of Beijing, Shanghai, Guangzhou, Wuhan, Shenzhen, Qingdao, Shenyang, Dalian, Changchun and Chongqing.*

connections is 2mbit/s + 256kbit/s; Shanghai's connection is 2mbit/s. How fast is that? Does the phrase, "Quick like a bunny" ring a bell?

CHINAFO169 (China Public Multi-media Communications Network) began service in December 1996. CHINAFO169 was built by the former Ministry of Posts and Telecommunications (now the Ministry of Information Industry). CHINAFO169 offers multi-media services including sound graphics, data and other integrated multi-media communication. Its early Web-sites included Guangdong Ling Tong, Tian Fu Hot Line and Shanghai Hot Line. By the end of 1998, CHINAFO169 had 525,000 clients.

www.21.cn.com

The next and inevitable step came in June of 1997, when the government finally created a body to oversee the development and administration of the Internet in China. The Information Project Office of the State Council and the Academy of Science established the China Internet Network Information Center (CNNIC). This acronym, regrettably, must be pronounced "Cynic," although it is built on faith. The CNNIC was given full powers to become the official National Internet Information Center. A Working Committee of the CNNIC was also established. Some of the CNNIC's duties include the registration of all cn domain names and a semi-annual survey of Internet users in China.

A hit. A very palpable hit!

I first became aware of the Internet in China in the summer of 1997. I was involved in a feasibility study trying to determine the market for an English-language magazine on business in China. One of my colleagues showed me a page from a Web site advertising rental accommodation in Shanghai. It was an English language Web site focused on the expatriate community. The page I saw carried various rental accommodation available in Shanghai. I was indifferent and unimpressed. My colleague pointed to a box at the bottom of the page. The box said that over 250,000 people had visited the site in the last four months. I almost fell off my chair. I don't know whether I was more surprised by the number of people on the Web—or the numbers interested in rental accommodation in Shanghai. Probably a combination of both.

The first semi-annual report from the CNNIC was released in November 1997. The report found that there were 299,000 computers connected to the Internet in China, 620,000 Internet users, 4,066 domain names registered under cn and approximately 1,500 Web sites. Total bandwidth of leased international connections was 18.64mbs.

1996

1— Order Number 195, for Internet control is promulgated
2— First offer of Internet Service to the public

China declared 1998 "The Year of E-commerce". In April 1998, The Information Infrastructure & Economy Development Research Center of the Academy of Science in conjunction with the Shanghai Information Port hosted the 1998 Shanghai International E-commerce Symposium, as part of this celebration.

www.gztelecom.com.cn

By this time, CHINANET, CERNET, CSTNET and CHINAGBN were all in operation and interconnected. Connectivity was beginning to reach critical mass. Conferences were being organized throughout China on e-commerce and the Internet. The Ministry of Electronic Industry and the Ministry of Foreign Trade hosted the second China E-commerce Application and Market Symposium. And the CNNIC's second report showed that the number of Internet users in China had almost doubled in only six months. The July report showed that there were now 542,000 computers connected to the Internet, 1,175,000 Internet users, 9,415 domain names and 3,700 Web sites. China was wired!

However, most of this activity was taking place in English, which seemed somewhat belittling and even pointless for a great many people. Accordingly, the next Great Leap Forward, excuse the expression, came when China Telecom, about this same time, decided to launch an all-Chinese 169 network. The existing 163 network was employing both Chinese and English, but now, at last, the audience was reaching critical mass and the audience was Chinese.

The early reports issued by the CNNIC were received by many in the Internet field with skepticism. First, the numbers seemed far too small. There simply had to be more people on the Internet than reported. The fourth report issued by the CNNIC in July, 1999 began to expand some of the criteria. This report broke the number of computers connected to the Internet into two categories. Of a total of 1,460,000 computers connected to the Internet, 250,000 were connected through dedicated lines and 1,210,000 connected to the Internet using a dial-up service. And of the 4 million users, as opposed to the computers they were using, the CNNIC claimed that 2,560,000 were using a dial-up service, 760,000 were using dedicated lines and 680,000 using a combination of both. In July 1999 the report claimed that there were 9,906 Web sites and 29,045 domain names ending in cn.

Many people think the CNNIC's numbers underestimate the actual amount of activity on the Internet in China. But no one can fail to recognize that each time the CNNIC has

1997

1— China Internet Networks Information centre set up
2— China has 620,000 Internet users

China's Wired!

www.cei.gov.cn

issued its report those numbers—in almost every category—have almost doubled. Internet use is doubling every six months. Never mind the specifics, the growth rate itself is staggering. The most recent report, issued in January 2000, showed some numbers increasing by more than 100%. The total number of computers hooked to the Internet was listed as 3,500,000, and the total number of Internet users reached 8,900,000. If Internet use continues to grow at this rate there will be almost 40,000,000 people on the Internet in China by the end of 2000. Phenomenal.

The first contact I had with somebody behind a Web site in China was in September 1998. I'd stumbled across Zhaopin.com while surfing the Web. It was one of the few sites in both Chinese and English that had a Beijing address and telephone number. I'd sent a few e-mails asking who they were and what they were up to. I'd found out that the two founders of Zhaopin were Mark Baldwin, an Englishman, and Steve Chiu, a Canadian. Mark had lived in China for years, spoke Chinese fluently and had spent most of his career in the head-hunting business. Steve is a Chinese Canadian who'd grown up in **Newfoundland**.[1]

www.confucius.com

At the time, Zhaopin was essentially a job posting site—a giant billboard if you were looking for work, or looking to hire someone. The site—and the concept—had grown out of Mark's primary business of recruitment.

I didn't think I'd have time to meet with Mark or Steve during my trip to Beijing in September 1998. The only free time I had was on a Saturday. Nevertheless, I phoned their office. I called several times over the space of a couple of hours. I was about to give up when Mark finally picked up the phone.

The wise man is not confused, the benevolent free of anxiety, and the bold has no fear.

—*Confucius*
551B.C. - 479 B.C.

[1] *The name was first used in 1497 in an English registry recording the "discovery of Terra Nova" or " new found land."*

Newfoundland is the most eastern and newest (1949) province in Canada. It is made up of two parts; Newfoundland, which is an island and Labrador, which is on the mainland of Canada.

It covers 405,720 sq. km. with population of 551,792. It has the lowest population density in Canada, About two people per sq. km.

It is about the same size as Gansu Province in China, which has a population of 24 million.

He sounded exhausted. I explained who I was and what I was doing in China. He wanted to know what I wanted from him. I said I was curious. I wanted to know how they had managed to build a Web site here. And why was it getting 100,000 hits a day? Were they really getting that kind of traffic? I asked Mark if I could drop by their office. He hesitated and seemed a bit suspicious of my motives. Finally, he said he and Steve would meet me in my hotel lobby for a drink.

It's not that you need them to say yes...you just don't want them to say no

We talked for over an hour before they finally invited me to come to their office. They couldn't quite understand why I was so anxious to see it. I said I wanted to know the conditions they worked under. As it turned out, their office was in a hotel only a block from mine. At that time in Beijing, many companies worked out of hotels. It was the only place you could be sure of having electricity, air conditioning, telephone connections and the general infrastructure necessary to conduct business.

Maybe I'm lucky to be going so slowly, because I may be going in the wrong direction.

—Ashleigh Brilliant

Their office couldn't have been more than 120 square metres in size. It was dark, stuffy and cluttered with computer equipment. Steve turned on one of the terminals, Mark lit up a cigarette, and we started talking about the Web in China.

At the time, they didn't have 'official' permission to run the Web site. They told me that people from various ministries knew all about what they were doing and would sometimes drop by and say hello. They were usually more curious than censorious. It was very much wait and see. In China, it's not always necessary that they say yes...you just don't want them to say no.

The office itself was rented in the name of Alliance

1999

400,000 Internet users

China's Wired!

Consulting, Mark's bread and butter business, and the business for which he had all the appropriate permits. Zhaopin was essentially an experiment that was taking more and more of their attention, interest and energy.

Most of the successful Web businesses I've seen started by turning to the Web as a support or supplement to an existing bricks and mortar business. (By bricks and mortar business I mean a business with an office, staff, desks, parking spaces and some sort of a product—something bought, sold and/or manufactured.) Somebody in the office figures the Internet is a better and cheaper way to advertise. Somebody else thinks it might be an effective way to source new suppliers—virtual comparative shopping.

You'd have to be crazy or brain dead not to turn to the Internet in China. This country has limited modern infrastructure for business; notably; a lack of effective media outlets for business promotion. This is a particularly acute problem for a business like Alliance Consulting, which is focused primarily on finding middle to senior level management for all types of Foreign Invested Enterprises (FIEs), including joint ventures, Wholly Foreign Owned Enterprises (WFOEs) or representative offices.

'This has to be worth money'

It started when the two men decided to allow companies to post their recruitment ads for free. That was the killer application. And that's when the tidal wave hit them. Hundreds of thousands of hits from every university-educated, English-speaking manager or administrator in the P.R.C. Everyone wanted more money and a better job. And not only was Zhaopin generating hundreds of

Human history becomes more and more a race between education and catastrophe.
—*H.G. Wells*

2000

thousands of hits, they were also generating extremely valuable market research data. Almost by accident they were gathering statistics on the most sought-after consumer demographic—single young professionals with disposable income.

Mark and Steve had planned to spend that Saturday putting together a formal business plan for Zhaopin.com. They figured they'd need it if they were going to try and raise some money to ramp-up the site. Instead, they spent most of the day trying to explain their vision to me.

The most vivid memory I have of that afternoon is the look in Mark's eyes as he stared at Zhaopin's home page. He kept saying, "I don't know how yet, but I know this has got to be worth a lot of money...It has to be..." ⇒

🔲 (go to...)

For additional information and updates to charts and graphs, visit: **www.flyingarmchair.com**
the China's Wired! *resource site.*

4

Through the looking glass

Modification becomes transformation

A lice fell through the looking glass into a strange and wonderful world. Lucky Alice. At least she knew it was a different world. Sometimes it seems as if the Internet is changing our world while we're in it—making it something new and magical before our very eyes. That can be exciting or terrifying or wholly transforming— sometimes all three at once.

NOTE

Through The Looking Glass by Lewis Carroll.

Chapter One - Looking-Glass House.

"...For instance, the pictures on the wall next the fire seemed to be alive, and the very clock on the chimney-piece (you know you can only see the back of it in the looking glass) had got the face of a little old man, and grinned at her."

A world of extremes

www.lewiscarroll.org

One of the most amazing things about the Internet is its ability to penetrate a vast country and reach deep into the lives of its people. Wherever there is electricity or a telephone line, there is the ability to be hooked up and plugged in to the whole wide world. In the West the process is redefining life, business and our understanding of our economy. In China, it's doing that and more. It's pumping life—and information—into the homes of what have been an extremely isolated people.

The first three chapters of this book have laid down a kind of foundation. They have answered a few fundamental questions. What is the Internet and e-commerce? Where is China's economy today and how did it get there? And what is the history of the development of the Internet in China? This chapter looks at some of the other forces at work shaping China's Internet development. Looming large over

Masa of the Internet

this scene are two Asian-based commercial entities: Richard Li's Pacific Century CyberWorks and Masayoshi Son's Softbank. Who are they and what is their agenda? We'll also visit China's Silicon Valley and examine Beijing's efforts to develop its own software and hardware industries. And finally, how are the visionaries? How do they nurture their dreams in such a hostile, confusing and fast-changing environment?

But what does the guy in dusty Taiyuan care about billionaires? His relationship with the Internet is grittier and more real. What he sees on his screen are flickering dreams—promises of things to come—at least in terms of the products offered for sale and his present ability to pay for them. Nevertheless, he knows it's 'message time.' The **Information Age**[1] is here and he wants to be part of it.

www.dictionary.com

For most people in China, the Internet's reality is directly related to its cost, and the sacrifices that must be made to pay for it. To get a sense of the real sacrifice necessary, I asked a friend in Shanghai to show me his monthly phone bill. My friend is a university graduate and has a very good job with a large State-Owned Enterprise.[2] He receives accommodation as part of his remuneration. His monthly income is approximately RMB1,200 (US$145) (US$1= RMB8.3).

The monthly Wage: US$36.00

The bill he received from China Telecom in March 2000 covered the period from January 26-February 29, 2000. The total bill was RMB83.80 (US$10). Ten dollars doesn't seem much until you realize that the average monthly wage in China hovers around RMB300(US$36).

China Telecom has a virtual monopoly on telephone service in China today. The only other company in this arena, China United Telecommunications, or China

[1] *Information Age - The period beginning sometime in the early 1970s which spoke to the availability, consumption and use of huge amounts of information. More of this information was becoming available through computers and computer networks.*

[2] *New State-Owned Enterprises do not offer accomodation as part of remuneration. More and more, State Enterprises are phasing out housing benefits. Soon, workers will be paid in cash only.*

Chongqing: 30 million people

www.chinaunicom.com

Unicom, has been trying to play a competitive role in the China market with little real success. China Unicom has laid down its own fixed lines and has significant coverage in cities like Tianjin and Chongqing. But the vast majority of the nation is hooked up to China Telecom. In March, Beijing finally allowed China Unicom to also offer IDD service. Well, a step in the right direction is better than no step at all. Isn't it?

Of the bill, RMB24 (US$2.90) goes to the basic line rental. For that he gets 50 free, three-minute calls within Shanghai. Additional calls cost him RMB.16 for every three minutes. The phone company charges in three minute blocks. If he places a call that is three minutes and one second he is charged for six minutes. Hey, sounds just like home!

There is no discount for local calls made in the evening.[1] For a direct distance dialing (DDD) call, or Internet use, the charge varies depending on the distance. For those calls, there is a 50 per cent discount if the call is made between 9pm and 7am. The discount also applies for calls made on Saturdays, Sundays and public holidays.

Discounts are also available through a relatively new product called an IP phone card. These cards offer discounts up to 70 per cent and can be purchased at supermarkets, grocery stores, or at the phone company offices. They're essentially a calling card with a Pin Number you key in through a touch-tone telephone. This service is very popular, but has limited capacity. In the evenings the lines are jammed and users are forced to redial endlessly. My friend explains calmly that patience is required. Not if it's my dime!

I was also curious about the cost of installation. Here he had good news. Today, it costs RMB300 (US$36) and takes about a week to get a new telephone line installed into a home. He said that last year, it took at least a month and

NOTE

Chongqing is reported to be the biggest city in the world with a population of 30,023,000. It covers an area of 82,368 sq. km. which makes it larger than the state of South Carolina but smaller than Maine. Chongqing is made-up of 16 districts and 27 counties.

The city is 1,500 km from the Chinese coast and handles 10 million tons of cargo annually.

Chongqing's nicknames are "hilly city," "foggy city" and "hot stove."

It was the capital of the Ba kingdom 3,000 years ago. During the Second World War, Chongqing was the war-time capital of China.

The city has more than 300 scientific institutes, 23 universities and colleges and 350,000 scientists.

[1] *At one time, Shanghai Online was the dominant ISP and ICP in Shanghai. Shanghai Online charges RMB100 as an installation fee on first-time dial-up subscribers and RMB4 per hour for Internet connection. Internet users must also pay for the phone line – discounted to 50% of standard rate for local calls. The same installation charge applies to ISDN (integrated service digital network) users and DDN (dedicated digital network) users.*

RMB 800 (US$ 96). Local families with an existing telephone line can have additional lines run into their home for free. In the past, people in rural areas had to pay higher installation rates. In 1998, his parents, who live in the country, paid RMB1,200 (US$145) to have a telephone line installed.

Paying the bills is also getting easier. Not long ago, customers were obliged to pay their bills by lining up in long queues at the neighborhood service kiosks. Today, the customer can open a debit card account at a local bank. The phone company sends my friend the monthly bill and as long as there are no complaints withdraws the amount from the customer's debit card account. He received his February bill on March 13, and had until March 17 to lodge any complaint about the charges. He told me the bill is generally accurate.

He made 245 local calls during the billing period for a total of RMB25.08 (US$3). During the month, he went on the Internet 11 times for a total of 62 minutes. Internet use at home for a one month period cost him RMB27.60 (US$3.35).

www.cwhkt.com

Public Internet

My friend has access to the Internet at work. There are also many Internet cafés in Shanghai, where you can go online for anything from RMB6 per hour (at the public library) to RMB30 (a more commercial café/bar environment).

NOTE

IDD rates from Cable & Wireless, Hong Kong per minute.

Standard rate

Shenzhen	HK$2.40
Guangdong Prov.	HK$3.70
Rest of China	HK$9.50

Off-Peak rate

Shenzhen	HK$2.40
Guangdong Prov.	HK$3.70
Rest of China	HK$9.50

Exchange rate
US$1.00=HK$7.79

FIGURE 4.1

Telephones in China
(Millions of subscribers)

	Total	Urban	Rural	Public
1998	87.4	62.6	24.8	2.6
1993	17.3	14.0	3.3	0.2
1988	4.7	3.5	1.2	0.03
1980	2.4	1.3	1.1	0.001

If my friend were living on an average wage he'd be spending close to 10 per cent of his income on Internet access. Nothing else—not on hardware, or online purchases—just access. As it is, he's spending about 2.5 per cent of his income this way. What do we spend for Internet access? Certainly not 10 per cent of our incomes. What about 2.5 per cent?

If he were living in the United States, my friend would probably be making about US$75,000 annually. The benefits he'd receive on top of that would probably offset the accommodation he receives as part of his package in China. Nevertheless, 2.5 per cent of US$75,000 is US$1,875. For Internet access? Wow, that's commitment! Now, can entrepreneurs find a way to get Chinese customers to spend that much while they're on the Internet? This is exactly what Richard Li and Masayoshi Son want to know.

And until they know for sure, Pacific Century CyberWorks and Softbank are going to continue swallowing up everything in sight.

The most common strategy of Internet start-ups seems to be to try very hard to figure out the killer application—or the angle that will make your mouse-trap better. The alternative road to riches is to be bought out by a bigger player with very deep pockets. Of course, you have to achieve one or the other before the seed money runs out.

Gone with the Warner

Consolidation seems to be a characteristic of the new Internet economy. Fast and furious and out of the blue consolidation. Just look at that late-century stunner—the merger between America Online (AOL) and Time Warner. It was so surprising that many seasoned business reporters were sure it was Time Warner that was taking over AOL.

The Warner merger was without question a merger of

NOTE

In January of this year authorities shut down 127 small unauthorized Internet cafés in Shanghai. Most were unlicensed. Laws now stipulate that an Internet café must have at least 20 computers, occupy 50 square metres and have at least two staff on duty at all times. New laws also ban unaccompanied children under 18 from spending time in Internet cafés during weekdays. Unaccompanied children under 18 are only allowed to spend three hours per day in Internet cafés on weekends and public holidays. There are approximately 777 government-approved Internet cafés in Shanghai. The number is increasing rapidly due to the relatively low start-up costs of approximately RMB70,000 (US$8,433).

www.timewarner.com

equals and a merger of giants. The more common consolidation strategy seems to be to cast a broader net—scoop up everything you can in the hope that something—anything—in the net comes up a winner.

Is this a strategy, or roulette? Are these people frantically placing bets on every number on the board only because they can? Rich enough to cover the board and greedy enough to want even more? Or are they simply entrepreneurs responding to a changing and charged economic environment?

If making money in cyber space is relatively new to Richard Li and Masayoshi Son, money itself isn't. Both have had huge commercial success and have enormous personal wealth.

www.softbank.com

Masayoshi Son made his first fortune shortly after graduating from the University of California at Berkeley. In 1981, Son used the proceeds from the sale of a hand-held organizer he had developed to start Softbank. Softbank began as a software distributor but quickly moved into sales of networking products. In 1994, Son took Softbank public. The company then moved into trade shows through the purchase of a division of Ziff-Davis. In 1995, Softbank took over the Comdex trade show and in 1996 purchased the remainder of Ziff-Davis. Son began to move into the Internet in a big way in 1996 when Softbank purchased 23 per cent of Yahoo for US$80 million. It's been expanding ever since.

www.forbes.com

Richard Li is about a decade younger than Masayoshi Son and has had a somewhat different ride to commercial success. He is the younger of Li Ka-Shing's two sons and sole heirs. He founded Star TV in 1990. Three years later, Star TV had 53 million subscribers and an audience of 220

NOTE

Time Warner Inc. is one of the world's leading media companies. Time Warner Inc. operates the following:

CNN News group

Cable Networks group

Home Box Office

Turner Entertainment

Sports Illustrated

Time Warner music group

Warner Bros.

New Line Cinema

Time Warner Cable.

PROFILE

MASAYOSHI SON

Son started taking a proactive approach to his life at a very young age when he moved from Japan to California. He attended the University of California, Berkeley where he graduated with a BA in economics. While attending Berkeley, he earned his first million by importing arcade games from Japan to be installed around the campus. He later invented and patented a multilingual pocket translator that he sold to Sharp Corporation. This became the prototype of Sharp's successful Wizard series.

million spread across 50 countries. In July 1993, Li sold 63.6 per cent of Star TV to Rupert Murdoch's News Corp. In July 1995, he completed the sale of Star TV; at the sale the valuation of the enterprise was US$950.5 million. The total investment in Star had been US$125 million. He was 23.

www.newscorp.com

The Billionaire Boy's Club

Looming large over any discussion of Richard Li is the legend of his father, Li Ka-Shing. It's hard to convey the awe with which K.S. is regarded. He's a legend in Hong Kong as well as on the mainland. In China, the wealthiest entrepreneurs in any city are often referred to as that city's Li Ka-Shing.

I interviewed Li Ka-Shing in the early 1990s for a book I was writing on Hong Kong. The week before the interview I met a Chinese-American entrepreneur who was doing a lot of business on the mainland. He was not convinced that I'd actually meet Li. At the end of my trip I called him to say goodbye. He asked if I'd met K.S. I told him I had and that I'd spent a couple of hours with him in his office. There was a long pause at the other end of the line. Finally, he asked, "Did you get his card?"

"Yes, of course I have his card."

"Do you want to sell it?"

www.cki.com.hk

I was baffled. Sell his card, it doesn't even have his signature on it? I was told it was worth a lot of money on the mainland because it proved you had contact with Li Ka-Shing. If you got his card, you had his ear. Showing this memento on the mainland was the best letter of introduction you could ask for. I still have the card. I'm not sure it would be as valuable on the mainland today as it was then. The myth remains strong, but the audience is a lot more sophisticated.

One of the most interesting insights I've heard about Li Ka-

NOTE

Cheung Kong (Holdings) Limited, chaired by Li Ka-Shing, conducts the real estate development investment holding company. It controls Hutchison Whampoa, Cheung Kong Infrastructure and Hong Kong Electric.

Shing came from his son. The younger Li was trying to explain his father's acquisition strategy. "He doesn't have a formal understanding of economics...What he does is examine small samples or aspects of the business, little slices here and there, looks at them closely and then makes his decision...He's right but right in a different way, and from a different perspective".

Bad *feng shui*

The elder Li is probably more intuitive and instinctive than his younger son. He also follows the instructions of *feng shui* masters when designing a new building or decorating his offices. The head office of Cheung Kong Holdings used to be located at No. 9 Queen's Road Central. At one point a new building sprouted up beside Li's headquarters. The corner of the building pointed threateningly at Li's offices. A *feng shui* master told Li he would have to deflect the bad forces of the neighboring building. Ultimately, two antique cannons were mounted on the roof of Li's building—their barrels aimed at the offending building's bad *feng shui*. This isn't unusual in China, where most entrepreneurs respect the same traditions.

I interviewed his son, Richard Li, in the spring of 1998. The cyber wars hadn't yet started. At that time, Li's focus was on the Pacific Century Group. This firm had three distinct sectors: digital technology and media, financial services, and infrastructure and property development. At the time, Li was just finishing a US$500 development in central Beijing that was a combination of office space, residences and a shopping centre. In hindsight it's interesting that Li commented, "I pay the most attention to the technology side of the business because it's so challenging. The fight is always for the best product... I'm torn between technology and the intellectual challenge of the macro game." At the time, I felt he was drawn to technology because it was the

A little slice of Li

greatest business challenge. How do you turn all this stuff into a business? Hardware, software or applications? No one was talking about portals and IPOs in 1998. Certainly not Richard Li. I also remember being struck by how intelligent Li was and by how proud he was of that intelligence. He wasn't showing off, he was enjoying the thrust and parry of intellectual exchange.

In the spring of 1998, Li had just moved into the Internet field in a partnership with Intel, the world's largest manufacturer of micro-processors. He told me they planned to work together to develop Internet and digital interactive services across Asia.

In late 1998, Richard Li began to lay the foundations of a high-tech strategy—literally—when his group purchased a relatively isolated piece of land on the back of Hong Kong Island. With great fanfare, they announced the development of Hong Kong's cyber port. The industrial park would hold research facilities, residences and office space. Microsoft, Intel and others all signed on. Will it work? Can anyone duplicate the environment that created the Silicon Valley? The answer, still to come, has taken a back seat to more pressing concerns—and more recent incarnations.

Li launched Pacific Century CyberWorks in 1999. Its stock has risen over 1,000 per cent since listing. And now everyone—especially his shareholders—wants to know what young Mr. Li is going to do to prove that valuation. In a move that seems a stroke of genius, but has yet to be concluded, Li used Pacific Century CyberWorks stock—and a little cash—to take control of one of Hong Kong's oldest and bluest of blue chips, Cable and Wireless Hong Kong Telecom.

www.intel.com

www.chinanewsletter.com

PROFILE

LI KA-SHING

Li Ka-Shing (above, with the author) was born in 1928 in Chiu Chow (Chaozhou), a city not far up the mainland coast from Hong Kong. Li moved to Hong Kong with his family in 1940. In 1950, he founded Cheung Kong Holdings with personal savings of HK$50,000. Li made his first fortune manufacturing plastic flowers and watch bands. In the early 1960s he moved into property development. In 1979, Li bought controlling interest in one of the great 19th century British trading houses or hongs, Hutchison Whampoa. Li purchased 37.8% of Hong Kong Electric in 1985. In 1986, he purchased Husky Oil, Canada's largest producer of oil and gas. Recently, Li realized a profit of US$24 billion from the sale of mobile phone operator Orange to the Mannesman Group.

There are things about Richard Li and Masayoshi Son that are extremely Western—both studied at universities in the United States. But there's also a lot about them that reflects the ground from which they come. In the East, so much depends on *guanxi* or connections. Your destiny is determined by who you know and how you know them. At least your commercial destiny. Richard Li inherited his father's business instincts—and luck—as well as his father's connections and the reputation that goes along with it. It could be argued that the net he casts as he invests small amounts in many fields springs from the same spirit. To cultivate or create a network.

www.cmgi.com

Of course they're not re-inventing the wheel. College Marketing Group Inc.(CMGI), the huge U.S. Internet conglomerate, has been following a similar strategy of investing in many different and varied Internet start-up companies. Curiously, one of the most lucrative investments Richard Li has made through Pacific Century CyberWorks was a share swap with CMGI. In September, 1999, the deal was valued at US$350 million; in February 2000, that value of the stake had risen to US$910 million.

Ultimately, it's hard to say which of these conglomerates will have the greatest effect on the development of e-commerce and the Internet in China. They both own pieces of each other and pieces of something the other has also invested in. There are tremendous synergies and a great unity of purpose. And they both want the same thing: to control the universe as it unfolds before us.

What is all this acquisitiveness about? Is it simply the nature of the free market system? And if so, is it good or bad for the Internet and the new economy it defines?

These two young billionaires have proven that they have

There was a time when a fool and his money were soon parted, but now it happens to everyone.

—*Adlai Stevenson*

What hath God wrought

the entrepreneurial genius—and the cash—to assemble all the tools necessary for building the new economy. The one thing neither has proven to any great degree, is a solid understanding of the content that will define and dominate the **Information Age.**[1] What is the sound of the Internet's voice? What colour is it? How does it make us feel?

The Information Age isn't just about technology, equipment and delivery speeds. It's the look and feel of the interaction itself. This is the gap in the conglomerates' defenses—and all the space David needs to slay Goliath.

There's an old saying in the study of art, 'The only thing that endures is emotion.' Ideas, technique and materials come and go. Great art survives because it continues to move us.

I remember asking Richard Li what he considered to be his greatest failure. At 33, he's had stupendous commercial success. But what—in his eyes—has he failed at? I was surprised more by how long he took to answer the question than the answer itself. He sat thinking for a good twenty seconds in silent contemplation. I remember stopping myself from interrupting or offering help. Finally, he said, "The worst failure isn't necessarily losing money on a bad investment. I think for me, missing opportunities is a greater failure."

Opportunity has a richer and more complex meaning in the East than it does in the West. The Chinese word for crisis is made up of two characters. One means danger, the other means opportunity. In the West we see crisis as a bad thing—governments fall and markets crash. In the East, crisis is a time of opportunity—dangerous—but full of opportunity.

A professor from Beijing University gave a speech on the

www.ckh.com.hk

1 *According to the National Museum of American History, the dawn of the Information Age began in 1837 with Samuel Morse's telegraph transmitter and receiver. This was followed closely by the Morse-Vail telegraph key which sent its first message in 1844 from Washington D.C. to Baltimore, Maryland.*

The famous message was "What Hath God Wrought."

The next step in the Information Age was the Edison Stock Printer followed by the Atlantic Cable of 1858 and the Telephone invented by Alexander Graham Bell.

The first Information Processing devices were believed to be the doctor's stethoscope, Hollerith Tabulating machine, sorter and Arithmeter.

Beijing bytes back!

development of the Internet in China at the University of Chicago in June 1995. In the transcript of his speech, he mentioned that many of the graduate students and research scientists involved in the development of the Internet in China were forced to use portions of their research grants to pay for e-mail accounts and telephone charges. At the time, an e-mail account cost RMB1,100, the dial-up cost was RMB25. The user was also responsible for all local or long distance telephone charges that might ensue. RMB1,100 was a fortune in 1995—it's still more than twice the average monthly wage.

How fast would the Internet have developed in North America if an e-mail address had cost twice the average monthly wage? Not fast. Perhaps not at all. And where would it be if just being connected cost us 2.5 per cent of our wages? Nowhere. Considering the economic sacrifice it entails, it's amazing that the Internet even exists in China. Of course, money for development of any sector is in very short supply in China. They have more pressing problems—like feeding 1.3 billion people.

But how can a country as poor as China compete with the resources of Richard Li and Masayoshi Son and others? How do you even begin? One of Deng's early economic innovations was the creation of Special Economic Zones (SEZs), where Chinese entrepreneurs and enterprises could mix with foreign business interests. It was a way of insulating the body of China from the capitalist virus. Some of these SEZs are also high-tech development zones. Today, there are 53 high-tech zones in China. The largest and most famous of these is Zhongguancun in Beijing. Zhongguancun is nestled between two of China's most important universities, Beijing University and Tsinghua University. They are also the universities that spearheaded

FIGURE 4.2

Cheung Kong Group
Total Market Capitalisation

HK$ 781 billion
(as of April 15, 2000)

GROUP STRUCTURE

Cheung Kong Holdings

HWL
Hutchison Whampoa

Cheung Kong Infrastructure

Hongkong Electric

Symbols for danger and opportunity form the word 'crisis.'

the development of the Internet in China. Their scientists and graduates are Zhongguancun's greatest resource and hope.

Zhongguancun has been growing at almost 30 per cent annually. Alongside this growth today, there are over 4,800 hi-tech companies with total revenues of US$5.5 billion. Some of the largest companies include Legend, China's largest manufacturer of personal computers; the Lixiang Group, which makes China's most popular office and word processing software; the Fang Zheng Group, also a software manufacturer; and the Beijing Stone Group, a manufacturer and distributor of personal computers. There are also 230 research and development centres. Last year, 916 companies began operation in Zhongguancun, of these 110 were foreign. Thirteen companies in Zhongguancun are listed on the Shenzhen and Shanghai exchanges. Zhongguancun is also a retail area full of shops selling all manner of software and hardware. But is it a 'Silicon Valley'?

Silicon Valley is the result of a confluence of a number of key elements. First and foremost is Stanford University. It has a tradition of innovation, research facilities and funding. Sun Microsystems, Cisco Systems and Novell were founded by Stanford graduates. The first Internet transmission occurred between UCLA and Stanford. The second element, is an entrepreneurial environment. A place where no dream is too big, and no idea too small. A place where anything is possible. Finally, and perhaps most importantly, Silicon Valley needed abundant capital. There are hundreds if not thousands of venture capital companies and angel investors in Silicon Valley—all ready to throw money at the next big thing. They're not reckless or crazy. They're a special breed. They know what to look for and how to handle it when they find it. Abundant but

www.legend.com

Where anything is possible

www.hkt.com

NOTE

Guangdong Province is a centre for electronics development and production. In 1999, Guangdong's gross electronics industry production grew 49.79 per cent to RMB188.60 billion (US$22.72 billion). Sales volume grew 51.54 per cent over the year before to RMB 111.80 billion (US$13.47 billion). Guangdong produces everything from cordless phones to fax machines, mini-computers, monitors, printers, colour displays and integrated circuits. Much of this production comes from three cities, Huizhou, Dongguan and Shenzhen. Shenzhen is responsible for 60 per cent of Guangdong's electronics production.

PROFILE

LIU CHUANZHI

Asia's Businessman of the Year, Liu Chuanzhi, CEO of the Legend Group, has been able to turn the State-owned, privately run corporation into the number one PC manufacturer in China with 23 per cent market share.

discriminating capital.

Portals

Zhongguancun is China's Silicon Valley but it's not Silicon Valley. Zhongguancun has had some successes. Shortly after graduating from Beijing University in the early 1990s, Wang Zhidong started a small software company called Stone Rich Sight. Wang developed one of the first programs for reading Chinese characters on the Internet. Today, Wang heads Sina.com, one of China's most popular portals. But that is a rare exception. It would be more accurate to say that Zhongguancun contains the greatest concentration of information technology research, development and manufacturing in China. It's where it is, but not where it's happening. Almost 20 per cent of the companies in Zhongguancun are joint ventures with foreign technology companies, including Microsoft, Intel, Sun Microsystems, Oracle, Dell and Compaq.

Creating Net value

What Zhongguancun lacks is capital, and commercial incentives. Scientists have little incentive to bring their innovations to market, since they are only allowed to own a maximum of 25 per cent of their own company. They can develop the product and raise the money to form a company but can only hold 25 per cent of the shares. Why bother? Or at least why bother In China? Why not take your ideas and ambition elsewhere—which of course has led to something of a Beijing brain drain.

www.altavista.com

In 1998, approximately US$13 billion was invested in hi-tech companies—80 per cent of it going to Silicon Valley. For the most part, credit, lending, profit sharing, issuing shares or bonds simply don't exist in China. It's not as if there isn't a lot of private capital in China's banks. One estimate puts individual deposits at RMB6 trillion (US$72 billion). Beijing is trying to make it easier for companies to raise capital, recently announcing the addition of two high-

NOTE

Shenzhen is sometimes called the Silicon Valley of South China. It began as a small village on the border of the New Territories north of Hong Kong. In 1990, it was predicted that Shenzhen's gross industrial output would reach US$6 billion by 1999. Gross industrial production in 1999 reached RMB207.81 billion (US$25 billion), four times the earlier estimate and a 25 per cent increase over 1998's figures. Information technology accounted for RMB120.5 billion (US$14.5 billion) or 58 per cent of the city's gross industrial output.

Shanghai trails behind Beijing and Guangdong province in high technology production. Total output in the information technology sector in 1999 increased 20.6 per cent over the year before to RMB 24.6 billion (US$3 billion).

Genius, yes; glue, no

www.sh.com

tech exchanges in Shanghai and Shenzhen. But is it enough?

It's not just about the money, it's also a way of thinking. There is a lack of a commercial culture around the development of high technology in China. All the elements are there to make it happen except the glue to bind it together. There's genius—both scientific and entrepreneurial—and there's desire. But it often strikes me that these separate forces are working away in isolation— each waiting for the other to knock on the door first. Zhongguancun lacks community, the magnet that pulls these disparate interests together.

There's also an indifference to protecting the ownership of ideas. Certainly, that's reflected in policies about scientists and company ownership. But it goes deeper than government rules and regulations; it's often absent from the consciousness of the very people who need protecting most.

I talked to a group of young e-commerce entrepreneurs in Beijing. One of them had an idea for a business but didn't want to tell me because he was worried I would steal the idea from him. I asked him how he was going to raise the money to get it to market if he wasn't prepared to tell anyone what it was? He was perturbed. But whom to trust? I told him about the poor man's copyright. Every writer knows this one. If you have a manuscript that you want to protect you send it to yourself by registered mail. When it arrives you leave it sealed and put it away in a safe place. If somebody steals it you can prove that you owned the idea or manuscript on the date when it was sent to you by registered mail. It works in courts in the West. It may yet have to be tested in a Chinese court. The point is that if you don't have some system to protect the ownership of ideas and inventions you won't have good people spending much

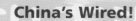

Stepping through the looking glass

www.zhaopin.com

time trying to think up those new ideas or inventions.

Pacific Century CyberWorks, Softbank and Zhongguancun are all about the Internet. They have real power. How, when or if they exercise it will not be up to us. In many respects we are at their mercy. But they're so big and so complicated it's hard to know if the person or persons at the top are leading or just trying to hang on.

I know who's been behind the growth of Zhaopin.com. I know something of the struggles they've faced over the past few years. It's been a tough and wild ride, but they've hung on.

Since I first visited them in Beijing in 1998 their Web site has gone through a number of incarnations. It began as a kind of directory or resource site. But directories in and of themselves don't keep people coming back. You need content, and content that counts. At one point they set up something called the "English Corner" where they posted reviews and articles in English. It was a huge success and brought them over a million visits a month. And then suddenly, in late 1999, I heard that they'd got some money and were ramping up their operations.

Zhaopin's new offices aren't very far at all from their old ones. They're located in the last building in a row of new buildings lining Dongzhong Street. From the outside, it's hard to tell if they're office buildings or condominium residences. The first thing that struck me—even before I arrived at the front desk—was the smell of fresh paint and new carpet— the cologne of Internet start-ups in China.

There was no one at the front desk, so I walked right in. Everything was pale—pale grey desks, pale walls, harsh neon lights and a grey-blue carpet. All new and bloodless. I found Steve sitting in an office by himself in the dark. I think the

NOTE

The Information Age continued with the NBC microphone, Magnavox loudspeaker and the Edison Stock Exchange Ticker.

The ENIGMA machine of the Second World War also became part of the history of this age.

The ENIAC, or Electrical Numerical Integrator And Computer developed by the U.S. Army filled a room 30 feet by 50 feet.

The 45 rpm record and player developed by RCA in the 1950s was another step.

The next step was the formation of the "Homebrew Computer Club" in Silicon Valley which hoped to give computing power to individuals. Two of the more famous founding members were Steve Jobs and Steve Wozniak, who created the Apple I computer in 1976.

office was half furnished—it certainly didn't seem like a place anybody had worked in for any length of time. Steve greeted me warmly and then led me around the corner to Mark's office. Mark has a real office. Books, photos, a round table, a big desk, chairs, bookshelves, phones—all that serious business stuff.

Zhaopin founders: Mark & Steve

www.east.net.cn

The odd couple

They're an odd couple, these two—Steve, the Chinese Canadian from Newfoundland, and Mark, the chain-smoking Englishman. Mark seems to take the lead in most discussions. He seems to be the boss. But every once in a while, if I ask a complicated or compromising question Mark will cast a glance at Steve before answering. Whatever the chemistry, it works.

I thought Mark looked five years younger than the last time I'd seen him. Steve hadn't changed much at all. Steve is one of those people who doesn't seem to be bothered by much. It's not that he doesn't have anxiety, he just doesn't show it. Mark's emotions are easier to read.

I asked them what it felt like to be in such grand surroundings and especially what it felt like to have staff. There were about twenty people working in the office the day I visited. They even had a new marketing executive. I didn't get her card. It was her first day and she didn't have one yet. I got the feeling they were still getting used to all this.

They told me that they'd started to talk seriously about raising some money for the business in December 1998. They needed to move to a bigger office and buy some new equipment. Initially, they were looking for US$40,000. And they wanted to borrow the money, they weren't looking for partners.

In early 1999, Mark made a trip to London to talk to some venture capital companies. This didn't go well at all. Not

NOTE

The English Corner is described as "indisputably China's most popular study guide for English, read by 2,000,000 people every month."

www.zgc.gov.cn

only did the venture capitalists want their souls, they also wanted Mark and Steve to carve off the recruitment side of the business. They wanted Zhaopin to be a pure Internet play—all virtual, no bricks and mortar. Mark only made two brief trips to meet with banks and investors. Most of the investment people came to Beijing to see them.

As word leaked out that they were looking for money, they started to get all kinds of calls and crazy offers. Finally, in the fall of 1999, they settled on a San Francisco-based company called Orchid Asia Holdings. They liked the people at Orchid. They liked the way the people at Orchid treated them, and they liked the valuation Orchid put on Zhaopin. By this time, investment money had grown out of the all-virtual model, and was beginning to warm to the bricks and clicks paradigm.

Ultimately, Orchid took a minority stake in Zhaopin for a few million dollars. A lot more than the original US40,000 they'd started looking for a year earlier, and enough to turn them into a very serious business.

What were they going to do with all that money? Advertising, marketing, staff? Mark explained that they planned to hire staff and focus on increasing business volume. Orchid was going to leave them alone to run the business as they saw fit. Orchid knows nothing about the realities of business on the ground in China—employee benefits and idiosyncracies, government regulations and taxes. Mark said that Orchid has offered to support Zhaopin should they need help in areas such as managing capital expenditures.

He went on to explain the agenda for the rest of the year. He said they planned to expand the number of 'products' Zhaopin would be offering. When I asked what he meant by

NOTE

It is reported that 40 per cent of the Chinese population is made-up of 10 major Chinese surnames:

Zhang, Wang, Li, Zhao, Yang, Wu, Liu, Huang or Zhou.

Rare surnames in China would be one of the following:

Mao, Jiang, Bai, Wen, Guan, Liao, Miao or Jia.

1,000 years ago a book called "Surnames of a Hundred Families" reported that there were 438 surnames of which 408 were singular with only 30 double surnames.

NOTE

Zhaopin comes from two characters, the Pinyin versions of which are "zhao" and "pin."

Essentially, Zhaopin means "recruitment" or "help wanted." These two characters appear in almost every print ad for employment.

www.sztdb.gov.cn

products, he explained that Zhaopin would offer online human resources management and software programs to help companies hire and train staff.

There are many hidden forces at work on the development of the Internet in China. Money is being pumped into Zhaopin in part because they've asked for it and in part because there's lots of it around. How will it change these companies and the people who are running them?

Mark and Steve built something viable with nerve, knowledge and experience. How will these new internal forces affect their judgement and the development of their company? Will it bring them success or will it choke them? Did the pump need priming, or was the universe unfolding as it should?

SIGN OF THE TIMES

You are very invited to take advantage of the chambermaid.

Sign in a Jilin hotel

go to...

For additional information and updates to charts and graphs, visit: **www.flyingarmchair.com**
the China s Wired! *resource site.*

S

Portals

Transforming realities

S cience fiction tells us that a portal is an entryway into another world. Alice entered Wonderland through the portal of her looking glass. The difference between science fiction portals and Web portals is that Web portals are a gateway to many different worlds. A place you go to – to go somewhere else.

[1] A portal is a doorway, entrance or gate, especially one that is large and imposing.

Also—A portal is a Web site that aims to be a " doorway or entrance" to the World Wide Web, typically offering a search engine and/or links to useful pages and content such as news or other information services. These services are usually free in the hope of attracting users to the site on a regular basis.

Transforming realities

The success of a **portal**[1] is measured by depth of penetration. The better the portal, the deeper you go and the longer you stay. And what do you do there? You go to find products or services or both. The portal is a shopping mall of options. It only succeeds if you find what you want, or stay long enough to notice all the flickering ads and promotions. The only thing a portal offers is access. It has no product. It makes money from commissions and advertising.

Unlike a book, you can't thumb to the last page to find out how the story ends. You have to experience a portal. You have to step inside it. You have to navigate through it.

www.portal.com

What the Internet does that no other mass medium can do is relate to its audience individually. Yaolan is one of the most interesting new sites in China. It offers information and products to China's twenty million pregnant women. Yaolan creates an intimate relationship with each and every visitor. Each relationship is defined—and initiated—by the

www.yaolan.com

personal data the visitor offers to the scrutiny of Yaolan's database. But Yaolan's audience is narrow and extremely focused. Yaolan gains the audience's confidence by offering free advice and abundant expertise. And then it sells them something. But Yaolan isn't a portal, it's a B2C. And that's how B2C works. That's the business model.

Fiery Portal of the East

Portals cast a broader net. Sometimes the net is so broad that it lacks cohesion. There's no sense of identity. There's no *there* there. The trick with a portal is to offer up an identity that appeals to a specific demographic. Do more young people go to Yahoo than go to AOL? Do young people go to Yahoo because of the funky name?

The AOL/Time Warner merger sounded solid. It felt solid—as solid as any digital business can seem. Some of that comfort might come from the feel of the name. After all, AOL is a variation on a theme: ABC, CBS, NBC, MSNBC etc. Would the merger have worked if it were Yahoo and Time Warner? I'm talking more and more about the feel of things because it's the experience that counts.

Business to Consumer B2C

We return to a restaurant because it was a pleasant experience and satisfied all our sensual and practical needs: good food, good service, nice atmosphere and reasonable price. Three of those criteria are wholly subjective. Some people might argue that they're all subjective.

See, see King Richard doth himself appear,
As doth the blushing discontented sun
From out the fiery portal of the east

—*Shakespeare*

FIGURE 5.1

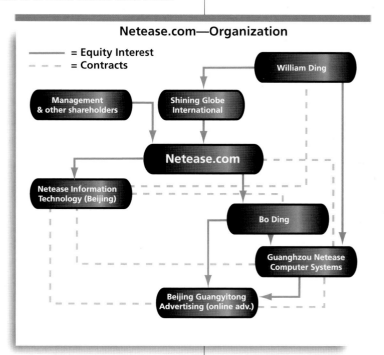

Netease.com—Organization

⎯⎯ = Equity Interest
- - - = Contracts

William Ding

Management & other shareholders

Shining Globe International

Netease.com

Netease Information Technology (Beijing)

Bo Ding

Guanghzou Netease Computer Systems

Beijing Guangyitong Advertising (online adv.)

A portal is an experience. It's an environment. Its construction and maintenance require as many separate skills as the construction of a successful bricks and mortar shopping complex. You want the best architect to ensure that people can move freely and easily through space. You need the best window decorators to make sure the products are displayed to their best advantage. And you need the very best staff to ensure the best customer relations and the greatest customer satisfaction. A portal is a huge challenge.

But the definition of a portal is always changing. This is because of technology and because the audience is becoming increasingly splintered and ever-more sophisticated. In some cases, they're changing because their business plan is no longer relevant.

A portal must be cutting edge

A portal has to be more than up-to-date, it has to be cutting edge. It has to be tomorrow, today. Portals are also different things for different peoples. Portals in China are not the same as portals in the West.

Sina.com, Sohu.com, Netease.com, etang.com, Tom.com and china.com are China portals. China.com is probably the most famous of these because of the tremendous success of its Nasdaq debut in July of last year. Tom.com might be running a close second because of the legend of Li Ka-Shing, the man behind it.

www.sohu.com

To some people, China.com and Tom.com are not China portals. They're Hong Kong portals. They're Western. They don't even use the 'correct' Chinese language. In the P.R.C., Chinese is written in a modern, simplified form. Hong Kong, Taiwan and the Chinese of South East Asia use traditional, complex characters. Of course, any Web site can carry its messages in many different languages. Just

When o'er the Aegean main Athens arose: a city such as vision Builds from the purple crags and silver towers Of battlemented cloud, as in derision Of kingliest masonry: the ocean-floors Pave it; the evening sky pavilions it; Its portals are inhabited By thunder-zoned winds.

—Shelley

NOTE

The GEM Exchange has only 23 companies listed as of this writing, including;

tom.com Ltd.

Sunevision Holdings Ltd.

Hongkong.com Corp.

iMerchants Ltd.

TS Telecom Technologies Ltd.

The current listing requirements include jurisdictions of incorporation as only Hong Kong, Bermuda and Cayman Islands. There are no specific winding-up provisions and no restriction on minimum transaction size.

click on the language of your choice. But some argue that Sohu and Sina will always have greater legitimacy as China portals. They say it's not just about language.

What then defines something as being a China portal? Is it that the founders were born in the P.R.C.? Or is it that the business model is original to the P.R.C.? Who is more Chinese than who? What are the criteria? Is identity and nationality relevant in a global economy and shrinking universe? Or is increased sensitivity to nationality the product of a smaller world? Whatever the cause, it continues to be an issue.

"Buyers beware" market for informed investors

Almost all the China Web sites want to list on the Nasdaq. Only a few are listed on China's two exchanges. Why Nasdaq? Why not Hong Kong's GEM(Growth Enterprise Market) exchange? Wouldn't that make them more Chinese? Perhaps, but this has less to do with nationality than money. The Nasdaq is the place to be if you want the pot of gold. Sina.com was the second (after chinadotcom) of the China-based portals to list here. The stock rose 22 per cent on April 13 2000, its first day of trading. It was astonishing that the stock rose at all, considering all the blood on the floor from an earlier sell-off of high-tech stocks. What was more extraordinary were the lengths to which Sina had to go to get permission from the China Securities Regulatory Commission (CSRC) even to try a listing.

Foreign investment in mainland Internet sites is prohibited in China. So, to get around this they took the elements that make up the value of the site and vested them in other related corporate structures whose ownership was not restricted. It's like listing a gold mine without any gold in it. The gold is in a warehouse. There's a contract between the gold mine and the warehouse saying all the gold belongs to the mine. Semantics or sleight of hand? It doesn't matter much until you want to sell your shares.

Well, whatever they did, it worked. And on April 13 2000 Sina.com raised US$68 million for working capital, marketing and general corporate purposes. Does this make them less Chinese? And what of Sohu and Netease? Sohu.com is registered in Delaware, U.S.A. and Netease.com is registered in the Cayman islands. Chinese?

There's a basic physics to commerce—it always finds the path of least resistance. These companies—or their corporate structures—belong to the global economy. Ultimately, they're owned by thousands of individuals and institutions around the globe. What makes them Chinese is their audience. If people in the People's Republic of China tune in, they're Chinese, if they don't, they'll soon be broke and gone.

Presently, the CNNIC lists the top three Web portals in the P.R.C. as Sina.com, 163.com (Netease) and Sohu.com, in that order. Another survey in April 2000 by www.cwrank.com lists the top three portals as Sina.com, Sohu.com and 163.com(Netease).

Is there anything that distinguishes any one of these portals from the others? Not much. Sohu.com seems to have the largest search engine, and has a few more categories to choose from, including employment opportunities and news on business. Sina.com seems to be faster and offers more news from a broader range of sources. And 163.com(Netease) has aspects of both. But there's nothing about any of them that suggests they've got the formula that will move them ahead of the pack. Unfortunately, money may be the ultimate deciding factor in the race to supremacy. Survival of the deepest pockets.

www.netease.com

Survival of the deepest pockets

www.163.com

FIGURE 5.2

TOP TEN CHINA WEB SITES	
1. SINA	Portal
2. SOHU	Portal
3. Netease	Portal
4. 8848.net	B2C
5. ChinaByte	Portal
6. CWW	Portal
7. Goyoyo	Portal
8. Yesite	Portal
9. Alibaba.com	B2B
10. Zhaodaola	Portal

Source: *www.cwrank.com as of April, 2000*

If it is, chinadotcom and Tom.com will be the horses to watch.

Ultimate success will also depend on the strategies and expertise of the CEOs behind these companies. Who are these people? What are their qualities? Why are they staking their careers and reputations on this new 'new thing'? The best answers about the Internet in China—or anywhere else for that matter—-come from the people behind it. My job isn't to tell you which laws are likely to be put into practice and when. Or the implications of those laws on China's Internet development. No one can say how that will all unfold. The best thing I can do is to convey an understanding of how the people building the Internet in China see its development—and their lives—-unfolding. What kind of people are they? What are their strengths and weaknesses? Why? Because that will determine the character of the Internet in China and its strengths and weaknesses.

The global community became aware of the Internet in China on July 13 1999. That was the day that **China.com**[1] made its debut on the Nasdaq. The initial public offering valued the stock at US$20. At the close of trading, the share price had risen to a phenomenal US$67 7/64. China.com raised US$86 million. There were many spectacular IPOs on the Internet at this time; this one, however, was the first such venture based on the launch of a Chinese-language portal focused on a potential audience of 1.3 billion people.

Everybody wanted to know who these people were and what they were going to do with all the money they'd just raised on the stock market. Their Web site certainly wasn't much to look at. At least not in July 1999. So, what's the story?

Did these guys even have a plan?

I met with Peter Yip, CEO of chinadotcom (as the company

NOTE

Netease, launched in June 1997, has achieved a number of firsts in services to its Chinese audience:

First

- free Web-based e-mail

- free personal Web site hosting

- free e-mail greeting cards

- personalized information services

- online auction

- major portal to be hosted on CERNET.

1. *China.com became chinadotcom. Cute,eh?*

www.corp.china.com

is now known) near the end of my Internet tour of China. I'd seen what was happening in Beijing, Shanghai and Guangzhou. I'd asked everyone what they thought of chinadotcom. What was it, who were they and what were they going to do? Nobody seemed to know. I'd even talked to someone on the inside, a friend who'd been hired to head one of chinadotcom's new businesses. He didn't know what was going on either. All he knew was that things were changing every day and that it was both the most exciting and most terrifying experience of his career. Was all this the normal chaos of a start-up, or something else? Did these guys even have a plan?

It took some time to arrange, but Peter Yip finally agreed to meet me at 11am February 23 at chinadotcom's office in Causeway Bay, Hong Kong. I'd been asked to send ahead a list of questions. Most of the time, this is a bad sign. It usually means a stiff interview with someone not altogether friendly or forthcoming. I'd sent along a list of the types of questions I wanted to ask. Nothing too pointed, nothing aggressive. All I really wanted to know was how this thing called chinadotcom came to be. I also wanted to know what they were going to do with the US$86 million they'd raised on the Nasdaq, and the US$395.25 million they'd raised through a second public offering in January 2000.

I was shown into an empty office and asked what I'd like to drink. Someone had just vacated this office, or was about to take up residence – perhaps both. Come to think of it, the whole atmosphere suggested process, movement and change. Nothing permanent.

Peter Yip entered the room alone, carrying a coffee and a few loose pages – probably my questions. He's a tall man. It's hard to tell exactly how old he is. Physically, he could be

www.hongkong.com

A visionary who sets the course

profile

chinadotcom corporation has over 1,900 employees in China and in the Pacific Rim. It has total of 24 offices in such key Asian markets as Australia, Hong Kong, Japan, Korea, Malaysia, Singapore and Taiwan. In PR China, it has twelve offices with another 550 employees.

The major corporate shareholders are America Online Inc., Mitsui & Co., Nortel Network, Sun Microsystems, New World Infrastructure and 24/7 Media Inc.

in his late thirties, but his eyes suggest he's seen more of life than that. He moves slowly and deliberately, his attention focused on the floor in front of him. There's a kind of professorial air about him, as if he's preoccupied by something. I didn't feel that he was aloof or arrogant. I was intrigued. This was no fast-talking hustler—or any kind of traditional salesman. A different kind of businessman.

He listened carefully when I explained the purpose of this book. I ended my introduction by asking how it all began. He paused for a moment. I felt he was giving serious consideration to my question. He ignored the papers he'd put on the desk in front of him and started to talk.

chinadotcom has gone through a number of incarnations over the years. Yip claims that the push toward the Internet was instigated by Xinhua News Agency, China's official media. Apparently, Xinhua approached Yip almost six years ago and began encouraging him to develop a China-focused Web portal. At the time – and until fairly recently – chinadotcom was primarily involved in web design and construction services.

This seems to be the way many Internet businesses begin. They start by offering Web design, construction, strategy and management services to businesses wanting to build a Web page or develop an Internet strategy. And then an opportunity comes along, the vision of the management expands, or someone buys them out and they move from designing Web pages to being a Web business. Zhaopin was built on recruitment; chinadotcom on Web services—both began with traditional cash flows based on services rendered.

The future in four books

I was intrigued by the mainland connection and the time frame. Yip said that Xinhua had approached him five or six

We represent a new breed of management; a team that combines transparency, passion and professionalism.

—*Peter Yip, CEO*

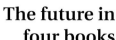
www.cww.com

years ago. In 1994 or 1995, there was very little happening on the ground in China. Plans were being made, but plans for infrastructure, not product. Foundation, not face.

Yip sent an assistant to find some early documentation. She returned with four books—each commemorating a conference for something called the China Wide Web. As Yip leafed through them he pointed to all the people who had dropped away over the years—all of whom now regretted leaving.

The first book announced the inauguration of the China Wide Web (CWW). The conference was held in Beijing in October 1996. It wasn't that surprising that I hadn't heard about it. In October 1996, most people were only concerned with the looming hand-over of Hong Kong. In Hong Kong itself at that time, all attention was on the November vote for Hong Kong's first Chief Executive. The Internet wasn't even on the horizon.

As the years passed, the style of the books changed. The first one began with an introduction by the President of the Xinhua News Agency, Guo Zhaoren. A number of pages followed carrying written calligraphic messages from high-ranking government officials. The calligraphy is quite beautiful and is displayed on the pages as if it were a photograph or an illustration, not a text. English translations accompanied each message. The tone and content of each message was much the same. Everyone wished the CIC well with the launch of the China Wide Web.

Endorsement from on high

The endorsements came from some very high-ranking officials including Guo Dongbo, Chairman, China Council for the Promotion of International Trade, Wen Shizhen, the Governor of Liaoning Province and Gao Xinmin, the President of the State Information Center. Gao Xinmin's

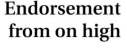
www.taiwan.com

NOTE

E-Commerce Spending
Estimates PR China

2003	US$ 6.5 billion
2002	US$ 2.4 billion
2001	US$ 820 million
2000	US$ 221 million

Source: IDC

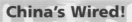

message was the simplest and most direct: Information facilitates modernization. Letters of support followed from people as diverse as Michael Bloomberg and former United States Secretary of State William Rogers. All big hitters with serious business interests behind them. There were also advertisement/endorsements from companies such as Sun Microsystems, Bay Networks, Bloomberg Financial Markets, Commodities News and Reuters.

What exactly were they trying to launch in 1996 and who was behind it? The China Internet Corporation was launching the China Wide Web. The Chairman and Chief Executive Officer of the China Internet Corporation is listed as Ma Yunsheng. Ma's biography states that he has been an official with Xinhua since 1975 and has launched a number of commercial enterprises owned by Xinhua, including Fortune China Development Limited and Fortune China Public Relations Limited. In the West, a news agency gathers news. In China, organs of the State such as Xinhua News or the People's Liberation Army were among the first to begin to develop commercial enterprises outside their specific field of expertise. Why? Because they could. They saw the opportunity and they had the resources.

Peter Yip is found on the second-to-last page of the first book and is listed as Executive Vice Chairman. His biography also mentions his MBA from Wharton School of Business. He also has a BA and an MA in Computer Science from the University of Pennsylvania. Impressive credentials.

Innovative leadership

In 1996, the China Internet Corporation under Ma and Peter Yip launched the China Wide Web. It is described in that year's volume as China's first nation-wide Intranet. The CIC is building the CWW to carry business information, Web Sites and electronic mail in both Chinese and English. They also propose offering a variety of other services to

NOTE

Liaoning Province covers 147,500 sq.km. with a population of 40 million. The capital of the province is Shenyang. The provincial GDP is US$38.1 billion.

Upstreaming

When our clients moved into China and began investing overseas, we were forced to follow...If you let a competitor service your clients overseas you risk losing that client to upstreaming...your competitor attaches themselves to the client in the field and then moves upstream, gaining more and more of the client's business. Eventually, if you're not careful, you end up losing the client at home.

—M.K.Tan, Partner Deloitte Touche, Hong Kong.

Source: China Business Monthly

their clients/subscribers including the annual conference, an annual directory and a magazine. Their market includes foreign businesses on the ground in China. Their goal is to be China's World Wide Web.

The most impressive and portentous achievement was probably getting then Vice-Premier Zhu Rongji to give a speech to the delegates at their first conference in 1996. I also noticed that one of the co-organizers of the meeting was the State Information Centre. The State Information Centre, the State Statistical Bureau and the People's Bank of China are the three principal parties to the Golden Sea Project, the network connecting all of China's top leadership. Well, you couldn't ask for a stronger endorsement than that, could you? Of course, just because the State seems to be endorsing something doesn't guarantee its success. Or else no one would have dropped out over the years, would they? And, as Yip pointed out, many had.

They just kept at it

www.cwrank.com

So what happened? Well, the CWW still exists and was in fact listed in April 2000 as the sixth most popular Web site in China by www.cwrank.com. But what really happened is that they just kept at it.

The second conference was held in Beijing in December of 1997. This is covered in the most substantial of the books, which includes endorsements from almost every entity anywhere that has any interest in the Internet, including AOL, Yahoo and Cisco Systems. The core players are the same but a new principal player is emerging. Raymond Chi'en, who is presently chairman of chinadotcom, is listed as one of the guest speakers at the conference. The title of his speech is, "The Importance of Information Infrastructure Development in Greater China." Chi'en is also listed as the chairman of a company called the China Information Technology Infrastructure (CITI). CITI is the

NOTE

Brander's beware!

The Chinese government has demanded that a cookie manufacturer change the name of its famous three-part cookie from " Xiao Lao Po Bing" to some other name. The cookie's current brand name is well known as "Concubine's Cakes."

result of an association between the China Internet Corporation and New World Infrastructure, one of the leading infrastructure investment companies listed on the Hong Kong Stock Exchange. Building bridges, or catch as catch can?

By the time the third conference rolled around in November 1998, it had become the China.com/CIC conference. The look and feel of the accompanying book changes. The tone of the text changes from a cautious and lofty regard for what the Internet might mean to China to being direct, confident and businesslike. China Telecom is now listed as a key organizer along with the CIC and Xinhua News. The opening address to the conference was given by Zhang Guoliang, Chairman, China Internet Corporation and Peter Yip, Vice Chairman. There is a page devoted to each of the new portals the China Internet Corporation has launched: China.com, Hongkong.com and Taiwan.com. The China Wide Web also has a page, but cww.com just doesn't carry the impact or have the resonance of a china.com. The conference was jammed with all kinds of events and seminars and included speeches from people from Cisco, Dell and China Telecom. William Ding, the founder and CEO of Netease Systems and netease.com was also giving a speech. The title? "How to Build a Successful Chinese Web Site."

The book mentions that China.com has entered into a strategic arrangement with AOL to act as AOL's exclusive partner in Hong Kong. It also quotes a study by the **International Data Group(IDG)**[1] that predicts that there will be 9.4 million Internet users in China by 2002. And it claims that the China Wide Web is now available in over 200 cities throughout China. Zhu Rongji, Xinhua News and the State Information Center may have started the ball rolling

1 IDG China has been working with the Ministry of Electronic Industry, Ministry of Information Industry and the State Science and Technology Commission since 1980.

IDG has more than one million paid subscribers each month through its18 joint-venture publications.

It has over 400 local reporters and editors in China with two product test labs in Shenzhen and Beijing.

www.idgchina.com

two years earlier but by 1998, the third conference is all corporate, or at least dominated by corporate agendas.

The final book, of the fourth conference, held in Beijing in November 1999, is all business. Or at least it feels as if it's all just about building a commercially viable Internet for China. The book looks and feels better organized. It's also apparent that this has become a chindotcom conference. Peter Yip appears at the front of the book. He offers an enthusiastic welcome to all the co-organizers, co-sponsors, speakers and attendees. His title is listed under his photograph, CEO of chinadotcom corporation. And he's wearing a smile that must be in part inspired by a very successful run up the Nasdaq.

www.zhaodaola.com

What is remarkable about this whole story is that Peter Yip has been part of it from its very beginning five or six years ago. That's a century in cyber-time. Yip says the company actually began in 1994, even before Netscape was a publicly listed company.

Xinhua News started the company and approached Yip to help them develop strategy, recruit partners like AOL and help convince other ministries in the Chinese government that the Internet was here to stay. It took two long years to gather sufficient support within the various ministries to finally get the approval to form the company. Finally, in 1996, with the direct support of then Vice-Premier Zhu Rongji, the central government gave permission to set up the China Internet Corporation.

The long road to Nasdaq

It took another four years to get the company listed on the Nasdaq. A long, frustrating journey. And one marked at every turn by expressions of skepticism. Yip tells me that those four years were incredibly difficult and impossible to compare with today. They had no money at all and worked out of a tiny office.

The first step in the corporate strategy was to convince the central government. Once that goal had been achieved Yip began focusing his energies on Merrill Lynch. They wouldn't be able to do anything without some serious money. They needed a company like Merrill Lynch to help them find it.

www.nasdaq.com

Initial financing for the company had come from Yip's friends, people who had invested in him in the past and done well. One of the first investors in the company—contributing to the seed money—was Dr. Raymond Chi'en, chinadotcom's current chairman. Seed money of approximately US$1million was enough to get them going. Yip wanted Merrill Lynch to help him raise US$20million.

Yip says that chinadotcom's successful IPO came in part because of the support of the people and organizations he'd been working with or talking to for the past three or four years. chinadotcom was not an overnight hit or some fluke. Everybody knew what Peter Yip was up to—if he hadn't asked them for money he'd asked them who he should talk to about finding some money.

He says that though there is a lot of excitement about China and the Internet now, most of the time he was met with skepticism. One of the reasons he thinks Wall Street took to chinadotcom is because it has the backing of the central government. Yip says a lot of people try to work without the government's support. The government is slow and bureaucratic—it's easier to just set up operations and hope for the best. But this only works for so long. Eventually,

FIGURE 5.3

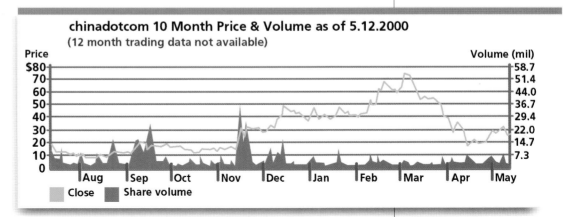

chinadotcom 10 Month Price & Volume as of 5.12.2000
(12 month trading data not available)

all those working without proper authority will be found out and closed down.

Yip went on to discuss the nature of the Chinese government, how it is reactive rather than proactive and how it is especially concerned about the cultural ramifications of a new technology like the Internet. It doesn't help that the Internet was in part developed by the United States Department of Defense. But is dealing with China's government any more

www.cgc21.com

or less difficult than dealing with any government anywhere? There are different obstacles, but the same smothering bureaucracy everywhere.

Yip began this journey before most of the China-based Web sites existed. He says he couldn't have done any of it without the support of Xinhua News Agency. Yip was born in Hong Kong and is not a member of the Communist Party. He says what China needs now are more people like Charles Zhang, the creator of Sohu.com, chinadotcom's competition. It's still a very small circle of players so everybody knows everybody else. Yip remembers meeting with Zhang a number of times over the years when neither had any money.

Yip believes that the Internet is forcing China to change its point of view toward the media, communications and business. The government now accepts that the Internet is here to stay and that it's a critical tool in China's economic advancement. But what does the government do when old rules about media, content and communication threaten to stifle the growth of this new, much-needed technology? Yip believes the government will change the rules as it goes— slowly, but inevitably. He believes that China's accession to the World Trade Organization (WTO) will lead to a release of new and thorough rules and regulations on the Internet. Yip thinks most people will be surprised by how progressive those new rules will be.

The Internet is an enabler

Reform isn't just about closing down inefficient state enterprises. It's also about new ways of inspiring initiative and rewarding talented people. In this way, the Internet is an enabler for China. It allows individuals to have big dreams. Ten years ago Yip gave a speech at Beijing University. At the end of his address, he asked the students what they wanted to do with their lives. The most ambitious wanted to be government ministers. Those who

NOTE

Netease.com Inc., the third portal attempting to list on Nasdaq, has had to postpone its US$120 million Nasdaq listing.

It is believed that regulatory issues surrounding the current and future rules on overseas investments in Web firms is at the centre of the delay.

www.wavdev.com

wanted to be rich wanted to be developers. But the new era isn't about infrastructure development. It's about ideas and innovation. It's about adding value to services—all the things the Internet brings. Most importantly, Yip says that the Internet allows a level playing field. It allows anyone with a good idea to enter the game. Yip is no longer explaining chinadotcom's strategy or evolution, he's selling the Internet. Perhaps that was his strategy all along?

China's weakness

Yip says that China has many brilliant entrepreneurs. They do not lack in spirit, ideas or discipline. Their great weakness is their inability to bring together a management team capable of executing their visions. Yip knows most of the top Internet players in China and has from time to time advised them. He says that there is a great reluctance on the part of these entrepreneurs to cede control to a proper management team. They don't understand why they should cede control, and what the benefits could be. Yip says that this is extremely dangerous as Wall Street will not forgive you if you miss your quota.

In hindsight, Yip is grateful that it took them four years to launch the IPO. Certainly, it separated the believers from the uncommitted. It also helped him understand the qualities needed to succeed in this new economy. Yip says the most important quality needed is the ability to accept change. Yip says they changed their business plan at least ten times. If something didn't work, they'd modify the strategy or tear it all up and start again. This kind of atmosphere of uncertainty can be extremely frustrating for some people—but it's fundamental to a new economy being shaped by evolving technologies.

www.feer.com

Yip notes they were always aiming for a Nasdaq listing. They could have listed in Shanghai, or in Hong Kong. They also could have bought a shell company and gained a back-

NOTE

China is ahead of the United States in wireless applications used by their consumers. More people will be gaining access to the Internet via wireless technology, such as cell phones, pagers etc.

WaveDev is one of the first to offer personal wireless Internet access and wireless Web site enablement.

door listing, as many have. But they wanted to do it on Nasdaq and they wanted to do it right. When I press Yip, he says he believes that that was what China wanted. China wanted the legitimacy a Nasdaq listing would bring.

Traditionally, Chinese stocks have not done well on Wall Street. China Telecom may be an exception but China stocks are received with tremendous skepticism. Added to the difficulty was the fact that chinadotcom was also a technology stock and an Internet play. More and more, the July 13 launch seems almost a miracle.

Show us the money

The skepticism has not subsided since July 13. If anything it has increased. Now the question is, "What are you going to do with all that money, Peter Yip, and when will I see some profit?" Yip laughs and says that's why the whole process is so much fun. Clearly, a different kind of businessman.

He explains that this is not the first company he's built. He's done it before and succeeded. He does say that this will probably be the last company he builds. Not for any other reason than the time and commitment it requires. He says it's not about the money. For Yip, building chinadotcom has been an enriching and hugely satisfying experience. He hopes he'll be able to look back ten years from now and see that they played a fundamental role in the development of the Internet in China and South East Asia. He sees chinadotcom as a pioneer, making the path easier for those that follow.

We start talking about the kind of real revenues chinadotcom is producing today—the real business. Yip says that chinadotcom had US$10.8million in revenue in the last quarter of 1999—up 100% from the quarter before.

He predicts they will reach US$100million in annual revenue in the next twelve to eighteen months. I ask if this is through acquisitions. Yip is quick to shoot that one down. He says

NOTE

China has set up a bureau to regulate Web content, enforce copyright standards and attempt to control sensational content which is deemed to be "harmful."

Sina.com, Sohu.com and Netease.com have already been barred from showing any foreign content on their sites.

revenue growth is a result of their own organic growth. The nurturing of the past four years is beginning to bear fruit.

But chinadotcom had a net loss in 1999 of US$18.7million, up 100%from the year before. When will they be profitable? Yip says he wants to see chinadotcom profitable by 2001. He believes that once they reach US$100million in revenues they can begin increasing their margins and operating efficiency. A man very much grounded in traditional business fundamentals, he says chinadotcom is not concerned at this time with the number of page views. They don't produce revenue. chinadotcom's core revenue business is Web Connections, a high-end Web consulting and design business. Twelve months ago they had about 120 employees. Today, they have a staff of 1,900 and offices in Hong Kong, Korea, Taiwan, Singapore and Australia.

At the end of our meeting, Yip comes back to a discussion of the quality of the people on his team. He says it is by far the most important factor for success. And it's increasingly difficult to keep those people. Yip says his top twenty people each get at least two calls a day from competitors or head-hunters offering them jobs. He says they stay with chinadotcom because they are treated well and rewarded generously. Yip is being modest. They also stay because of Peter Yip. They believe in his vision and admire his tenacity.

Yip told me that his investors stuck with him because he'd made them money before. People had faith in him and I understood why. Perhaps that's what it's all about, faith. If you believe strongly enough it will happen. Well, Yip did, and it has—as far as it goes. On July 13 1999, investors around the world said we believe in Peter Yip and his firm. The real trick, and the guts of the story to come, is how Yip and his team hope to turn faith and promise into a business with cash flow and profits.

History is the version of past events that people have decided to agree upon.

—*Napoleon Bonaparte*

Your notes

 go to...

For additional information and updates to charts and graphs,
visit: **www.flyingarmchair.com**
the China's Wired! *resource site.*

Business to
Business
B2B

Business to Business
B2B

From soup to nuts on the Web

NOTE

"Thousands of Dragons Ploughing and Weeding."

This is the corporate slogan for the Kelon Corporation. It defines their corporate culture by expressing "the thousands of Dragons" as the strength of their 12,000 employees. The "ploughing and weeding" expresses the meaning of cultivating within each employee the seed of the enterprise and that all staff are involved in this endeavour.

Business to Business
B2B

Always be the best

www.kelon.com

The day I began writing this chapter the Internet version of the South China Morning Post ran an article about Guangdong Kelon, the largest refrigerator manufacturer in the P.R.C. Kelon announced that it would be launching an e-commerce platform shortly. A spokesman for the company was quoted as saying that they hoped going online would cut inventory levels and increase the amount of component parts the company bought from outside suppliers instead of making themselves. The company also believes their online strategy will make after-sales service quicker and cheaper. So far, so good.

The company's strategy is to put all of its suppliers and distributors online. They would then post the company's needs for parts or components and invite bids. The spokesman admits that few of their suppliers and distributors are presently on the Internet. Kelon's Internet strategy will only work if its suppliers and distributors get wired. So who's going to pay for all that?

It's about the supply chain

www.dell.com

There's no lack of enthusiasm in China for the Internet, just the means to make it happen.

B2B is about the supply chain. It exists in the transactions between the supplier and the manufacturer, the manufacturer and the wholesaler, and the wholesaler and the retailer. B2B cuts transaction costs and increases efficiency. But B2B does more than affect the supply chain, it also changes the role of the consumer.

In the old days, a manufacturer would decide how much product to make based on past sales, projected sales and general market conditions. The manufacturer would make an educated guess. Based on that guess, production lines would be set up, staff hired and raw materials ordered. The manufacturer was at the centre of the process—pulling resources in to make a product they would then push out at the consumer. B2B changes that dynamic dramatically.

The more B2B e-commerce in the supply chain, the more crucial the role of the consumer is. Dell Computers is a good illustration of this role modification. Dell doesn't build a computer until a customer orders it. When it's ordered, it's built and shipped within 48 hours. Dell keeps a minimum amount of inventory on hand. If they don't need it they don't order it. The consumer drives the supply chain. The supply chain is no longer a chain, it's a circle. The consumer is both the starting point on that circle, and the end point.

In February, GM, Ford and DaimlerChrysler announced a joint venture to establish one enormous B2B Internet exchange. The auto makers hope to move 60,000 suppliers and US$250billion onto the Net. In the neutral atmosphere of cyber space, suppliers will be forced to compete exclusively on price, quality and delivery. In time,

NOTE

Dell's China pricing for desktops starts at RMB9,388 or about US$1,154. Notebooks on sale start from RMB29,818 or US$3,664. This represents a substantial amount compared to the salary structure of RMB300 per month or US$36 per month.

Build your car on the Net

consumers may order their cars based on the options available on one huge database. What kind of wheels from this menu of thousands would you like? What kind of suspension? Two door or four? How about a Cadillac front end and a Beetle out back? Whatever you want. The consumer builds what he or she wants in virtual reality. The manufacturer assembles real parts and delivers.

There is probably more potential in China to reap immediate financial rewards from B2B activity than any other e-commerce model. Guangdong Kelon knows that. If they're smart they'll cover the cost of getting their suppliers online. They'll easily recoup the expense from the savings realized by holding lower inventories.

Alibaba.com [1] is probably the best known of China's B2B sites. Alibaba.com claims to be the first global Internet brand to emerge from the P.R.C. It's certainly moved far and fast since beginning operations in March 1999. Presently, Alibaba.com has 180,000 commercial users. The company claims 1,000 new members join every day. In addition to being a huge trading platform for at least 27 specific industry groups, Alibaba offers free e-mail, commercial news and information exchanges. How does it work? Manufacturers or suppliers post a description of goods available and a desired price. Purchasers place orders. Alibaba takes a commission. It's an extremely simple and elegant use of the Internet. All Alibaba needs is a deep, well-organized data base. It's also the kind of business model where first-to-market wins all. In the beginning, anyway. It's hard to tell what may happen when Tom.com makes its move.

In January 2000, Softbank invested US$20million in Alibaba.com. Other investors include Goldman Sachs, Fidelity Capital and Investor AB of Sweden. Alibaba's head

www.alibaba.com

NOTE

Cyber space was first used in the 1984 science fiction novel by William Gibson. The novel titled *Neuromancer* speaks to the global information network called the Matrix.

Cyber space is a world wide network of computer networks, or a state of mind, or metaphoric location in the mind.

[1] *John Wu has joined Alibaba.com as its Chief Technology Office(CTO). Wu was previously with Yahoo where he developed their directory search engine technology. Wu holds the patent for this technology.*

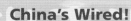

office is in Hong Kong; it also has offices in Beijing, Shanghai, Hangzhou, Seoul, California and London.

Is Alibaba.com Chinese? If it is, why isn't it Alibaba.com.cn? Presently, it has sites in English, simplified Chinese, complex Chinese and German. It seems more an international amalgam than anything that might have grown out of China's unique business environment.

Alibaba.com was founded by Jack Ma Yun, a 35-year-old English lecturer from Hangzhou. Ma's Web career began at a Web hosting company called Chinapages.com. Three years ago, the Ministry of Foreign Trade and Economic Cooperation asked Ma to become the head of the China International Electronic Commerce Center. Presently, Ma serves as Alibaba's chairman and CEO. Apparently, Alibaba was launched with official approval.

www.meetchina.com

Alibaba means business, any size Business.

There are similarities between the emergence of Alibaba.com and chinadotcom. Both appear to be very international. But there's a broad mix of forces at work. The face and the business model seem foreign, but the State is the instigator.

FIGURE 6.1

Alibaba is a success because it's serving a need. But how is B2B e-commerce affecting small to medium companies on the ground in China? What is its level of penetration into the supply chain?

A friend of mine decided to start a food business in China

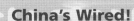

Alibaba has over 150,000 registered members in 188 countries. It has branches in Shanghai, Beijing, Hangzhou, Seoul, London and Silicon Valley.

in 1993. The economy was booming and more and more foreign businesses were entering the market. He left a very good job and a wonderful lifestyle in Hong Kong for five years of hell. Nothing worked the way it was supposed to. Reality made the worst-case scenarios in his business plan look like success. But he'd raised a lot of money from people who trusted him. He wasn't going to let them—or his staff—down. He stuck with it.

It was so tough that he moved his family back to the United States. Every five weeks he'd fly 24 hours to spend four days with them. Finally, five years later, it all worked out. The business survived and now prospers. His investors got their money out and a little profit. His family still loves him. It's a story with a happy ending. It's also a story about one of the most vital and sensitive supply chains in any economy— the production, distribution and sale of food.

This is how it started. My friend had heard that someone with a lot of money was going to build a big Disney World-type amusement park on the outskirts of Shanghai. Wouldn't every little emperor in Shanghai want to attend? At the time, almost every child in China was wearing something or other that was Disney-inspired. They were just nuts for American culture. People eat food at these parks—lots of food. And not just any food. It's got to be fresh and good and plentiful. At the time, no one in Shanghai could supply that kind of food to the numbers of people they were projecting. An opportunity. And since commerce—and nature—abhor a vacuum—my good friend stepped in.

The developer of the theme park had a big ego and deeper pockets. But he hadn't done his homework. There wasn't a mass transit service to bring the crowds from the city. And the cost of admission was going to be prohibitive. Not long

www.chinae.com

Focus on technology

after my friend set down his bags, his biggest client packed up and left. Well, that's China. So, what next?

Very soon—fear, adrenaline or both—delivered up another opportunity. There are many Fortune 500 businesses operating in Shanghai. There are hundreds of factories housing tens of thousands of employees. They need to eat, don't they? Maybe he could sell his services to them?

It wasn't such a hard sell. Most of the factories had between 100 and 300 employees. The companies that let employees bring their own meals were having problems with sanitation. The companies that tried to supply meals weren't doing a very good job. It looked as if my friend was in the right place at the right time.

I visited his factory in Shanghai shortly after they became fully operational. They'd turned the corner. They had clients and cash flow. They'd also started to spin off the businesses they'd had to build to supply the products they needed. They'd been in the same position as Guangdong Kelon—they had to build their supply chain, or parts of it.

Thought for food

The company, Asia Foods, was preparing thousands of meals a day. That meant tons of produce—some requiring more processing than others. They had started a processing plant to produce the tons of cole slaw they served every day. Soon, the plant was supplying Shanghai's Kentucky Fried Chicken outlets. They built a meat-processing plant to handle all the fresh chicken they bought. That company also became a supplier to other food companies. In China, if you can't find it, you build it.

On the way to his factory on the Hu Qing Ping Road he told me all about his latest scheme. It woke him at four a.m. He'd done the math and figured it would bring US$20million annually to the company's bottom line. He

Menu
星期二
上海熏鱼
或
宫保鸡丁
辣白菜
时蔬
番茄蛋汤
水果

Tuesday
Smoked Fish of Shanghai Style
Or
Gongbao Chicken
Cabbage
Seasonal Vegetables
Tomato & Egg Soup
Fruits

Sample of daily menu offered by Asia Foods

NOTE

736 million KFC chickens are consumed annually world wide. The chain served 1.914 billion pounds of chicken in 1998.

Laid head to claw, KFC chickens would chicken-out at 209,000 miles long. This means that they could circle Earth 8.5 times, like the rings of Jupiter, except that Earth would have chicken rings.

The second job is the first priority

was going to offer box lunches of roast chicken to Shanghai's hungry workers. Fresh cooked and taxi-delivered. He said there was first-class production in China and an extremely sophisticated consumer, but no easy way to bring the two together. But he figured he'd solved the distribution problem. There are over 33,000 taxis in Shanghai and most of them are going broke. He was going to give them RMB1,000 (US$120) a month for three hours of their time each day. He was going to have them park in his factory's parking lot between 11 a.m. and 2 p.m. As the lunch orders came in, the food would be passed to the taxis to be delivered.

He was convinced he had it right. Why? Because he was hiring the drivers for their second job. He'd learned that you always get the best effort out of someone if you were their second job. Apparently, many employees take their first jobs for granted. They show up and do the time but remain indifferent. The second job is the money that makes a difference in their lives and the job they work hard to keep.

Taxis that chicken out

I toured the factory and met most of his key people. Everyone had his own supply-chain nightmare to tell. The plant manager took me to the cooler to show me how the lettuce was shipped. Several dozen heads of lettuce are wrapped in newspapers and packed into a cardboard box. To keep the produce cool, old style Coca-Cola bottles are filled with water and frozen and packed amongst the lettuce.

Traditional market stall selling fresh produce in Beijing.

I was told that the produce would sometimes arrive on the back of some sputtering, heaving machine that seemed about to expire. There was no real difficulty in actually getting someone to pick something up from Shanghai and deliver it to Beijing—that wasn't the problem. The weak link in the supply chain was the hand-off. The plant manager told me that they'd have no problems if they could use the kind of hand-held scanners courier companies used in the West. He said that the guy driving the truck could always get it there but never knew what he was supposed to sign or leave behind.

Tasty and enjoyable

That was the first time B2B e-commerce was mentioned in relation to his business in Shanghai. This was the late summer of 1998—early days yet. A few months later, my friend contacted me about an idea he had for a market research company. He'd found a behaviour-scaling software system he thought might work well in China. One of the problems with market research in China is that the Chinese actually have a greater than normal interest in trying something new. This can be misleading for companies introducing new products to the market. They may experience tremendous initial sales that then seem to evaporate for no apparent reason.

www.
thecocacolacompany.com

www.handheld.com

Soon, my friend began introducing B2B e-commerce systems to his company. The first thing he did was put all his order processing online. Every day his clients would fax in their food orders. He had over thirty major clients. Every day the pile of faxes would be added to the pile from the day before. At the end of the week, someone would spend half a day reconciling the accounts. He had them put it online. Now they e-mail their orders. Reconciliations are completed in seconds. That's B2B.

But the real B2B story here isn't about my friend's factory in Shanghai. It's about one of his employees. Someone he hired in Hong Kong and who was with him from the beginning. Someone who took all that he saw and learned

NOTE

"Tasty and enjoyable"

Chinese equivalents for western names can either be transliterations (i.e. phonetic equivalents) or translations (i.e. meaning equivalents). Think of the good marketing fortune when both work. "Coca-Cola is translated as "tasty and enjoyable. "

It certainly bodes better than a soda called Libido, or maybe not.

from that first experience and bundled it into an on-the-ground B2B start-up. This new company, China Supply Chain, might just change the way the food business operates in China. If it does, it'll change everything before anyone knows it's happened. Why? Because it's deep in the supply chain, where consumers rarely tread.

I'd made arrangements to meet with Steven Yaung in a bar/coffee shop called On the 97, on the edge of Fuxing park in the old French Concession of Shanghai. It took me a while to find it. The door I opened had no clear markings. It was dark, and jazz was being played on a very good sound system. There were a few people seated at scattered tables. It almost seemed closed, or about to close. Steven was the only person facing the front door. He looked as if he was waiting for someone.

No more coleslaw for Steven

I started by asking Steven to bring me up to date on Asia Foods. First, he wanted to make it very clear that his new venture, China Supply Chain, was a completely new and separate company from Asia Foods. Then he told me that Asia Foods had been broken into three separate entities. Those entities were in the process of being sold off. The contract catering business was being sold to Compass, the world's largest contract catering company. Sara Lee was purchasing the Beijing factory, and negotiations were under way to sell off the cole slaw and salad business.

Steven had been recruited in Hong Kong and had been with Asia Foods from the very beginning. In the early days he'd worked at the factory. Eventually, he was involved in sales and marketing. One of Asia Food's biggest clients in Shanghai is Kentucky Fried Chicken. KFC has 55 outlets in Shanghai and is much more popular there than McDonalds. Asia Foods also supplies the local Pizza Huts.

NOTE

Shanghai means "go up the sea" or "leave for the sea" and is called "the dragon head" of East China.

It is on the same latitude as Cairo and Jacksonville, Florida.

• Shanghai dishes are noted for their use of strong flavoured sauces. All food items tend to be cooked in deep fat and soya sauce.

• Shanghai specialities:

Songjiang Perch,

Longhua Honey Peach,

Chongming Crab and Dianshan Lake Crab,

Sheshan Orchid Bamboo Shoots,

The Fermented Bean curd for the Capital.

Just the fax, ma'am

Steven tells me that even KFC is stuck in the past when it comes to order processing. Store managers at each KFC write out their daily orders on a piece of paper that is then faxed to the KFC head office. There are people at the head office whose full-time job is to take those faxes and copy the instructions onto other pieces of paper that are then faxed to the appropriate suppliers.

The store managers are working day to day. They have no way of knowing how this month's quantities compare to last month's orders. There's no central system enabling them to do any kind of ongoing reconciliation or analysis. Steven said it wasn't unusual for the store managers to call him to ask how much lettuce they'd purchased from Asia Foods over the past month, the past six months, even the past year. Steven said that the whole supply chain was inefficient and expensive.

www.china-window.com

The food industry throughout China is still extremely unsophisticated, even archaic. I told Steven how surprised I was to see a shipment of soya sauce at their factory that had been delivered in clay pots sealed with mud and straw stoppers.

Steven had been with Asia Foods for three years. One way or another he was going to be leaving as soon as he became vested in June 1999. The one thing he was not going to do was sell any more cole slaw or lettuce. They had been tough years for Steven and everyone else at Asia Foods. They'd come as close as any company can to bankruptcy—a number of times. There was even a ten-month stretch where they all worked without salaries. All through it Steven's boss—and mentor—had taught him to look at Asia Foods as the mother ship. The mother ship got them here, the mother ship might not survive, but take the opportunities and experience the mother ship has provided

Suppliers deliver soya sauce in traditional clay pots

No salaries for ten months

and put them to work somewhere else. He was always told to think of Asia Foods as a starting point, not an end.

Steven's boss also told him to find the crossroads. Find the intersection of two major forces—that's where opportunity waits. China and the Internet are Steven's crossroads. He thinks he's there at the right time with the right tools.

Steven started formulating his ideas for China Supply Chain in March and April of 1999. But very few people were talking about B2B back then, not even contacts in the United States. And fewer software companies were working on B2B applications. Steven spent five months travelling around the United States, visiting dozens of different software companies and B2B **verticals.**[1] He visited with I Two, Logistics, Commerce One—all the big players working on B2B vertical supply chain applications. Essentially, he picked up the phone and introduced himself as someone who'd been running factories in China. He'd tell them he'd had a lot of China business experience and was looking for Web-based supply chain solutions for the China market. He said his first call was usually to the Chief Operating Officer and that most of the time he ended up speaking to the top people in the company. He said there's something magical about China that appeals to almost every entrepreneur. It's the size, the market, the challenge—something—but they were all interested.

He found out very quickly that B2B was still in its infancy in

1 A vertical is a vertically-integrated entity, specializing in one field. General Motors, for example.

Asia Foods kitchen and preparation area.

www.chinasources.com

the United States. Everybody was still just trying to figure out the U.S. market. There was certainly no such thing as an international strategy or approach. He narrowed his search down to what he considered to be the two biggest players, Commerce One and Tradex.

I asked Steven how he found Commerce One and Tradex. Who or what recommended them? E-commerce is still not yet institutionalized. Steven said most of it came from reading magazines like Red Herring or Business 2.0, or surfing the Net, or sometimes just happening to come across something in the newspaper. He says he still spends a couple of hours on the Internet each night—usually after 10p.m., when it's a bit faster. When I mention the slow speeds he tells me that there is actually a rumour afoot that China Telecom has a lot more capacity than they admit to but that they're holding it back until the government sorts out more of its Internet rules and regulations. Everybody's got a theory—or heard a rumour—about the Internet in China.

www.commerceone.com

Old Hongs meet the new Hongs

There were a number of reasons why they finally decided to go with Commerce One. Most importantly, it had existing software that was very close to what Steven was looking for. He says they could have designed and built their own software. But his experience in China taught him not to try and re-invent the wheel every time. Take the path of least resistance—the business is hard enough as it is.

China Supply Chain agreed to pay US$2million for the world rights to the B2B software Commerce One developed. When they signed their contract in January, no software company in the world had yet developed a B2B platform in Chinese. China Supply Chain would be the first. Delivery was expected in early March.

Steven pulls out a pad of paper and starts mapping out the

NOTE

Global Trading Web, the world's largest B2B trading community, and Commerce One are creating a joint-venture with seven leading China businesses. The partners include Beijing Enterprises, i-CABLE Ventures, Jardine Internet, New World China Enterprises Projects, Sunevision, Swire Net Ventures and WI Harper Group. They are prepared to invest up to US$40 million to develop a B2B portal for exchanging goods and services among businesses world wide.

structure of China Supply Chain. Essentially, what he's building is a clearing house or trading platform for the food industry. It's an Alibaba-like concept but focused on a very narrow vertical chain. China Supply Chain is about order management within this structure. He agrees when I tell him it sounds as if he's playing the role of a go-between or an old fashioned **comprador**[2].

And of course, the concept for China Supply Chain sprang from the mother ship, Asia Foods. In the old days, when he was looking for meat suppliers in a telephone book, he'd find listings such as Number One Meat Factory, Number Two Meat Factory, Number Three Meat factory, etc. There was no way of knowing what kind of meat they were selling— let alone if it was for human consumption. This assumes you can find a telephone book. Until very recently, there were no Yellow Pages in Beijing or Shanghai. There are still no White Pages. If you don't know someone's number, you're out of luck.

China Supply Chain has three segments or levels of operation. The first is order management. This will appear on the Web site as a list of suppliers and buyers. Suppliers will detail their products, prices and quantities. Buyers will post their needs. Everything will be done electronically, eliminating all paperwork.

The second level of operation will be a news and information centre. In China today the food industry is incredibly fragmented and disorganized. If you want a commodity price, you have to go to the post office and look it up and call. There are few trade shows or professional organizations. Steven wants China Supply Chain to be the best source of information on the food industry in China. Of course, that sort of information will also draw buyers and sellers.

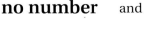
www.tradex.com 1

www.ariba.com

Sorry, no number

[1] *Ariba acquired (March 10 2000) TRADEX shortly after Arthur Andersen Partners (February 22 2000) made an equity investment in TRADEX.*

Ariba Inc. is a publicly-traded global leader in B2B e-commerce solutions.

[2] *Comprador has been defined as a native-born agent in China employed by foreign businesses to serve as an intermediary.*

The third part of the structure is what Steven calls a catalogue exchange or directory. Here he will list, categorize and qualify all the buyers and sellers. The directory will tell you how big the company is, how many employees it has, years in operation, products, clients, contact numbers, etc. I ask Steven how different this might be from something like Alibaba.com, or some of the other B2B platforms. He says that there are a number of similar Web-based businesses in China that follow this model but they're trying to cover all the industries—trying to be everything to everybody.

Steven believes that the key to success is the quality of the information they will offer. He says an e-business is only 20 per cent about the Internet, the rest is about all the basic business fundamentals that make or break any business anywhere: customer service, management, vision, finance etc. They also plan to support China Supply Chain's Web site with traditional media initiatives. He wants to have a strong presence in trade shows, magazines and newspapers. He wants China Supply Chain to become known as the very best source of information on food in China. He notes that Commerce One has designed their system so that other applications can be incorporated easily once the necessary volume is achieved.

The catalogues, directories and news will be made available for free. Revenue will come primarily from commissions on sales. Once they get enough traffic coming to the site, they'll start running auctions. With volume, advertising revenues will also become a significant revenue source. Additional revenues may also be realized from the sale of data generated off the site itself. Clearly, the business plan is evolving.

Everything to everybody

What Steven is trying to do is to create a community. He's trying to institutionalize the food industry. This is a huge

NOTE

Branding in China

A brand so popular that the government was forced to ban it!

Why?

A famous brand-name popsicle in Beijing is called:

Xiao mi bang da kuan

The literal translation is as follows:

xiao - little

mi - honey, same pronunciation with Chinese character - secretary

bang - help, assist

da - catch, get hold of

kuan - money, referring to a well-established man, who makes a fortune over-night, older, richer, married boss.

• Problems can arise if you don't check the meanings and translations. For example the following Chinese brand names:

Clean Finger Nail = hand-tissue

Swine = chocolate

Fduhy Sesane = snack food

task because it's never existed in China. If he succeeds, the rewards could be phenomenal. Steven says the initial incentive was to eliminate inefficiencies in the food supply chain. But China Supply Chain has become a lifestyle centre, a place where people in the food industry come to learn more about their own business. This seems to be the way with e-commerce. First, it provides a simple and highly economic solution—like a virtual farmer's market. Soon, the simple solution suggests other profitable options— virtual catalogues and industry guides. Before you know it, you've created a new world.

Now he's really excited. Now he's trying to sell me shares. He tells me Asia Foods used to get calls all the time from other food companies in China. They'd get a call from a company with five tons of frozen meat. They could have it for the cost of shipping. China Supply Chain could sell those opportunities. They might even eliminate the inefficiencies in the supply chain that led to five tons of unwanted meat.

When we met in February, Steven wanted to keep a low profile for China Supply Chain. He didn't want to be scooped by another player, or draw too many clients before they were ready to handle them. He already had a list of clients wanting to use the service—clients he'd developed a relationship with through Asia Foods. His biggest problem at the time was finding good staff.

Steven's experience at Asia Foods taught him a lot about the kind of people you need for a start-up. A start-up is unlike any other business venture. Nothing's fixed in stone. Change is the only constant. Steven says he looks for intuitive people who are strong lateral thinkers. They'll get lost if they can't keep the big picture in focus. He also looks for bright people, but says that emotional intelligence is

Before you know it, you've created a world

Tsingtao beer is the number one imported Chinese beer in the United States. It is also the number one consumer branded product exported by China.

more important. After all, the food industry is a service industry.

www.chinatradeworld.com

Steven had recently hired a former PricewaterhouseCoopers consultant to be on his team. He was particularly pleased with the guy because he'd already had seven years in China and was an e-business specialist. What more could you ask for? Steven then asked me if I could help him find someone to manage content on their site. He was asking me because I'm a writer and he needed a writer or an editor. Steven's smart enough to know that managing content is complicated and requires a specialist. As it turned out, I did know a writer in Shanghai and arranged for the two of them to meet.

The longer I stayed in China the more this sort of thing happened. For the first ten days I'd been asking all the questions; then more and more, my subjects were turning to me for information, advice or referrals. This is as much a product of the fast evolving e-commerce revolution the Internet brings as it is a product of China. The oldest Internet working hand-in-hand with the newest.

Nothing's fixed in stone

Finally, I asked Steven if China Supply Chain was going to be the name of the Web site. Would their address be in Chinese or English or both? He said they would probably be running both versions of Chinese and English. They had played around with a couple of names but were thinking of going with *gongxiaoshe*. This is the name of a firm that no longer exists. In the old days in China, you went to the *gongxiaoshe* to buy everything. It was a one-stop shop, that carried anything and everything—from cigarettes to salt, to food, to tractors. It was the only place to shop. Ironically, few people in China under the age of thirty will even know what it means. Deng Xiaoping's reforms made it obsolete. ▤

www.sh.com/dish

NOTE

China International Electronic Commerce, the electronic arm of the Chinese Ministry of Trade, has launched its own e-commerce initiative.
-- ChinaTradeWorld.com

BREAKING NEWS

As of June 2000, the company's name has been changed from China Supply Chain to Transfood.

Steven has a new investor behind him. Funding is now coming from an incubator headed by Moses Tang, former chairman of Goldman Sachs Asia.

Steven has a new technology partner: iAspec. iAspec has over 300 people in Hong Kong and Asia.

Your notes:

go to...

For additional information and updates to charts and graphs,
visit: **www.flyingarmchair.com**
the China s Wired! *resource site.*

Business to Consumer
B2C

Business to Consumer
B2C

Mother's milk

When Zhaopin began looking for money in early 1999, venture capital firms told the company to dump their traditional executive search business and go totally virtual. Smart money wanted virtual action—bricks and mortar need not apply. Six months later smart money had changed its tune—it wanted bricks and clicks.

Business to Consumer B2C

B2C topped the charts in December of 1999, when Amazon.com founder Jeff Bezos became *Time Magazine's* Man of the Year. And then came winter. And B2Cs began to falter. Observers began to ask if the model could ever turn a profit before running out of money. Attention began to shift to B2B. They pay their bills, don't they? And you don't have all that fussy hand-holding. And they're not fickle. Right? And then came April—the cruelest month—and everyone wanted out of everything, as world markets bounded up and down.

The last twelve months has seen a parade of evolving e-commerce business models hit the fashion runway. You don't like B2C, how about B2B? Doesn't fit? How about C2C—or E2B? Better yet, come up with one of your own design.

One thing is certain: the Internet and e-commerce are here to stay. The only thing that's likely to change are the names we use to describe it.

www.amazon.com

The B2C e-commerce business model has probably received the most attention, investment and scorn of all e-commerce forms. Initially, it's where everyone thought the big money would be made. It seemed so easy and cheap. You advertise goods on the Net, people place orders and in comes the money. A department store without staff, or real estate. Wow!

Is B2C finished? Hardly. The possibilities and permutations of the B2C business model remain largely untapped. It's true that there's too much out there that's too much alike. Many firms will hit the wall and die. It'll come down to survival of the richest, fittest and most clever. But the capacity of the Internet to create a new retail world has hardly been touched. It's early days yet.

www.barnesandnoble.com

The B2C models most familiar to North America are Amazon.com, barnesandnoble.com, eToys, Ticketmaster Online and EMusic.com. They all sell the kind of stuff we throw our "mad" money at. Entertainment, music, books and toys. Feel-good stuff.

It's not mad money, but smart money

The highest profile Chinese B2C sites are 8848.net; dangdang.com; eBid.com and CyberBJ.com. Chinese consumers go to B2C sites primarily to purchase electronic goods and goods not available locally. The range of products available is still fairly narrow: books, electronic goods, software and information on technology. The products that sell on the Internet in China today are those that will help to increase the Internet. Curiously, it's building its own audience and infrastructure. The clients are primarily young professionals with a high degree of disposable income. It's not mad money they're spending, it's smart money. It's message time and they've heard the call.

China's online shoppers

Who are China's online shoppers? The January 2000 CNNIC report found that 79% of all Internet users were male with

The secret of life is honesty and fair dealing. If you can fake that, you've got it made.
—*Groucho Marx*

75.6% falling between the ages of 18 to 30. A total of 64% are single, 52% have university degrees, and 36% claim incomes between RMB1001-2000 (US$120-240) per month. Of the almost nine million Internet users in China, 8.99% claim to have bought something over the Internet in the preceding twelve months. In spite of all the problems, this is significant economic activity.

China's top B2C Web sites follow the same basic business model as B2C sites in North America. They also—by and large—create a similar business-to-customer relationship. And they share similar problems. Shipping costs can be greater than the cost of purchase. And methods of payment are limited and cumbersome.

www.etoy.com

In China, few people have true credit cards. Those that have plastic carry what is essentially a debit card. They go to their local bank and deposit a few thousand RMB into an account. The bank issues them a card that debits money against that account. They're not extending credit—the bank's not taking any risk—they're simply offering something of a 'service.' The cards can usually only be used in the city in which they were issued. You can't use your Taiyuan debit card in Guangzhou.

The most common form of payment is with a money order purchased at a post office. The next most popular is to deposit cash directly into the Web site's bank account. Again, this only works if you happen to live in the city where the Web site does its banking, or in a city that has a branch of the Web site's bank. A few Web sites also offer COD payment—if you happen to live within their city limits.

A very good friend of mine in Shanghai told me that 8848.net.cn was the best B2C site in China. He was so enthusiastic that he said it before I'd even finished asking

www.8848.net.cn

NOTE

Deferred-debit cards in circulation amount to about 30 million. In China, you need to open an account and deposit RMB10,000 in a secured interest bearing account. This gives the card-holder RMB10,000 spending power. The secured deposit is never touched by any spending activity, it just acts as a security deposit against spending. The card-holder incurs interest on his spending of 55 per cent if he pays within 15 days or up 110 per cent with 30 days payment. Imagine going past 30 days and having to pay 165 per cent on the unpaid balance!

the question. He told me he'd bought some items from the site and was very satisfied with both the price and the delivery. Other friends and contacts also rated 8848.net.cn as the top B2C in the country.

8848.net.cn is the Web site for a company called Beijing Everest E-Commerce Network Service. They chose the Web address because the height of the Chinese side of Mount Everest is 8,848 metres. It doesn't hurt that eight is also a particularly fortuitous numeral. The site became operational in the early fall of 1999. By February 2000, it claimed 20 million registered users. The company sells electronic goods, software, DVDs, multimedia, health products, digital equipment and books. They even sell gloves, coats and bullet-proof vests. It's an all-round online shopping centre. Sales in November 1999 reached approximately RMB12.5 million (US$1.5million). One quarter of these sales were to overseas customers.

The Web site is uncluttered and all business. Once you've decided what you want to buy, you complete a virtual form with your name, address and contact numbers. You are also offered a choice between regular postage rates or express post service. 8848.net has recently signed an agreement with United Parcel Service (UPS) to deliver goods to customers overseas.

www.ups.com

A question of payment

Presently, 8848 delivers to 160 cities in the P.R.C. In 18 of those, the company has set up COD delivery capacity. However, this is only available for certain products. Payment can also be made by money order, or by making a direct deposit into 8848's bank account. Customers are

FIGURE 7.1

INTERNET WORLD

Top 10 sites
unique visitors

1.	Yahoo	35.4 M
2.	AOL	30.9
3.	MSN	30.8
4.	Microsoft	22.9
5.	Geocities	21.8
6.	Netscape	20.8
7.	Go	19.2
8.	Amazon	14.8
9.	Passport	14.7
10.	Hotmail	14.5

Top 10 e-commerce sites
(US$)

1.	eBay	1.1 - 1.3 B
2.	Amazon	1.0 - 1.1
3.	Dell	500 - 600M
4.	Buy.com	350 - 400M
5.	Onsale	300 - 350M
6.	Gateway	250 - 300M
7.	Egghead	150 - 200M
8.	Barnesnoble	125 - 175M
9.	CDnow	125 - 175M
10.	AOL	100 - 150M

Source: www.iconocast.com

notified by phone or e-mail as soon as the payment is received. Shipping instructions are confirmed and the product is sent out. Customers can return goods within seven days without penalty. The site has contact numbers for after-sales service and proudly guarantees the high quality of its products.

What makes it so special? My friend claims that it has the best and broadest choice of electronic products and software. He also praises the order management and delivery. But success probably has more to do at this point with good financial backing and sound business planning. They also hold a first-to-market advantage.

There's not a lot of difference between the way 8848.net.cn operates and the way some of China's other B2C sites operate. The only interesting distinction I found was a posting board for delinquent accounts. If you send them a bum cheque, the whole world's going to hear about it!

At the time of writing, 8848 was edging toward a Nasdaq listing as a way to raise funds through a share offering. Money will always be needed—in great quantities—for those B2C sites that want to cast a broad net. Selling software and bullet-proof vests is casting a very large net indeed. My guess is they'll start to specialize in those products that sell in the greatest volumes and at the highest margins. In all likelihood, they'll aim at software and small electronic goods.

www.8848.com

An online bookstore

FIGURE 7.2

DOMAIN NAMES BY CITY OR PROVINCE	12.1999	6.1999	
1. Beijing	17,871	10,661	(1)
2. Guangdong	7,043	4,349	(2)
3. Shanghai	4,284	2,245	(3)
4. Jiangsu	2,362	1,480	(4)
5. Shangdong	2,353	1,430	(5)
6. Zhejiang	2,094	1,132	(6)
7. Liaoning	1,223	798	(7)
8. Fujian	1,167	703	(9)
9. Henan	1,130	779	(8)
10. Hubei	891	605	(10)
Sub-total	40,418	24,182	
Other	8,277	4,863	
Total	48,695	29,045	

NOTE

UPS is currently lobbying the U.S. Department of Transportation for the right to fly directly into China. United Airlines, Northwest Airlines and Federal Express are the only companies with direct flights into China.

 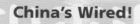

"Dang dang" is **Pinyin** [1] for "perfect perfect." The company behind dangdang.com is called Science & Culture Book Information Company.

Peggy Yu and Li Guoqing began strategizing for the launch of dangdang.com in 1996. Yu has an MBA from New York University. Before returning to China, she ran a corporate acquisitions advisory firm in New York. In 1996, Li was running the largest book distribution business in China. They both recognized the potential of the market and the lack of competition. But 1996 was the Stone Age for the Internet in China. Nevertheless, they decided to prepare to launch an online bookstore as soon as Internet use in China reached 3 million. The CNNIC's first report—in November 1997—put the number of Internet users in China at 620,000.

Yu and Li laid the foundation for dangdang.com by building a comprehensive data base of all the Chinese books in print. It took years, as no such database had ever existed. They also reasoned that the database would remain an extremely valuable asset whether or not the Internet in China could support an online bookstore.

In January 1999, the CNNIC report claimed 2,100,000 Internet users in China. dangdang.com was launched in November 1999. Sales in the first two months of operation were more than RMB1 million (US$120,000). Second month sales were 30% higher than first month sales. By the end of the year they had processed approximately 30,000 orders. And all this with limited

[1] *Pinyin*

In the past, Chinese words were usually transliterated into English according to a phonetic spelling system called Wade-Giles romanization.

However, beginning in 1958, the more easily-understood romanization called Pinyin (literally, spelling) was given official standing in the People's Republic of China. The replacement of traditional Chinese characters by Pinyin has been proposed, but is being adopted very slowly, because of the threat it poses to literature and culture in the classical language. The New China News Agency has used Pinyin in all dispatches to foreign nations since 1979.

Bookstore on Nanjing Road, Shanghai

advertising and promotion.

dangdang.com's strength is its rich database. The site lists approximately 200,000 titles. Customers can search for a book by subject, author, publisher or by International Standard Book Number (ISBN). The Boston-based International Data Group (IDG) and Luxembourg Cambridge Holding Group presently hold the majority equity stake in Science & Culture Book Information Company. At the time of writing there was no move afoot to take the company public.

dangdang.com will deliver books COD within Beijing city limits. Other payment options include money orders, direct deposits into dangdang's accounts, debit cards and Visa or Mastercard. If you use a debit card, dangdang will deliver the book to you in Beijing within 24 hours. Processing overseas credit cards slows delivery to three days.

It's a dangdang good business

Dangdang has strong business fundamentals and a very linear business strategy. It feels right. It looks as if they've got it worked out and should be able to turn it into a profitable business. ('Should' still leaves a lot of room for surprises.)

Dangdang's main competitor has a completely different feel about it. First, it hasn't been rolled out as an e-commerce strategy. It's happened. And it wasn't conceived by a business mind but by an artist and teacher who loves books. It's also got that magical and charged word "community" floating around its parameters.

The highest art form?

To some, calligraphy is the highest art form. The calligraphy of great painters is often more highly valued than their paintings. It's certainly a complex art as it combines both

NOTE

A sample survey of 110 Beijing bookstores revealed that 50 per cent of urban residents spent anywhere from $US12.00 to $US60.00 a year on books.

FIGURE 7.3

Question asked of Chinese Web users by CNNIC, Dec., 1999

What is the major problem of online shopping?	
1. Poor quality of products and service	37%
2. Lack of transaction security	28%
3. Lack of transaction convenience	18%
4. Price is not attractive	8%
5. Poor delivery service	9%

language and painting. Calligraphy is traditionally taught in two stages. First, the student masters *kaishu*. Learning *kaishu* is like learning how to print. Learning to print provides the foundation upon which we build our writing skills. After *kaishu* is mastered the student moves on to *xingshu*. *Xingshu* is like writing in that it is cursive and expressive. Most believe *xingshu* cannot be mastered without a solid foundation of *kaishu*.

In the mid 1980s, Xi Shu developed a system of learning *xingshu* without having to spend all that time mastering kaishu. In 1992, Xi Shu published a book on his methods. It sold over one million copies. He formed a club for calligraphy enthusiasts. Soon, it had 100,000 members. And then he started selling other books on other topics to the members of the calligraphy club. The calligraphy club became a book club. In 1995 Xi Shu registered Beijing XSH Books Company Ltd. In 1996, he opened his first book-store. Presently, XSH Books Company has a warehouse outside Beijing holding 150,000 different titles and 10 million books. Xi Shu has decided to go online—not to start a new business, but to support an already successful and lucrative business. Xi Shu's partners in this e-adventure are Longyuan Publishing of Canada and China International Books and Periodicals Import-Export Corporation. No talk of IPOs here!

Will dangdang.com beat aba.com.cn? That's not the point. There's plenty of room for both. The significant difference here is community—aba.com has it, dangdang.com doesn't. Xi Shu is using the Internet and e-commerce to bring greater efficiency to an existing community and an existing

www.beijing.gov.cn

www.bjbb.com.cn

NOTE

Beijing Book Building, the largest state-owned book retailer, has sold over 5,000,000 books since opening in May 1998.

FIGURE 7.4

Question asked of Chinese Web users by CNNIC Dec., 1999.

Which Internet activity do you wish to use in the near future?	
1. Information service	56%
2. Order books/magazine	38%
3. Online shopping	35%
4. Online ticket sales	35%
5. Delivery of flowers	30%

commercial exchange. He's wiring up a smooth-running business model. dangdang.com hopes to build what aba.com already has. It will do that by making itself known as an entity that represents qualities people are drawn to. It's not only about the product—it's about look and feel and reputation. Dangdang needs brand recognition—aba.com.cn has it.

Birth of a notion

There's a real horse race here to become the Amazon.com of China. They both have strong management and clear vision. They both have something the other could use. Together, they'd be unstoppable.

China is a tough place for business of any kind. Survival is success. I think most of the businesses I talk about in this book will survive in one form or another. But there are few businesses or business models here that truly illustrate the full potential of the Internet. There are few anywhere. Yaolan.com comes very close to explaining why some people remain incredibly excited about the Internet's potential. It certainly goes a long way toward explaining what this whole digital, global economic revolution is about. It's the kind of idea that will make many skeptics say, "Oh, now I get it!" It certainly made a believer of me.

In January, I met with the head of Andersen Consulting in Beijing to discuss the development of the Internet in China. I asked if he knew of any interesting e-businesses I should look at. He couldn't think of any off the top of his head. He said he'd think about it. But just before I left his office he told me there was one business I might want to take a look at. He wouldn't give me the name—or give me any details—he wanted to check with the CEO first to see if he was prepared to meet with me. It all seemed very cloak and dagger.

The head of Andersen called me later that day. He said that Matthew Estes, chairman of Yaolan.com, was prepared to speak to me but was extremely busy. He passed along Estes' contact numbers and told me Estes was expecting my call.

"Yaolan" is Pinyin for "cradle." Yaolan.com is a Web site that offers support, information, advice and community to the 20 million women in China who give birth every year.

The soundest businesses are those with the deepest roots in China. Again, it's about community, or the interpenetration of a series of communities over time. Steven Yaung has deep roots in China—as do the Zhaopin boys. Matthew Estes, the chairman of Yaolan is no different.

Over the phone, he sounded a bit like Henry Kissinger. I could tell that it was an old voice

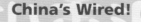

on a young man, but that's all it told me. Estes said he was very busy and could only spare 30 minutes. He set the meeting for 8a.m. the following Monday. It was clear that he was meeting me reluctantly. I came very close to cancelling. I didn't think he wanted to talk, and I didn't want to waste his time or mine.

For whatever reason, the best interviews and experiences always come from meetings I've almost cancelled. I liked Estes immediately. He's a brilliant and highly articulate man. And no simple businessman—not that there's any such thing in China. He'd been reticent because he didn't want his business to be misrepresented. He didn't want it to be just another story. He sees the big picture—life and success is more than a black and white bottom line.

Estes was born in Hong Kong. He was raised in both Hong Kong and the United States. He speaks Mandarin, a bit of Cantonese and Spanish. Estes has a BA in Economics as well as a BA in International Relations from Pomona College in California.

Estes' father is an Episcopal minister and professor. The senior Estes served as vice-Headmaster and Chaplain at St. Stephen's College, Hong Kong.

Estes arrived in China in 1991. His first job was as marketing and sales manager-hospital division for SmithKline Beecham. Estes moved to Wella, the German cosmetics firm in 1993. When he left Wella in 1998, he was Managing Director for Greater China.

Estes claims his success at SmithKline Beecham was all about distribution. His predecessors believed all they had to do was get the products into retail outlets. Estes understood that doctors are the drivers of pharmaceutical sales, not retail outlets. He sent his people out to build

Marketing is lateral thinking

www.babyhood.com

20 million expectant mothers on their own

SmithKline Beecham's reputation one doctor at a time. Convince the most trusted member of the community to take your product and everyone else will follow. It worked. Total sales increased at more than 80 per cent per annum.

Marketing is all about lateral thinking. It's about emotion, culture and sensibility. It's not rational. An accountant's bottom line reality is irrelevant to the marketer's big picture vision. Estes is a master of marketing—and marketing in China. He also has senior management skills and is an astute strategic thinker. Finally, he's launched two start-ups in China. Estes has had about as much on the ground business experience—and success—in China as any one person can claim.

Our first meeting was very brief. I learned that there were two different but allied businesses—BabyCare Ltd. and Yaolan.com. Estes is president and CEO of BabyCare, and chairman of Yaolan.

You don't have to be first to market to win. You just have to be first in the consumer's mind.

— *Matthew Estes*

FIGURE 7.5

Even with a declining birth rate, China produces 19 million babies annually

Population comparison

	CHINA				UNITED STATES	
	Total pop (millions)	Women of child bearing age (millions)	Births (millions)	Birth rate	Total pop (millions)	Birth rate
1999	1,259	343	19	15.1	273	14.6 est
1998	1,248	340	20	16.0	270	14.6
1993	1,236	337	20	16.2	268	14.5
1988	1,224	333	21	17.1	263	14.8
1980	1,201	330	21	17.5	249	16.7

I returned to Beijing briefly in late February to meet again with Estes and have a tour of his facilities. Of all the businesses I looked at BabyCare and Yaolan were the most intriguing. It was such a simple—and beautiful—idea. Their strategy is impeccable. It's also being executed with the precision of a military campaign. The most exciting part is seeing how the strategy—and idea—for a bricks and mortar business called BabyCare, has been expanded and adapted so naturally into a brilliant B2C business called Yaolan.

BabyCare was conceived four and a half years ago—inspired in part by the pregnancy of Michael McNabb's wife (McNabb is a non-executive director of BabyCare). Who did all the pregnant women in China turn to for advice and support? Who helped them through the pregnancy and the child's early months? There was no such person or organization. There was no community. For the most part, China's 20 million expectant mothers every year were on their own.

BabyCare is a support organization for pregnant mothers and the parents of infant children. BabyCare is also a business as it sells baby products, nutritional supplements and educational toys. And BabyCare is a lifestyle. Estes and his team have created a community environment that also happens to be a commercial enterprise. The products were the easiest part of the equation. The tough part was educating the market and creating community.

One child, one treasure

If you're only allowed to have one child, that one child will carry heavy expectations. All the hopes and dreams of the child's two parents and four grandparents rest on that single child's shoulders. And all the disposable income from those two parents and four grandparents will be dedicated to that single child's upbringing. If this toy will make him learn faster, I want it. If those vitamins will build stronger bones, I'll buy them.

www.babycenter.com

THE DRAGON–BOAT RACE

The Americans and the Chinese decided to engage in a dragon-boat race. Both teams practised hard.
On the big day, they felt ready! The Chinese team won by a mile.
Afterward, the American team was discouraged. Morale sagged. Corporate management decided that the reason for the defeat had to be found. A consulting firm was hired to recommend corrective action.
The consultants' findings were as follows:
  - the Chinese team had eight people rowing and one person steering, the American team had one person rowing and eight people steering,
After a year of studying the problem, the consultants concluded that too many people were steering and not enough were rowing on the American team.
So as the race day neared the following year, the American team was completely reorganized. The new structure was as follows:
  - four steering managers
  - three area steering managers
  - a new performance review system for the person rowing the boat to provide work incentive.
The Chinese team won by two miles.
Humiliated, the American corporation laid off the rower for poor performance and gave the managers a bonus for discovering the problem.

Estes says that most of the manufacturers of baby products in China have had an extremely difficult time. He says production in China is terrific and the consumer is extremely sophisticated. The problem is with marketing and distribution. How do you educate the consumer—especially about a subject as complicated as child rearing?

Traditionally, baby care products are sold at retail outlets. In China, price is not the issue when it comes to baby products—consumers will spend whatever it takes to get the best for their only child. But they'll only spend it if they know why they should have it. Mass advertising is ineffective because the information is too complicated to relay in a small space and the audience far too broad. And consumer's questions are generally too complicated for retail staff to answer. Ultimately, there's no method to inform the consumer about the products—and why their babies need those products.

BabyCare is the strategy Estes and his colleagues developed[1]. They started by doing a huge amount of research into child development and rearing. They went to international experts as well as China's top pediatricians and scientists. There are a number of Web sites which specialize in child care in the West, but only this one in China.

www.baby-place.com

A Mothers' Club

Estes and his team have organized child development in phases. They've produced literature explaining the key phases of a child's physiological and intellectual development. And for each phase there is a product. From vitamins for the embryo—to toys for the toddler.

NOTE

In 1949 China's illiteracy rate was 80 per cent of the population. By 1998 the rate of illiteracy had fallen to 14.5 per cent, thanks in part to the forced elementary education.

FIGURE 7.6

1 *A key player on the team is Vivek Kapur, a founder and non-executive director of BabyCare. Kapur is something of a marketing guru in China. He worked at Proctor & Gamble and Heinz in the early 1990s.*

BabyCare's literature is comprehensive and impressive. BabyCare's objective is 'To become the pre-eminent source of credible advice and products satisfying a wide range of physical and mental development needs for mothers and children.' Estes gave me a brochure and a beautifully bound book. They're both printed in full colour and carry images of both Chinese and Caucasian mothers and children. Caucasian women and children inspire confidence in the products. Consumers read it as an indication of quality.

The brochure talks about a BabyCare Mothers' Club where pregnant mothers or mothers with young children can come together to share their experiences. It also shows a range of products from nutritional supplements to educational tools, to breast pumps. And there is a picture of the BabyCare Centre, the retail centre and gathering place. The retail centre is open for members only. A one-time purchase of RMB450 (US$54) of BabyCare products entitles the purchaser to membership. The centre is also open at select times for non-members. It sounds and looks more like a community centre or club than a retail outlet. But the

www.babysoon.com

The products sell themselves

www.babycare-direct.co.uk

FIGURE 7.7

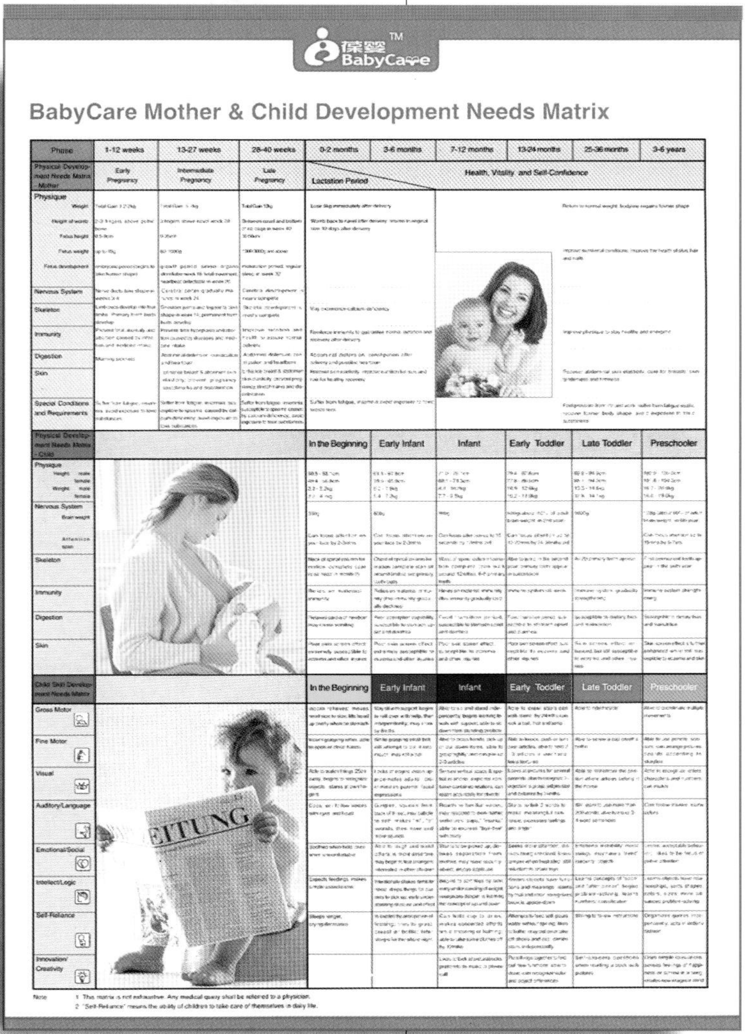

BabyCare Mother & Child Development Needs Matrix

Above is the development chart that forms the key to the BabyCare strategy.

most interesting part of both the brochure and the book is the development chart upon which everything is based.

The chart is entitled the BabyCare Mother & Child Development Needs Matrix. The chart is divided into three basic sections. The first section addresses the mother's physical development needs from conception to birth. The second section charts the physical development needs of the child from birth to two months, 3-6 months, 7-12 months, 13-24 months, 25-36 months and 3-6 years. The third section covers the same development period for the child but focuses on the child's skill development needs. When will the child begin to speak? When will the child be able to ride a bike, talk, socialize and become self-reliant?

By being the bearer of quality information and support, BabyCare becomes a part of the child-rearing process. BabyCare becomes a member of the family and a part of the community. The information, the charts and lectures by specialists is offered free of charge. The products sell themselves.

The products BabyCare sells are produced by established manufacturers but carry the BabyCare 'private' label. Competitive brands as well as BabyCare brands are sold on Yaolan's e-commerce site.

Pregnant women are invited to come to BabyCare centres to hear specialists talk about nutrition and exercise. Pregnant women meet other pregnant women. A community is born.

Four and a half years ago, when Estes and his marketing gurus devised the BabyCare strategy, B2C did not exist.

Fortunately, they didn't need it, because BabyCare had been an almost immediate success. And then, about two

www.hbs.edu

All women become like their Mothers, that is their tragedy. No man does. That's his.

—*Oscar Wilde*

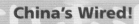

and a half years ago, the Internet started to take off in the United States. Estes and his colleagues recognized the potential for China immediately. They also recognized that the Internet would allow them to offer an even richer source of information in ever-greater detail.

The retail strategy

But BabyCare is a different company than Yaolan and a different retail strategy. BabyCare is bricks and mortar, Yaolan is all virtual. Estes makes the separation clear. At most, BabyCare is licensing its information to Yaolan, otherwise the companies are separate entities entirely.

They built Yaolan in two stages. Once again, they brought together a team of experts on child rearing to begin assembling and organizing the data. They also assembled a design and content team to organize and prepare several thousand pages of licensed content from BabyCare for the Web. Finally Yaolan out-sourced the database architecture to DAE Interactive, a Web design company in San Francisco that had built the Charles Schwab Chinese language site.

In April of 1999, Estes, and his business partner Christopher Mumford, CFO and COO of BabyCare, began to assemble the pieces necessary to bring Yaolan to life. Mumford had left a career in Investment Banking in the U.S. for what he considers the more meaningful work of an e-commerce start-up in the P.R.C. First round financing was arranged and Mark Levine, a Lotus veteran was brought in to oversee the development of the Web site. Tony Jin joined as general manager with a particular focus on establishing portal distribution agreements and increasing traffic. Larry Wang, an MBA from Harvard Business School was hired as CEO. Construction of the Web site began in June 1999.

The Yaolan site follows the format of the BabyCare Mother &

Every kind that lives, Fomented by his virtual power, and warmed.
—*Milton*

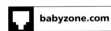

How Yaolan works

Child Development Needs Matrix. First-time visitors are invited to fill out a form and become members. Members can input their membership number. The membership form asks for name, sex, state of pregnancy or age of child. It also requests level of education, profession, income, address and phone number. And it asks if you're breast feeding your child and if someone else is helping you take care of your child. Finally, it asks if you've ever shopped on the Internet.

Yaolan has been designed to be an infomediator between the consumer and the manufacturer. What is infomediation? It's the ability to search the Web to find the best product at the best price for the consumer. How does it work? A consumer describes a simple rash. The Web site provides information on the probable cause and possible treatments. The consumer asks to see products that could treat the rash. Yaolan searches the Web and offers up a selection of manufacturers' products at a variety of prices. Yaolan is a sourcing mediator—it reaches out to other sites, scans their content and reassembles a selection of the most appropriate products for the consumer's needs. The consumer can click on a button and buy the product through Yaolan, or directly through the manufacturer. Yaolan charges a commission. Talk about virtual!

Tabs along the top of the site list each child development or pregnancy phase—from preparation for pregnancy to labour and lactation, baby, infant and pre-school. Yaolan covers the period from conception to about age six. Members receive free e-mail, current news on child development, a personalized home page for the child, access to Yaolan's specialists and a guarantee of confidentiality. They also have access to other Yaolan members who may have already gone through the experience they are entering. There is also a RMB5,000

FIGURE 7.7

Top Ten U.S. Boy Names

1. Jacob
2. Michael
3. Matthew
4. Nicholas
5. Christopher
6. Joshua
7. Austin
8. Tyler
9. Brandon
10. Joseph

Top Ten U.S. Girl Names

1. Emily
2. Sarah
3. Brianna
4. Samantha
5. Hailey
6. Ashley
7. Kaitlyn
8. Madison
9. Hannah
10. Alexis

(US$600) prize for the person who submits the best story about his or her own childhood.

Its all very soft sell

Yaolan creates a virtual community. Yaolan and BabyCare are the flip sides of the same coin, or perhaps parallel universes. A bricks and mortar universe, and a virtual universe. So much is similar yet dramatically and substantially different. As of April 2000, the only commercial aspect of the Web site was a button at the bottom of the form for product information. It's all very soft sell. I was told that they want to get the environment and information right before they start pitching anything.

www.babytrader.com

There are a number of subtle but significant differences between BabyCare and Yaolan. BabyCare, the bricks and mortar business, is a lifestyle retail center. BabyCare has solved the marketing and distribution problems which Estes says every consumer company in China faces. Yaolan is a second generation of BabyCare—the digital version. What Yaolan misses in one-to-one touch and feel it makes up in depth of knowledge. It's also available at any time of the day or night.

Curiously, Yaolan is also more intimate than BabyCare. Yes, it's intimacy with a database, but it's your intimacy. Yaolan remembers each and every consumer in more detail than any retail clerk could. BabyCare creates trust by bringing like-minded people with similar interests together. Staff— real people—deliver information that then drives sales. That's a huge service in China, where information of this kind is difficult to come by. But not everyone has the means to find their way to a BabyCare centre. Nor is everyone comfortable discussing such personal issues with strangers in public. Yaolan offers the shy or embarrassed a chance to ask any question on any subject without judgement. Just the facts.

NOTE

Go to this Web site, www.cgibin.erols.com and find-out what your Chinese name could be. For example, William Gates, born October 28, 1955 could be:

Kong Wang Lan or

Kong Wanglan.

This means as follows:

Kong - surname

Wang - look forward, hope, expect

Lan - look at, inspect, perceived.

www.cgibin.erols.com

A Web site as a wise elder

The one real advantage Yaolan has in developing relationships with consumers is privacy. A pregnant woman can ask the site any question she wants without fear of embarrassment—and it can do this as effectively for a woman in Mongolia as it can for one in Beijing. Yaolan is also scalable in a way BabyCare could never hope to be. Will Yaolan make BabyCare obsolete? Not likely, there's room and need for both.

Yaolan will probably be the first contact these new children will have with the Internet. As they grow, they will watch their mothers and fathers turn to the Yaolan site—as they might have once turned to a wise elder—for advice on health and education. Soon, Yaolan will develop the capacity for direct interaction with those children three, four or five years old. It might begin by showing them toys their parents can then buy. And as the child gets older, it'll find a way to offer more products and services—perhaps through games, perhaps through education.

Yaolan will create the first Internet generation—the first generation that will not be able to remember life without it.

I asked Estes what he planned to do after Yaolan. He said that he came to China because he was good at building companies and solving all the problems building companies entails. He says the job isn't finished just because it works and makes a profit. Estes wants to be with BabyCare and Yaolan until they reach maturity. A mature and accomplished staff, a mature and stable structure, a mature place in the community. Estes isn't only interested in profit, he wants meaning. ➡

BREAKING NEWS

BabyCare & Yaolan Merge!

The 'all-virtual' Yaolan joins with 'bricks and mortar' BabyCare for 'bricks and clicks' synergies.

Why it'll work:

The 'clicks' of Yaolan scales quickly, while the 'bricks' of BabyCare creates enduring client relationships.

Yaolan.com is China's leading parenting Web site with 120,000 members, five million monthly page views and 25,000 unique visitors daily.

In less than two years, BabyCare's management team has developed 64 high-margin private label products, two network centres and a team of forty-five commissioned sales people.

BabyCare's off-line client relationships generate an average RMB 2,400 annually.

Yaolan's on-line members generate an average RMB100 annually.

 go to...

For additional information and updates to charts and graphs, visit: **www.flyingarmchair.com**
the China's Wired! *resource site.*

Consumer to
Consumer
C2C

Meeting Madam X and
going C2C

Barter or buyer beware ?

Consumer to Consumer
C2C

On April 26 2000, the Wharton Business School in Philadelphia held a seminar called East-West.Com: The e-Revolution in Greater China Business. The seminar was chaired by Dr. Ming-Jer Chen, founding Director of the Global China Business Initiative at Wharton. More than a dozen guest speakers were listed, including Jack Ma, founder and CEO of Alibaba.com, Shao Yi-bo, CEO of Eachnet.com and Edward Zeng, Founder and Chairman of Sparkice.com. Wharton's literature claimed that this was the most complete gathering of China's Internet leaders ever organized in the United States.

www.paulallen.com

The topics discussed at the conference included the challenges facing a dotcom CEO, an examination of B2B in Greater China, and a look at incubators, Venture Capitalists (VCs) and Initial Public Offerings (IPOs). The seminar aimed to serve two distinct purposes. First, to discuss the development of e-commerce in China. Second, to provide a forum for those contemplating a China Internet start-up.

> *" The reasonable man adapts himself to the world; the unreasonable man persists in trying to adapt the world to himself. Therefore all progress depends on the unreasonable man."*
>
> —*George Bernard Shaw*

China Going Digital

Wharton may have been the first but Harvard came in an extremely close second. The third annual conference of the Harvard China Review was held on Saturday May 6, 2000. The title of the conference was Going Digital: The Future of the Internet in Greater China.

The conference was held at the Kennedy School of Government in Cambridge, Massachusetts, and was co-chaired by York Lo and Jin Chen. Co-organizers of the conference included the Harvard China Forum, the Berkman Center For Internet and Society at Harvard Law School, the China Initiative of the JFK School of Government and the Boston chapter of I&I Asia, a forum for Internet professionals doing business in Asia.

Registration for the conference began at 7 a.m. with opening remarks scheduled for 8 a.m. Presentations on different topics were to be held throughout the day at the Weiner Auditorium and the Arco Forum—sometimes simultaneously. This meant sometimes having to choose between such interesting topics as Enabling E-Commerce at the Weiner or Content at the Arco. Closing remarks were scheduled for 6 p.m.—followed by a cocktail reception and a VIP dinner for all sponsors and speakers at the Harvard Faculty Club.

Peter Yip, CEO of chinadotcom, had been listed as the first speaker. Unfortunately, Yip had cancelled as his wife was about to give birth. I did a quick count and came to the conclusion that the Yips had probably conceived this child in August of 1999—one month after chinadotcom's Nasdaq première. Once the war was won, attention turned to more personal matters.

Andrew Miller, Senior Vice President-Sales and Marketing, chinadotcom corporation, stood in for Peter Yip, delivering

cyber.law.harvard.edu

www.ksg.harvard.edu

When written in Chinese, the word 'crisis' is composed of two characters— one represents danger and one represents opportunity.

—*John F. Kennedy*

one of the keynote speeches. He began his remarks by referring to the chinadotcom people as the grandfathers of China's Internet revolution. Men in their forties, just starting their own families—the grandfathers of an economic revolution? Amazing but true. Internet time is the blink of an eye.

NOTE

Andrew Miller has been appointed President for the Americas, chinadotcom corporation

The Harvard seminar had a very impressive list of guest speakers—probably from a broader field of interests than those at Wharton. Harvard's speakers included specialists in e-commerce, connectivity, emerging technologies and venture capital. There was even a high-ranking official with China's Ministry of Information Industry. Madam X turned out to be something of a blast from the past. The old China struggling to be heard above the roar of the new. Madam X was one of three speakers on a plenary panel titled Internet in Greater China: Policy and Social Changes. The other two panelists were men in their mid thirties who were professional consultants on the Internet in China.

www.chinalabs.com

Eloquent stone-walling

Madam X seemed to answer even the most innocent questions defensively. And she began each of her responses with something of a lecture on how far-sighted China's government has been in its commitment to the Internet. What was so odd was that this defensiveness was completely unnecessary. None of the questions was critical of China, or China's policies. They were serious, well-shaped questions about the Internet. The only question that might have caused her to wrinkle her brow was about finance. When would China allow its citizens to enjoy the evils of credit? And this was asked as a joke—perhaps in an effort to break Madam X's icy demeanour. Unfortunately, the only chuckles occurred when Madam X began to answer questions that had been directed to the other panelists—before the other panelist had a chance to

Computers are useless. They can only give answers.

—*Pablo Picasso*

 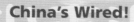

answer for himself. It was her show, and she wasn't going to let anyone think otherwise.

The great Lean forward

Her whole demeanour spoke of another place and another time. She would listen to a question wearing a neutral but severe mask. She would sometimes show impatience—or register disapproval—when her translator stumbled. Before she answered a question her torso would stiffen, her neck lengthen, and her face take on an expression that telegraphed disapproval edging towards rage. Her voice was shrill and her gestures sharp—a demon figure from some ancient Chinese opera. It was a fascinating—and riveting—performance.

Some people in the audience chuckled, some shook their heads in despair, others listened with their heads bowed—the muscles in their cheeks clenching. Chinese students from Harvard were deferential and nervous. Her fellow panelists cowered. The entourage that surrounded her sat in silent prayer.

www.digiark.com

If Madam X had been saying something original or interesting no one would have minded—as it was, she often answered each question with more or less the same answer. Her attitude had nothing to do with bad translation as some of the most thoughtful questions came from mainland Chinese students studying at Harvard. Other questions were asked by members of her entourage. It was a surrealist nightmare. Madam X—and her entourage—vanished shortly after the end of her panel discussion.

Inadvertently—and unknowingly—Madam X revealed more about the problems facing the Internet in China than any other single participant. And she did so with an eloquence beyond words.

Madam X had graduated from Tsinghua University in 1969.

NOTE

The Cultural Revolution began in The People's Republic of China in May of 1966 with the publication by the Central Committee of the 'May 16th circular.' It continued in one form or another until Mao's death in 1976 and the overthrow of the 'Gang of Four.'

The Chinese Communist Party divides the Cultural Revolution into three phases. The first phase begins in May 1966 and ends with with the 9th Party Congress in April 1969. This was perhaps the most violent period of the Revolution and led to the purge of a large number of senior revolutionary leaders.

The second stage lasted from April 1969, until the 10th Congress in August 1973. This period was dominated by the Lin Biao affair. Lin had been Mao's designated heir. But Mao's designated heirs had a very short shelf-life. Lin ended-up accused of treason and died in a plane crash while trying to "escape".

The final phase lasted from 1973 until the arrest of the Gang of Four. This period is preoccupied with the complex power struggles to succeed Mao.

www.tsinghua.edu.cn

The Cultural Revolution began in China in 1966. Traditional university curriculi were suspended between 1966 and 1976. University students spent their time arguing politics or suffering increasingly strident and sometimes violent indoctrination.

The Class of 2,474[1]

Madam X probably entered university in 1965. She would have completed a very thorough secondary school education and passed rigorous entrance exams. She would also have had to do very well on those exams as Tsinghua is one of China's top universities. In China, the entrance exam determines the university you attend. The higher the grade, the better the institution.

Madam X studied electrical engineering. But at the end of her first full year of study the books would have been chucked out the window. She would have spent the next three years in a violent and terrifying revolutionary environment. Deng's son attended Tsinghua and was thrown from a third floor window on the campus and paralyzed. Others suffered worse fates. Upon 'graduating,' Madam X would have been sent to do manual work—hard labour—in the countryside for a period of three to five years. No wonder she lost her sense of humour!

The perils of Paranoia

Madam X is now in her mid fifties and will probably retire in a year or two. But there is a whole generation in China that act and react exactly as Madam X did in front of the Harvard audience. To their credit they do have some education—high school and one or two years of real university education. To their detriment they're rigid, controlling, strident and paranoid. And they're in charge.

www.netalone.com

The generation that followed Madam X into China's universities is even more 'complex.' They're called the WPS (workers, peasants, soldiers) and they entered China's

NOTE

During the Cultural Revolution, children's names reflected the current fever in the revolutionary air. For example, Jianjun, which means 'Building-the-Army' or Xiao Hong, which means, 'Little Red,' or Mujun 'Army Admirer'. Post revolution, these names became embarrassing reminders to their owners and were often changed.

1 *Tsinghua University proudly proclaims that 45,888 students graduated from 1949 to 1981. A special category exists for the Cultural Revolution graduates; 2,474 graduated during this period.*

Tsinghua resumed national college entrance examinations in 1978.

universities between 1973 and 1977. Generally, they had only rudimentary education and were certainly not obliged to write the gruelling entrance exams Madam X's generation had had to endure. To make matters worse, the WPS gained entry into the universities only on the recommendation of a Revolutionary Committee. Every commune, factory or bureau had its own Revolutionary Committee—usually the most strident, severe and committed revolutionaries. You had to be even more strident to catch their attention; and more fervent still to gain their recommendation to enter university. The WPS didn't study in university—they criticized. Their goal was to inflame an already intolerable environment.

www.tenderbuttons.com

Today, the WPS are in their mid to late forties and occupy the highest administrative levels in the government, the military and industry. They, too, are in charge—not because of talent, but because of loyalty to the party. They've paid their dues—and heavy dues they were. If you ask them about their education they'll tell you where they studied—but not the year they graduated. They know that their generation is not held in high esteem.

A lost generation

The Cultural Revolution also left behind a lost generation— the students who resumed a traditional university curriculum when the universities were reopened in 1977. They have completely different psychological characteristics. Most educated themselves privately. That they were able to pass China's rigorous entrance exams without a traditional secondary school formation attests to both their discipline and intelligence. Unfortunately, this group had little to look forward to after graduation. China's economy was in ruins. What little there was rested—by and large—in the hands of people like Madam X and the WPS. Many chose to leave China to pursue careers and build

www.idominc.com

> *We have two ears and one mouth so that we can listen twice as much as we speak.*
> —*Epictetus*

> *You are all a lost generation.*
> —*Gertrude Stein to Ernest Hemingway*

lives in the West.

Most of China's top bureaucrats are cast in the mold of Madam X or the WPS. They've survived the system and the system has rewarded them. They cling to their power tenaciously. The only thing that's likely to diminish their stifling influence is time. They too grow old. In time, they will retire and make way for fresher minds.

The characters of the men at the top of China's government were not shaped by such pernicious forces. Jiang Zemin and Zhu Rongji were mature men before the Cultural Revolution struck. One of their most difficult tasks must be reconciling the forward movement of reform with the intransigence of this complex generation.

Why does this generation continue to have such influence in China? Why aren't they forced into retirement? Because that would be an admission that there was something wrong with them—something for which the party is responsible. They earned their positions of authority through loyalty. To condemn openly the conduct or nature of this generation would be to question the authority of the party. The same party that brought Jiang Zemin and Zhu Rongji to power. And they're not about to do that. This is the complicated landscape from which China's Internet grows. These are some of the forces pushing and pulling its development.

The Harvard conference was incredibly well attended—an overflow house. Normally, in these sorts of things guest speakers do their bit and then head off to the bar. But almost all the speakers attended each others' presentations. People were there to learn, participate and connect.

Some of the panelists proved more controversial or inflammatory than others. Nicholas Lee, CEO of Pacific Internet, argued that China's total number of Internet users

www.csfisc.com

www.chinaren.com

www.pacfusion.com

FIGURE 8.1

TOP 10 U.S. EDUCATION SITES

(by number of unique visitors)

1. BERKLEY.EDU	1,803
2. UTEXAS.EDU	1,531
3. UMICH.EDU	1,516
4. UIUC.EDU	1,479
5. MIT.EDU	1,289
6. WISC.EDU	1,237
7. UNC.EDU	1,216
8. HARVARD	1,156
9. CORNELL.EDU	1,123
10. UPENN.EDU	1,050

Source: Media Metrics

Momentum is where it's at!

could only be 1.2 million—nothing near the 8.9 million the CNNIC has claimed. Lee based his estimate on a calculation of bandwidth. Others argued that the numbers were much higher still—20 or 30 million, at least. Sager minds reminded everyone that size isn't everything—momentum is where it's at.

There was no feeling that April's worldwide stock market correction was in any way going to affect the development of China's Internet. A panel of venture capitalists barely touched on the subject even though at least one of them admitted that several hundred million dollars had been wiped off his fund's valuation.

The majority of the attendees were Chinese—many of them students at Harvard or MIT. When Joseph Tzeng, Managing Director of Crystal Internet Venture Funds, got up to speak, he first asked those in the audience involved in some sort of start-up—or contemplating a start-up—to raise their hands. Half the audience responded. Tzeng beamed and invited them all to meet with him later to deliver their pitch.

www.crystalventure.com

Was it worth the trip to Boston? Absolutely. Did I find out anything I didn't already know? Nothing that made me want to race back and re-write the manuscript of this book. Nobody can claim to have the full story—not yet—perhaps never. This economic revolution is still in its infancy, its history has yet to be written. Which is perhaps the point. History is the past recalled. We're still living the Internet's first steps. Conferences such as the ones at Wharton and Harvard legitimize the Internet, they begin to institutionalize it and give it context. They begin to make the virtual world real.

The most striking aspect of the conference was the enthusiasm that was expressed for China's Internet future.

Statistics are like bikinis. What they reveal is suggestive, but what they conceal is vital.

—*Aaron Levenstein*

NOTE

The United States will generate $US3.5 trillion by the year 2004 in e-commerce revenue.

source: Forrester Research

Consumer to Consumer
C2C

C2C:

Barter, or buyer beware?

NOTE
Crystal Internet's portfolio of companies includes the following:

about.com

babycenter.com

cobaltnet.com

eccubed.com

ejasent.com

interdyn.com

kaverintworks.com

magnifi.com

mypersonal.com

netgenics.com

opensolutions.com

rowe.com

sina.com

There is great optimism and building momentum—in spite of brutal market corrections. And it's probably the first time so many gifted Chinese students studying overseas look forward to returning home. They have the skills China needs. For once, the opportunities are greater at home.

The conference also showed that it is increasingly difficult to drop e-commerce into clearly defined categories. Certainly, there will always be businesses out there that are strictly B2C or B2B. But there are more and more that seem to be hybrids of several different categories. Is Zhaopin.com a B2C business or a C2C business? Is eBay a C2C business or a B2-two-Cs?

What is C2C? It should mean a direct exchange between consumers. I have something that you want. I'm a consumer and you're a consumer, we're not retailers. Tighten up the supply chain and cut out the middle man. But does the middleman ever really disappear? Not quite. If that were the case, Pierre Omidyar wouldn't be worth five or six billion dollars.

eBay is probably the best known and most successful C2C business in the world. It's also profitable. And its history is brief and astonishingly simple—perhaps the archetypical model for all Web dreamers. After graduating from Tufts University in 1988 with a degree in computer science, Pierre Omidyar and his wife Pamela moved to California. Omidyar built and sold a small computer company before going to work for General Magic, a software company specializing in information gathering and sorting programs.

eBay began life in 1995. It was inspired by Pamela Omidyar's passion for collecting and exchanging Pez candy dispensers.[1] eBay stands for Electronic Bay Area, an effort to add a virtual dimension to the Omidyar's real Bay area

1 If you go to www.thegoodnamesweretak en.com you will find the Prozac Web page. It pronounces that, " The world would be a happier place if antidepressants were distributed in Pez dispensers."

A click-of-the-mouse flea market

www.ebay.com

www.goodwill.org

www.sothebys.com

www.christies.com

neighbourhood. Traffic on the site exploded when collectors realized how easily they could source or exchange desired items.

Collectors are an odd but extremely passionate bunch—the sort of people who show up at a flea market site at 4 a.m. to make sure they get the first look. We've all heard the stories of million-dollar finds in dusty attics. What we don't hear about are all the other dusty attics and damp basements the poor soul has crept through before hitting the motherlode. This is where the Internet comes into play—and what it does particularly well. ebay is a weatherproof, 24-hour, click-of-the-mouse flea market.

Traditionally, collectors search for items or 'collectibles' at garage sales, used furniture stores, Church sales, Goodwill or Salvation Army used goods outlets, flea markets and traditional bricks and mortar auction houses. The more valuable the item, the more likely you are to find it at a traditional auction house.

For a time after finishing university I worked in an art gallery that sold early 20th Century American and European art and decorative objects. Twice a year we'd go to Europe to bid at auctions in Paris and London. These would be our blue chip items—expensive objects of high quality. Big investments of time and money that built the gallery's reputation.

We had to go to Paris and London because that was where the auctions houses were. But we found the bulk of our inventory much closer to home. Nevertheless, it required considerable time and included travelling long distances. One 'hunting' route would take us across northern New York State. We'd start at Buffalo and follow the I90 across to Rochester, Syracuse and Albany. These cities had been

FIGURE 8.2

TOP TEN E-COMMERCE COUNTRIES YEAR 2000
(US$ BILLION)

1.	United States	$488.7
2.	Japan	$31.9
3.	Germany	$20.6
4.	Canada	$17.4
5.	UK	$17.2
6.	France	$9.9
7.	Italy	$7.2
8.	Australia	$5.6
9.	S. Korea	$5.6
10.	Taiwan	$4.1

Source: Forrester Research

NOTE

There are numerous sites which offer free classified advertising for whatever you may want to sell. For example, www.illinoishorse.com has a 1999 Buckskin filly for sale at $3,700 or best offer.

Or if you're more into Mattels Hotwheels, go to Peter's Hotwheels at:

www.peterswheels.com

extremely prosperous in the early part of the century. Many great families had filled grand homes with even grander collections.

The stock market crash of 1929 ruined many of these families and the cities went into decline. But their collections remained—sometimes intact, but generally dispersed amongst an ever widening circle of heirs. By and large these heirs had little understanding of the value of some of the household goods they'd inherited. In the 1980s, it was not uncommon to hear of a Tiffany dragonfly table lamp turning up at a flea market in the area. We once missed four original Frank Lloyd Wright dining room chairs by a few days.

auctionauction.com

www.franklloydwright.org

What I've just described is the traditional supply chain for fine art and collectibles. It required building a network of contacts with dealers in the area who would watch for the items we wanted. It meant regular visits to the street or boulevard in each of these cities that held all the junk stores and antique shops. And it meant hours and hours of driving. Success seemed to depend as much on luck as anything else.

How to spend a billion!

Why was eBay successful from the start? Because it gathered everything together in one location and made it possible to find, purchase, or sell anything and everything with the click of a mouse. No more scouring row upon row of junk-laden tables at a flea market at four in the morning. Hallelujah!

Why did something so obvious not develop sooner? Because it required a collision of two different perspectives, personalities and interests. Pamela Omidyar is a collector. Pierre watched his wife collect. He saw the process I described above and knew the Internet could streamline

You can get much farther with a kind word and a gun than you can with a kind word alone.

—Al Capone

the process. Omidyar didn't create anything new, he introduced a new technology and a new protocol to an ancient human passion.

eBay's site has an almost Ikea-like feel to it. It's colourful and very rational. The first thing you're asked to do is to register. This is how they begin to build your profile—who you are and what you want—extremely valuable consumer information.

Selling online

If you want to sell something, you begin by putting your credit card on file. Then you assemble the data that will be required to describe your item properly—including a photograph. If you agree to eBay's terms—a posting fee and a percentage of the sale price—the item is posted in the appropriate category and the fun begins. Insertion fees usually run from 25 cents to US$2. (The insertion fee is based on the minimum acceptable bid for the item you're listing. The insertion fee is also non-refundable.) The final value fee is only charged if your item sells. This fee ranges from 1.25% to 5% of the final sale price. (Traditional auction houses usually charge 15% of the final sale price.) Additional fees may also be charged, according to how you want your posting to appear.

Your object remains open for bids for a specific and limited period of time. All bidders are informed daily by e-mail of the current highest bid. When the auction closes you contact the winning bidder, confirm the final cost, shipping charges and payment arrangements. eBay doesn't get

Bidding online

involved between you and the purchaser; they're the platform and the conduit and they're all virtual.

Bidding requires the same initial registration process. There is no charge to browse or bid on something on eBay, only sellers are charged. If you find something you want, you

www.auctionguide.com

WHAT WOULD YOU DO?

If you had US$ 1 billion what would you spend it on? Cars, boats planes or estates?

Prince Alwaleed of Saudi Arabia spent a quick billion on America Online, Compaq, Kodak and Xerox. As an after-thought, he decided to invest another US$ one billion on 15 stocks. They are in order of investment, in US$ millions;

WorldCom	$200
AT&T	$150
Gillette	$50
McDonald's	$50
Proctor&Gamble	$50
Coca-Cola	$50
Pepsi	$50
Ford Motor	$50
Walt Disney	$50
Amazon.com	$50
eBay.com	$50
DoubleClick.com	$50
Priceline.com	$50
Infospace.com	$50
ICGE.com	$50

I guess he likes the Internet?

enter a bid. You'll be sent a daily e-mail informing you of the highest bid. If you're the highest bidder at the close of the auction you e-mail the seller and arrange to claim your item.

An online neighbourhood watch

Most businesses offer general disclaimers warning customers of potential hazards. On some level they're concerned that if they're too specific about all the bad things that could happen they'll actually scare the client away. eBay addresses these issues with a button on the front page of the site called "Why eBay is safe." The page that comes up has a list of issues and links for additional information. Everything is presented with the kind of candour and conversational tone one expects from one's doctor: "Breathe easy because the vast majority of buyers and sellers at eBay are honest and reliable." Cold comfort, of course, if you hit the exceptions.

The first point talks about the site's Feedback Forum, a place where eBay users can leave comments about each others' buying or selling experiences. Essentially, it's the community posting board or general store gossip circle. eBay also reassures nervous buyers that they're all covered by an insurance policy that will re-reimburse them if they don't receive something they've paid for (up to US$200 with a $25 deductible). And if there's any funny business going on, you can always contact eBay's SafeHarbor where eBay's 'safety staff' will step in and sort out the bad guy.

eBay also offers an escrow service called i-Escrow which will hold your payment for the seller until you've received the object and had a chance to inspect it. If you want to keep the item, you authorize the release of the payment. If you're dissatisfied you return the object. Finally, there's also a dispute resolution service called SquareTrade.

All these services are less about protecting property than

www.aisa4sale.com

*I hear and I forget.
I see and I remember.
I do and I understand.*

—*Confucius*

FIGURE **8.3**

about generating a sense of security. If someone's going to rip you off, they're going to rip you off. But it'll feel better if it 'seems' as if everybody's doing everything they can to play their part in the neighbourhood watch. This is feel-good stuff, it's about community and eBay does it very well.

Payment systems hamper auctions

China's auction sites follow much the same sort of model as eBay. Their greatest difference—and disadvantage—right now is in payment systems and product delivery. They also seem to be a bit more chaotic and random as to what they offer on the site and how they arrange the categories. Much of this may be cultural.

Eachnet.com and hot100.com.cn are two prominent Chinese C2C auction sites. Eachnet.com is a clever amalgam of English and phonetic Chinese. The Chinese name for the site is made up of two parts: "yi", which can mean "easy" as well as "exchange", and "gu" which means "interesting, delightful". Together these parts can be pronounced as "ee-chuu" (close to the English word "each"). The name means "the pleasure of exchanging". The word for the Net in Chinese sounds like wan. Eachnet is meant to signify an easy and interesting experience on the net.

www.eachnet.com

The most striking item on the front page of Eachnet.com consists of two rows of four icons illustrating the buying and selling process. Each is represented by four icons. Buyers and sellers must first register. Sellers must also negotiate the fee they will pay for the privilege of selling

Dial-a-lawyer

TRIVIA

1-4-8 hike

What call centre is manned by 31,000 government legal consultants and receives 1.35 million calls annually as well 400,000 visitors in person?

1-4-8 —"Yao Si Ba."

The Ministry of Justice in China set-up a hotline called 1-4-8 to deal with legal issues. It operates in 2,938 counties or 96.2% of all counties in China.

Some of the services provided are free and others are billed to the client.

Hot seats for sale

In China, you don't sell on price

their goods on eachnet.com. The second step for buyers is to submit a bid. The second step for sellers is to arrange to have their goods properly described and displayed on eachnet's site. The third icon for both shows a hand reaching out as if to shake another's hand. This is where eBay and its Chinese counterparts differ. It's called *wangxia* and it means "under the net." It's where buyer and seller meet to verify the goods and exchange money. The virtual world hands the process back to the real world.

The two parties are brought together when the auction closes. The top five bidders are sent the seller's e-mail address. The five finalists are encouraged to contact the seller to verify the goods and complete the transaction. The seller chooses whom he might meet and to whom he sells his goods. This of course can only occur face to face. Upon completion of the transaction, both buyer and seller are asked to submit an evaluation of their experience. eBay could never have run up the Nasdaq with such real-time and real-world logistics strapped to its back.

Eachnet has three bricks and mortar locations in Shanghai where buyers and sellers can arrange to meet. They also have locations where sellers can have photographs of the objects they want to sell scanned. Eachnet offers the scanning free of charge. Eachnet also makes it possible for consumers who are not yet online to use their service. Off-line sellers provide all the basic information except for an e-mail address. Instead, they supply a pager or cell phone number. Off-line buyers can also order a catalogue.

Eachnet succeeds because China is not North America. It's all about consumer's expectations. No one in China expects Eachnet to be able to handle online payment, nor do they expect China's distribution system to operate cheaply and efficiently. They go to Eachnet because it's a sourcing and

SIGN OF THE TIMES

An entrepreneur inmate on death row in Texas offered a special auction item to eBay bidders.
Michael Toney, convicted killer of three, wanted to sell the five seats to his execution on eBay. He put the seats up for bid at $100 to start. The posting was removed four hours later with no bids on the hot seats.
The money from the auction was to go to his family.

selling tool.

Eachnet claims to have sold a total of 312,748 items. They also claim 618,809 regular clients and 33,020 registered members. The day I last looked at their site they had 31,615 separate items for sale.

One of the first things I wanted to know from Eachnet.com and hot100.com was how much they were going to charge. It would be the first thing I'd want to know if I were thinking of selling something on their sites. I was looking at the sites with our translator, and I became increasingly frustrated when he couldn't find the information quickly. I kept telling him how easy it had been to get that information from the eBay site. That's when he reminded me that they weren't eBay sites. They were Chinese sites, they were designed and built for a Chinese audience. In China, the last thing you talk about is the actual price. You don't sell on price, you sell on quality and reliability and reputation.

hot100.com.cn struck me as being more closely modeled on eBay's site. It lacked the charming chaos of Eachnet. It also offered a range of general economic and commercial news. Categories included a second-hand shop, a flea market, business opportunities, airline tickets, personals, toys, clothes and real estate. I was told that the real estate section was probably their most successful and lucrative section. This section has a bolder, more sophisticated feel about it. It's also a lot faster than the other sections. All manner of commercial and residential real estate is listed on the site. I was particularly impressed by the prices. There was one commercial space in Shanghai being offered for lease at RMB280 (US$33.00) per month. Most businesses in the West spend more each month on old-fashioned postage stamps. ⇥

NOTE

Shanghai is quickly becoming a gateway for returning entrepreneur Chinese students.

The Student Services Centre in Shanghai has announced that over 758 new enterprises have been set up by these returning students.

These students have received their education abroad and are returning with new technology, patents and the desire to found and develop hi-tech companies.

"What is the use of a book," thought Alice, *"without pictures or conversation?"*

—Lewis Carroll

Your notes

 go to...

For additional information and updates to charts and graphs,
visit: **www.flyingarmchair.com**
the China s Wired! *resource site.*

Winners and Losers on the road to a virtual China

And life in a cybercafé

The last few chapters have examined some of the different forms e-commerce is taking in China. Some of the companies we looked at will succeed better than others. Some might fail. This chapter tries to identify the elements that distinguish a successful e-commerce strategy from an unsuccessful one. What works and what doesn't. Most successful Web sites or e-businesses are those that are clearly focused on the needs of a specific community. Their strength is directly proportional to the depth of their roots in that community.

www.community.com

A traditional community is a collection of individuals who share similar values and interests. They come together because the presence of others of similar mind and spirit affirms their values and enriches their lives. The community begins to grow when its values become known beyond its physical boundaries. Like-minded people are drawn together. Traditional communities are earth-bound and real. They are bricks and mortar and a dot on the map.

Traditional communities also contain other communities. The travel club, the yoga society and the volunteer fire

www.excite.com/travel

We are all brothers all In honour, as in one community, Scholars and gentlemen.
—*Wordsworth*

An unreserved community of thought and feeling.
— *W. Irving*

department are communities operating within the structure of the traditional community. They wouldn't exist without the framework of a traditional community and rarely extend beyond the community's physical boundaries.

www.chinabooks.com

The Internet is a virtual universe composed of individuals, organizations and communities. It's not defined or contained by a physical location. It's out there—wherever there is. The Internet is part of the earth's atmosphere.

www.eduasian.com

We enter the Internet as a single individual. We search out that which is familiar, or that which satisfies a need. Quickly, we become part of a community, or a series of overlapping and interpenetrating communities. Yaolan.com, eBay.com and our favourite source for news and information are virtual communities. Our presence is felt and recorded. What we do or don't do affects the virtual communities we travel through. Our existence on the Web changes the Web.

A community of book lovers

aba.com.cn evolved from a series of different but related communities. Xi Shu began as an expert teacher of **calligraphy**[1] The first community he created around himself were his students. Then he developed a new system of instruction. Xi Shu published this new system. The book sold over one million copies. Xi Shu brought those people together by forming a calligraphy club. Soon, it had over 100,000 members. He then began offering other books on calligraphy and books he thought the community might enjoy; thus, he slowly transformed the calligraphy club into a book club. He added a bricks and mortar bookstore. And then the bookstore went online. aba.com.cn is now a virtual community of book lovers.

www.abookloversshoppe.com

Sunevision has evolved much faster than aba.com.cn but follows the same principle of developing out of what it

The illiterate of the 21st century will not be those who cannot read and write, but those who cannot learn, unlearn and relearn.

— Alvin Toffler

[1] *Calligraphy can be described as writing as an art. The derivation of the word is from Greek meaning "good" or "beautiful" and for "writing."*

In Asia, calligraphy has long been considered a major art form equal to drawing, painting and sculpture.

knows and does best. It succeeds because it respects the needs and dynamics of its community—both traditional and virtual.

Sun Hung Kai Properties is one of Hong Kong's largest property development companies. Tak-sing Kwok founded the company and ran it until his death in 1990. Since then, the company has been run by his three sons, Walter, Thomas and Raymond.

www.shkp.com.hk

Tak-sing Kwok's first company had been an import/export business in Guangzhou. When the Japanese invaded China in 1937, Kwok moved his family and business to Macau. The family settled in Hong Kong after the Second World War. In Hong Kong, Kwok expanded his import/export business and moved into manufacturing. At one point, Tak-sing Kwok was the agent for YKK Zippers, which accounted for almost seventeen per cent of the world's zipper market.

A giant land bank

By the early 1970s, Hong Kong was beginning to move away from a manufacturing-based economy into financial services and property development. The stock market crash of 1972 pulled down property prices and Kwok began to buy land. Today, Sun Hung Kai has a land bank of 51 million sq. feet and 16,000 employees.

His son Walter was born in Hong Kong in 1950. He is the eldest of the Kwok brothers and is Chairman and Chief Executive Officer of Sun Hung Kai Properties. Thomas Kwok was born in 1951 and is a Vice-Chairman and Managing Director of the company. Raymond Kwok was born in 1952 and is also a Vice-Chairman and Managing Director. Sunevision is Sun Hung Kai's Internet play. It's also the brain child of Raymond Kwok.

I first met the Kwoks in late 1992. I've come to know Walter

SIGN OF THE TIMES

Pepsi Comes alive.
It was originally translated into Chinese as "Pepsi brings your ancestors back from the grave."

NOTE

Sunevision has merged AsianE2E.com and eei-X.com to create the dominant electronics e-commerce market place.

and his wife Wendy quite well. I've enjoyed many Sunday cruises on one or another of Walter's boats with their three children, family and friends. They are warm and generous people.

The biggest land baron

In 1992 Hong Kong was experiencing a property boom and Sun Hung Kai boasted the largest property bank of all the great Hong Kong developers. Sunevision is a subsidiary of Sun Hung Kai Properties. Raymond Kwok is Chairman and Chief Executive Officer of Sunevision.

I was hoping to be able to interview Raymond Kwok for this book. I almost caught up with him in Beijing in late January. At the time he was incredibly busy preparing for the GEM listing of Sunevision. Walter, Wendy and Raymond had flown in from Hong Kong for some high-level meetings—including a dinner with Jiang Mianheng, the 47-year-old son of Jiang Zemin.

I had heard that Jiang Zemin's son was involved in the high technology sector and was intrigued to hear that these two powerful families had come together. Intrigued but not surprised.

Guanxi is the term used to describe connections of blood and belonging. Success determined by who you know and how you're connected. A network of acquaintance based on reputation and blood. The original wireless Internet.

We add to this the fact that almost all Chinese harbour a great affection for the motherland. Many continue to send money back to ancestral villages. China's economic rebirth has been fueled in part by investments from these 70 million overseas Chinese. And Hong Kong's wealthiest families have financed some of China's most ambitious infrastructure projects. The connections between Hong Kong and Shanghai are particularly strong and deep. Many

WALTER KWOK

Walter Kwok attended the Imperial College, University of London. He has a Master of Science in Civil Engineering. For the past 10 years, he and his brothers Raymond and Thomas Kwok have been the driving force behind Sun Hung Kai Properties.

DID YOU KNOW?

We get a hint that the Internet is likely to prosper in China from a recent report in *Science* magazine noting that President Jiang Zemin himself likes to exchange e-mail with other world leaders. Jiang made the comment while denying stories that Chinese citizens cannot gain free access to the Internet. He called this notion "nonsense." However his embrace of the Web carried the caution that, "One thing must be ensured: That facts should not be distorted. And I think this should apply to the Internet." How this would come about, he did not say.

A new morning

www.fudan.edu.cn

www.chimeb.edu.cn.org

of Shanghai's great industrialists moved their families and businesses to Hong Kong in 1949. Jiang Zemin and Zhu Rongji were mayors of Shanghai. Hong Kong's current Chief Executive, C.H. Tung, was born in Shanghai, as was his second-in-command, Chief Secretary for Administration, Anson Chan. Given this background, a business link between the Kwoks and Jiang is a natural. Jiang Mianheng is a graduate of Fudan University in Shanghai. He began his post-graduate degree at Drexel University in Philadelphia in 1986. Jiang's field of study was high-temperature superconductivity. After graduation, he spent a year in California at Hewlett-Packard. When he returned to China in 1992, Jiang was awarded a senior position as vice director of the Shanghai Institute of Metallurgy.

In 1993, Jiang was asked to help create a commercially viable company from some of the Institute's activities. The company Jiang helped create is called Simtek (Shanghai Simtek Industrial Ltd.). Simtek was quickly followed by the formation of a holding company called SAIL (Shanghai Alliance Investment Ltd.). SAIL owns stakes in such diverse companies as the publisher Shanghai Xinhui Disk Group Co. and the Shanghai Audio-Visual Press.

In 1997, SAIL took a 30 per cent stake in the newly-formed Shanghai Information Investment Company, a company designed to spearhead telecommunications development in Shanghai. Other shareholders included a cable TV company, the telephone bureau and the government department in charge of cable TV. One of the Shanghai Information Investment Company's first projects was to begin laying the **fiberoptic**[1] cable that will provide Shanghai's Internet **Protocol**[2] backbone.

Shanghai recently approved the formation of three companies to operate the three key aspects of the network:

NOTE

Fudan University was founded in 1905. Fudan means "a new morning." The phrase is from a Confucian classic entitled, "Shang Shu" "The Book of History", written about 3,000 years ago.

The complete quote is as follows: "Brilliant are the sunlight and the moonlight; Again the morning glory after a night."

[1] *Fiberoptics is the science of light transmission through glass or plastic fibers.*

[2] *Protocol is a standard procedure for regulating data transmission between computers. These standards will assure that different network products can work together. For example, POP3 is Post Office Protocol version 3.*

e-commerce, Internet access and cable TV. The Shanghai Information Investment Company has significant interests in each of these new companies.

Jiang also sits on the five-member board of China Netcom Corp. China Netcom is building a fibre-optic network that will eventually connect fifteen cities along China's prosperous east coast. China Netcom is set to become a very strong competitor of China Telecom and plans to offer inexpensive telephone service over the Internet to 50 million people in the region.

www.netcomsystems.com

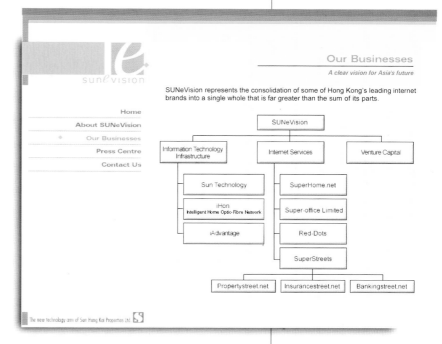

FIGURE 9.1

Below: Sunevision's corporate structure.

I did manage to have lunch with Wendy Kwok, Walter's wife, before she returned to Hong Kong. She said she'd try and set something up with Raymond, or arrange for me to talk to one of Raymond's deputies. A few days later, Wendy faxed me David Kwok's phone number. David Kwok is not related to the Sun Hung Kai Kwoks, but his card lists him as *Assistant to Vice Chairman of the company.*

What's in a name?

Sunevision is described as the new technology arm of Sun Hung Kai Properties. Its mission is "To be the best provider of premium-quality Internet infrastructure and services in Asia, enabling businesses and individuals to thrive in the "Information Age."

www.igigroup.com

NOTE

A partnership with Commercial Press E-Business Holdings Ltd. and Sunevision (25 per cent share) CP BookNet will develop the world's largest online Chinese language bookstore with over 250,000 titles. Initially books will be offered as well as audio-visual and multi-media products, computer software. etc.

Sunevision estimates the market value to be $HK100 billion in China alone.

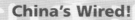

Could a big company like Sun Hung Kai accommodate a technology arm? Could they afford not to? Peter Yip had told me that Raymond Kwok was one of the people he'd tried to interest in chinadotcom. Three years ago he wasn't interested. And then suddenly something happened. Apparently, about eighteen months ago, Kwok decided to jump in with both feet. To his credit, he was still well ahead of the pack.

I met with David Kwok in his office in the Sun Hung Kai Centre at 30 Harbour Road in Wanchai. Kwok's office overflows with paper and documents. There was paper everywhere—and it all seemed to be in motion. Kwok assured me that none of it would stay long enough to gather dust.

David Kwok was charming, open and modest. I was confused about what Sun Hung Kai was doing, how they were going to do it, and why. Apparently, Raymond Kwok had spent about a year doing research before launching Sunevision. He'd spent a lot of time talking with CEOs in Silicon Valley. He wanted to forge the right alliances with the right partners. Partners whose businesses and business philosophies complemented Sun Hung Kai.

After Raymond had done his research, he invited a number of people to pitch him business ideas. (When I met with David Kwok in February they were still receiving between five and ten proposals every day.) One of these pitches was for Red Dot, an auction site similar to eBay. During the pitch, Raymond began to realize that a secure and reliable infrastructure was going to be essential if any e-commerce activity was going to succeed. You can't sell much if a power surge knocks out your site. This is the world—or community—Kwok knew better than anything else.

The pitch was successful as Red Dot is now a subsidiary of

www.red-dots.com

When I'm working on a problem, I never think about beauty. I think only how to solve the problem. But when I have finished, if the solution is not beautiful, I know it is wrong.

—*Richard Buckminister Fuller*

Sunevision's Internet Services. More importantly, Kwok was able to find a way to apply his expertise—and the expertise of Sun Hung Kai—to the new digital universe. The result is called iAdvantage, a subsidiary of Sunevision's Information Technology Infrastructure.

iAdvantage[1] is a 20,000 square foot state-of-the-art facility located in one of Sun Hung Kai's newest and most sophisticated building's in Kowloon. It is a facility that offers consistent, uninterrupted 24-hour server operation and high speed Internet connection over a fibre-optic system. The power supply is guaranteed by two back-up systems, an Uninterruptable Power Supply System (UPS) and two stand-by diesel generators.

Raymond Kwok's first step was to do what he and his family does best—create on infrastructure. In the months following the launch of iAdvantage, Kwok began adding on subsidiaries that reflected all the corollary activities of his core property development business.

All-intelligent buildings

Propertystreet.net sells real estate. Insurancestreet.net sells insurance. And all the new Sun Hung Kai developments—both residential and commercial—are being wired with their own Intranets. Currently, Sun Hung Kai has 32.1 million square feet of properties in various stages of development. It also holds the largest completed investment property portfolio in Hong Kong, with 18.9 million square feet of attributable floor area. That's a lot of cable and one heck of an audience.

Raymond Kwok's Sunevision is as rational and as elegant a digital evolution as Xi Shu's. Both men shaped the Internet around their core strengths. Both men will succeed because they use the Internet to help them do what they do best. The only difference may be one of scale.

[1]   *iAdvantage is working towards becoming the leading facility Management and Co-location Services Provider in Asia. It plans to open six new data centres in China and Hong Kong totaling 600,000 Sq.ft. of space. These service centres are to be completed by year-end 2000.*

Sunevision is the first company in China and Asia to integrate and leverage the entire Internet value chain to achieve critical mass with significant economies of scale.

- Raymond Kwok

The younger generation in China have embraced the Internet. They see it as their greatest hope for the future. Those a little older aren't so optimistic. Many of the people I talked to in China over 30 were skeptical that the Internet would ever change their lives. A few bright young entrepreneurs were raising a lot of money and getting a lot of press, but how's that going to affect me? Many of these people were professionals who used the Internet at work. They just couldn't see how it would change their lives.

www.superhome.net

If my only contact with or knowledge of the Internet came from Sparkice I might feel the same way. Sparkice tries to do too much for too many different people. By trying to embrace the universe it loses all focus. The universe is an idea, community has meaning.

Sparkice: A bridge too far?

Edward Zeng is the president and CEO of Sparkice. Zeng is one of China's most famous and visible Internet entrepreneurs. Zeng opened the first Sparkice E-commerce Service Center (ESC) in the fall of 1996. ESC was initially founded to provide Internet access and e-commerce training to local businesses. Over the next few years Zeng added the Sparkice International Trading Network which is described on his Web site as, "The world's most comprehensive e-commerce powered service for global purchasing and trade to, from and within China." Essentially, Sparkice International Trading Network[1] aims to connect everybody to everybody else.

Sparkice has also developed—in co-operation with the China Statistics Bureau—a database containing information on one million Chinese companies. The Sparkice family also includes a site called JadeMall which sells traditional Chinese crafts, a global online charitable donations site, and a source of industrial reports called ChinaRep.

When the president does it, that means it is not illegal
—*Richard M. Nixon*

[1] *The current number of companies listed with Sparkice according to their Web site is 3,706.*

Clinton surfs the Net

www.cnmall.com

Finally, Sparkice claims it is about to expand the "Sparkice International Trading Network to include four new vertical communities—Machinery and Hardware, Electronics and Communications, Home and Office, Textiles and Accessories."

I first heard of Sparkice and Zeng through the international media. President Clinton had visited Zeng's flagship cybercafé at the New World centre in Beijing during his 1998 trip to China. I went there to check it out for myself and to access my e-mail. Sparkice charges RMB 30 per hour for e-mail—much less than my hotel and on a much faster system.

Sparkice's literature is full of high profile celebrity endorsements. There are written plugs from people like Clinton, Canadian Prime Minister Jean Chrétien, the American futurist Alvin Toffler, Charles Schwab, and U.S. Commerce Secretary William Daly. The brochure also displays the signatures of Jiang Zemin and Zhu Rongji, as well as the chops of a number of government bureaus including the China State Development and Planning Commission[1], the China Statistics Bureau and the Bank of China. And Zeng's picture is everywhere.

Corporate literature is supposed to summarize and clarify a company's operations. Sparkice has lots of literature about a lot of different kinds of activity. But it confuses rather than clarifies. I kept thinking, 'Yeah, but what do they do?'

I very much liked the cybercafé. It was very well run and convenient. But I couldn't see how he was making any money—let alone paying the rent.

There are about 30 terminals lining the walls or on circular

NOTE

According to "The Cybercafé Search Engine," the database contains 4,702 verified cybercafés, public access points and kiosks in 144 countries.

A search of China indicates over 2,000 cybercafés, which is almost 45 per cent of their entire database.

Reuters film crew at Sparkice Cybercafé, Beijing.

[1] *Succeeded the State Planning Commission (SPC) in 1998.*

Computer: a million morons working at the speed of light.
—David Ferrier

tables, a couple of printers, a section for computer training sessions, three or four staff and a bar serving beer, liquor, coffee, tea and snacks. It's what any average North American expects a cybercafé to look like.

I visited the cybercafé several times during my stay in Beijing. I never saw any training sessions, nor were there ever more than a maximum of seven or eight people accessing the Internet at any one time. And most of these people were expatriates using the cybercafé for the same reason I was using it.

Sparkice charges RMB30 per hour for Internet access. An experienced hotel worker might earn RMB1,000 per month—and that's considered a high wage. Sparkice isn't something the local surfer can afford—especially when competitors offer Internet access for anything from RMB5 per hour to RMB14 per hour.

A government crackdown

I happened to be in the Sparkice Cybercafé in Beijing in January when the government announced that it was going to impose strict controls on the content of both local and foreign Web sites. The Associated Press crew arrived just before noon. I asked the producer what they were up to. He seemed a bit nervous by my question and dodged it by saying that journalists—and producers—were generalists. He said he really didn't know very much about the Internet. All he'd been told was that they were going to be shutting down Web sites.

Left: television film crew at work during the January crisis— Sparkice Cybercafé, January 26, 2000.

One of the reasons this particular cybercafé is so famous is because it actually looks like a cybercafé. As the Associated Press producer told me, it's the only thing they can film in China that looks as if it has anything to do with the Internet.

www.netcafeguide.com

FIGURE 9.2

An hour or so later, a Reuters crew arrived to film the same story. Later that night, I watched the Reuters clip on the TV in my hotel room. I noticed that they had been careful to film only Chinese or Asian clients. No one would know that most of them were expatriates. Nevertheless, it felt as if they were talking about another country and another time.

I returned to Sparkice the next day. As I expected, it was

Below: Sparkice Web page.

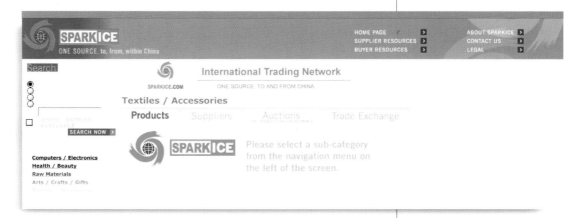

open and as busy as usual. I decided to call up the *New York Times* site. Perhaps they actually were blocking sites and imposing restrictions? But then I noticed that the fellow at the table adjacent to me was busy perusing a pornographic site called blowjob.com.

To be fair to Zeng, I decided to spend some time looking at his Web sites—perhaps the cybercafé was something of a loss-leader? As I navigated Sparkice.com I kept asking myself if I were a manufacturer would I want to sell my products on this site? Would I buy something from one of these sites?

When something really works—when it connects—it gets hot. There's a buzz about it and a building momentum. Success draws people. It becomes a self-fulfilling phenomenon. Think of eBay or Yahoo or even Yaolan. There's a palpable sense of a community's needs being

NOTE

Sparkice.com Inc., announced that it has been selected by Metro AG, the world's third largest retailer, as its strategic e-commerce procurement partner for Asia.

"We believe our partnership with a company as respected and as well known as Metro AG validates our business model in the strongest terms possible," said Edward Zeng, President and CEO of Sparkice.com.

Open for business, nobody home

served faster and more efficiently than ever before.

Sparkice.com offers a range of products for sale on its site. I chose sporting goods, as China probably manufactures more sporting goods than any other country in the world. How much would a pair of running shoes cost? Unfortunately, when I finally got through to the sporting goods section a sign popped up saying, *Sorry, there are no products in this category at present.* No sporting goods in China?

I tried *Travel Accessories.* The only products offered under travel accessories were umbrellas. The first umbrella displayed was for golf. All together, there were ten different types of umbrellas on sale, all from the same manufacturer. There was nothing in *Software* and *PCs/Components* had only one item, something called a U-Beley-assistant tool for computer operation. The manufacturer was Beijing Hanson Technology Ltd.

How does Sparkice survive? I don't know. I can't look through their literature and get a clear sense of what they do. Are they B2B, B2C, a production house or a cybercafé? Unfortunately, they're all those things and more. A successful B2B or B2C not only requires a sophisticated understanding of the digital world, it also requires a solid grounding in whatever industry it is focused on.

Will Sparkice survive? Zeng has been at this since 1996. He's not likely to give up easily. The great advantage of e-commerce is that it can turn on a dime. It has no baggage—no leases to break. Re-program the system, refine the process, rededicate and focus, focus, focus.

ChinaNow.com is one of the more intriguing entries in the China Internet field. Like both Sunevision and Sparkice it doesn't fall into any single easily described category. It is—

 Business to Consumer B2C

Business to Business B2B

 www.chinanow.com

NOTE

The following is a list of just a few of the many cybercafés in Shanghai:

Shanghai Library

Cost: RMB 5 per hour.

Address: Hua Hai Xi Lu.

Note: Lots of computers. Need membership card.

Internet Café

Cost: RMB 7 for 30 min.

Open: 1 pm -11pm

Address: 3/F hao Du Plaza, 400 east Jin Ling Lu

Tel: 63355-7070

Note: coffee(RMB 15), beer(RMB10), no smoking.

Infohighway

Cost:RMB 5 per hour

Open: 9am-6pm

Address; 181 Rui Jin Er Lu.

Tel: 6415-5006

SC & T

Cost: RMB 10 per hour

Open: wkdys:10am-2 am wkeds:10 am- 6 pm

Address: 1/F 238 South Shanxi Lu.

Tel: 6473-0874 ext. 229

By August 2000, the sporting goods section of Sparkice.com held 41 products from 8 suppliers. Products included in-line roller skates, skateboards, ice skates, air guns, darts and dartboards.

but really isn't—B2B, B2C or C2C. It doesn't grow from some long-established commercial entity or industry vertical like Sunevision. And though it's aimed at an extremely broad audience, it's not trying to be everything to everybody, like Sparkice. ChinaNow is about content. If anything, its roots are in the shifting fads of pop culture and mass media. ChinaNow delivers information.

ChinaNow: news and nightsoil

I stumbled upon ChinaNow in the late fall of 1999. My first reaction was astonishment. Most of the China-based sites I'd seen were well designed but serious and heavy looking. It was clear that the people behind the sites cared less about the look of the site than its function. ChinaNow certainly cared how it looked, and it looked attractive.

I stayed at the ChinaNow site because I found a terrific story about housing in Shanghai by a writer named Titi Liu. Ms. Liu and her husband (Eric Rosenblum, COO of ChinaNow. My, what a small world!) had recently relocated to Shanghai. Most accommodation for foreigners is high-rise non-descript modern. Ms. Liu and her husband wanted to find something a little more interesting, and something closer to the ground.

Shanghai is undergoing a huge amount of infrastructure development and residential and commercial construction. Tragically, many of Shanghai's older buildings—remnants of another time, and the product of another culture—are being lost.

Obviously no historical society

Liu and her husband wanted a home with character and history. Eventually, they found a six-room longtang house (a lane house, or townhouse). Liu describes the challenges such a residence presents. Their new home isn't connected

ChinaNow currently shows the cities of Shanghai, Beijing, Nanjing and Chengdu on its Web site.

Features are covered under the following titles: Then, Music, Travel and Rock Talk.

Rock Talk covers what is described as 'old time' on the Beijing rock scene, which apparently saw its heyday in the late 80s and the early 90s.

Travel China shows air tickets, embassies, photo tours, travel info, tourist offices and sights.

to a sewage system; once a month an old fashioned night-soil truck called a *choufen che* comes rumbling down the narrow laneway. There's no set schedule. The truck shows up when sewage starts to back-up into someone's home. Fortunately, the Rosenblum's home is on slightly higher ground then its neighbours.

The article introduces the patron saint of Shanghai's colonial architecture—and a legendary figure in the expatriate community—Tess Johnston. Johnston offers all sorts of wonderful—and extremely practical—advice. Before you sign anything, make sure you see the ownership certificate for the property. A green ownership certificate means it can be rented to anyone. If it's red it can't be rented to foreigners

That was my introduction to ChinaNow. What drew me in? Initially, curiosity. But I stayed because I found something I couldn't have found anywhere else. Why did I respond so strongly? Because it touched something in me that has meaning. Something very important to me. ChinaNow hooked me because their content had meaning.

ChinaNow was founded by Tony Zhang and Graham Earnshaw. Zhang was born and raised in Shanghai, but left at 17 to study in the United States. He completed a degree in Mechanical Engineering at UCLA and worked for a few years in the automotive industry before returning to Shanghai. In 1996, Zhang teamed up with Graham Earnshaw to produce Shanghai's first English Web site, www.shanghai-ed.com. Together they also founded Park 97, one of Shanghai's top night spots, on the edge of Fuxi Park. Zhang and Earnshaw also founded two English language magazines, *Travel China Shanghai Edition* and *Buzz*.

Zhang is listed as the CEO of ChinaNow, Earnshaw is

www.121.com

www.ucla.com

The Rosenblums

If the automobile had followed the same development as the computer, a Rolls-Royce would today cost $100, get a million miles per gallon, and explode once a year killing everyone inside.

—Robert Cringely, Infoworld

Founder and Creative Director. Earnshaw has more than 23 years experience as a journalist—most of which he spent in Asia. For five years Earnshaw was Asia Bureau Chief for Reuters news service. Earnshaw and Zhang both make their homes in Shanghai.

ChinaNow aims to create an information-intensive guide to city life. The model for ChinaNow is U.S.-based CitySearch. Their first priority is to become the best and most comprehensive source of information on any one particular city. When they get the content right, and the right audience, they'll add something called a "virtual shopping centre."

www.citysearch.com

Virtual shopping centre

ChinaNow's first sites are focused on Shanghai and Beijing. They're also in both English and Chinese. Eventually, the English sites will operate relatively independently and be focused on foreign tourists. ChinaNow's primary goal is to develop a city by city information resource site aimed primarily at Chinese **yuppies**.[1]

There are very few content sites in China that generate original material. Most of the sites discussed in this book draw content from other sources—if they have content at all. ChinaNow's literature points out that China lacks compelling content in all media. Yes! Everything has the same limited depth, breadth and tone. That springs in part from China's desire to control information that might incite political dissent. Content is one of the most contentious issues for China and the Internet. How do they hope to go where no one has gone before?

www.yuppy.com

Zhang and Earnshaw launched ChinaNow in July of 1999. chinadotcom had rocketed up the Nasdaq but dot com hysteria had yet to take hold. ChinaNow's fortunes—and future—changed shortly after the U.S. and China signed a

1 Yuppy=Young Urban Professional.

In China, yuppies are sometimes called 'little Emperors' because their parents and grandparents provide for all the wants of this 'only child' generation.

ChinaNow emerges

WTO agreement in November 1999. China dot coms became all the rage. By early 2000, ChinaNow was able to secure investments from both an international high technology company and a Chinese government venture capital firm. This funding will allow ChinaNow to expand to 15 or 20 cities by the end of 2000. The identity of their investment partners also explains their confidence in venturing into China's dangerous and murky content rules and regulations.

The first physical contact I had with anyone from ChinaNow was in Beijing. I called Kaiser Kuo shortly after I arrived in Beijing to arrange a convenient time for me to stop by their offices.

www.arizona.edu

Tangs for the memories

Kaiser Kuo is a rock star. He founded China's leading hard rock band, **Tang Dynasty**[1] in 1989 ,then took a short break from his musical career to complete a graduate degree in Chinese History at the University of Arizona. He returned to China and Tang Dynasty in 1996. Kuo left Tang Dynasty for good in June 1999 and now runs ChinaNow's Beijing office.

All I had to do to find the ChinaNow offices was to follow the smell of new carpet and fresh paint. The offices were 'evolving.' Lots of people, lots of noise, and urgency. Nevertheless, Kuo was able to give me some time and some helpful insights into ChinaNow and his role in it. And everything was happening very quickly. Kuo was particularly happy to tell me that a top writer from the *Lonely Planet Guide* had just agreed to come on board. Caroline Liou would be in charge of the travel section and books, while Kuo would oversee all English language editorial.

When I first sat down in Kuo's office, I asked him to tell me something about his background. Without even the blink of

SIGN OF THE TIMES

Please drop your trousers for best results.

A sign in a Wuhan dry cleaners.

[1] *The Tang Dynasty (A.D. 618-A.D. 907 is recognized as the period when China became one of the wealthiest and most powerful countries in the world.*

This period was called the Golden Age of literature and art and saw Buddhism become part of the Chinese culture.

an eye he pointed to a guitar standing in a case in the corner, "That's what I am. That was my life, until now."

Eric Rosenblum, the Chief Operating Officer, has made almost as radical a shift in careers as has Kaiser Kuo. Rosenblum is ChinaNow's Chief Operating Officer. He completed a degree in East Asian Studies at Harvard University (where he met his wife Titi) before refining his Chinese language skills at the Johns Hopkins program[1] at Nanjing University. He then went on to earn a Masters of Business Administration degree from MIT. No slouch here.

www.nju.edu.cn

Rosenblum had been with the Boston Consulting Group in Hong Kong for four years before a growing restlessness and the offer from ChinaNow prompted him to leave.[2]

www.mit.edu

I arrived in Shanghai just before Chinese New Year and the week-long Spring festival holiday. I left a few messages at the ChinaNow offices as soon as I got in. Rosenblum was out of town but called me as soon as he returned. I suggested we meet at ChinaNow's offices. Rosenblum said the heat wouldn't have been turned back on yet. Apparently, heat is turned off during holidays to prevent employers from forcing their employees to work. Rosenblum went on to say that they were presently occupying their offices rent-free. For some reason or another, the government had seized the landlord's chop. As a result, the landlord couldn't 'chop' any rental agreements and was therefore unable to collect any rent. Imagine Donald Trump losing his chop!

www.bcg.com

The landlord lost his chop

We arranged to meet at a small restaurant near Rosenblum's home. Rosenblum is a tall man and solid, but comes across as gentle and deferential. He has the face of a serious scholar—intense, curious, probing but cautious. His mind seems to be operating at several different levels at once—perfect for the digital world.

[1] The Center for Chinese and American Studies is operated by Nanjing University and the Johns Hopkins University. At Nanjing, each year, up to 45 Chinese students are taught in English about international affairs by American faculty. At the same time, a similar number of outside students, mostly American, study Chinese political, economic and social issues in Chinese. They are taught by the faculty of Nanjing University.

[2] The Boston Consulting Group officially opened their Shanghai office in 1993.
"Not only were we the first multinational consulting firm with a joint venture in China, but in 1999 we converted to the much sought-after status of wholly-owned foreign entity allowing us to operate freely in China."

We began by talking about the big issues. When would the dot com bubble burst? We agreed that it wouldn't burst, it'll only recede a little. What does the Internet mean to our lives? It means a complete transformation of who and what we are and how we live our lives. I'm sure we sounded like a couple of over-enthusiastic caffeine-cranked undergrads.

We also talked about the practical side of running ChinaNow. I asked how much he paid his staff. Web monkeys—the young ones fresh out of university who love everything about the Web—earn RMB1,500 to RMB2,000 per month. Managers are usually between 30 and 33 and can earn RMB2,500 to RMB4,000 per month. A really good manager can end up making up to RMB6,000 per month. Rosenblum puts this in context by saying that a Master Law Professor in Shanghai is lucky to earn RMB700 per month. The average age of ChinaNow's staff is presently 26.

Rosenblum seems confident that ChinaNow is developing at the pace it should. He really believes tough, rational management is the only route to take; that and focus. I ask him what his greatest strength is. Rosenblum claims to have a good solid knowledge of all the fundamentals necessary for building a business from the ground up. He's good at financial analysis and management. He's good with people. Finally, he says he's good at a lot of things but not great at any one thing. He feels his strength is also his weakness. A **Jack of all trades and master of none.**[1]

Creativity is a wild card

Rosenblum expresses some anxiety about his evolving management skills and the challenges ahead. He says he did a lot of project management while he was at Boston Consulting Group but that was always only overseeing four or five people. In February, ChinaNow's staff had already reached 40. Rosenblum was also concerned about

1 *The phrase was originally coined and mentioned in various poems by Walt Whitman, William Wordsworth and William Butler Yeats.*

www.creativity.com

www.matrix.com

managing the complex, multi-dimensional nature of the company's growth. ChinaNow operates across a series of sometimes interpenetrating planes. The first is language, as ChinaNow operates in both English and Chinese. The second is geography, as ChinaNow intends to be as city-specific and regionally-focused as possible. Finally, there are channels that operate across the system, delivering entertainment, travel services, e-commerce and other information services. Rosenblum describes ChinaNow as a three-dimensional **matrix**. In his mind and to his eyes, the virtual is real.

It's hard to say how effective ChinaNow will be in creating content that its Chinese audience will find compelling. Creativity is always something of a wild card. And popular taste is fickle. The final product is uncertain. But the process is focused and the execution impeccable. ChinaNow is doing everything Sparkice isn't. And doing it very well.

Finally, I asked Rosenblum if it had been difficult to leave the security of a career at Boston Consulting Group for the madness of a China Internet start-up. He said that the decision was actually quite easy. He'd been thinking about it for some time. I asked if he was working longer hours at ChinaNow. Was the job consuming him? He said he'd always worked hard. He liked to work hard. When he was at the consulting group he'd work late but sleep through the night. Today, he works the same hours but often wakes in the middle of the night and worries. Will our second-round funding arrive in time? Where will we find the skilled staff we need? He says he never worried about those kind of issues before, he never had to. He wasn't complaining, it was just an observation. ➡

1   A rectangular array of elements set out by rows and columns. It could also be an enclosure which something originates or develops from, derived from the latin for womb.

Update:

ChinaNow added a fourth dimension to the matrix in June: product. ChinaNow is now producing magazines and books. Adding print production creates a fourth dimension that Rosenblum claims is "virtually impossible to keep straight in an organization chart."

All that openth the matrix is mine; and every firstling among thy cattle, whether ox or sheep, that is male.

— Exodus 34, 19

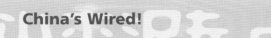

Your notes

 go to...

For additional information and updates to charts and graphs, visit: **www.flyingarmchair.com** *the* `Chinas Wired!` *resource site.*

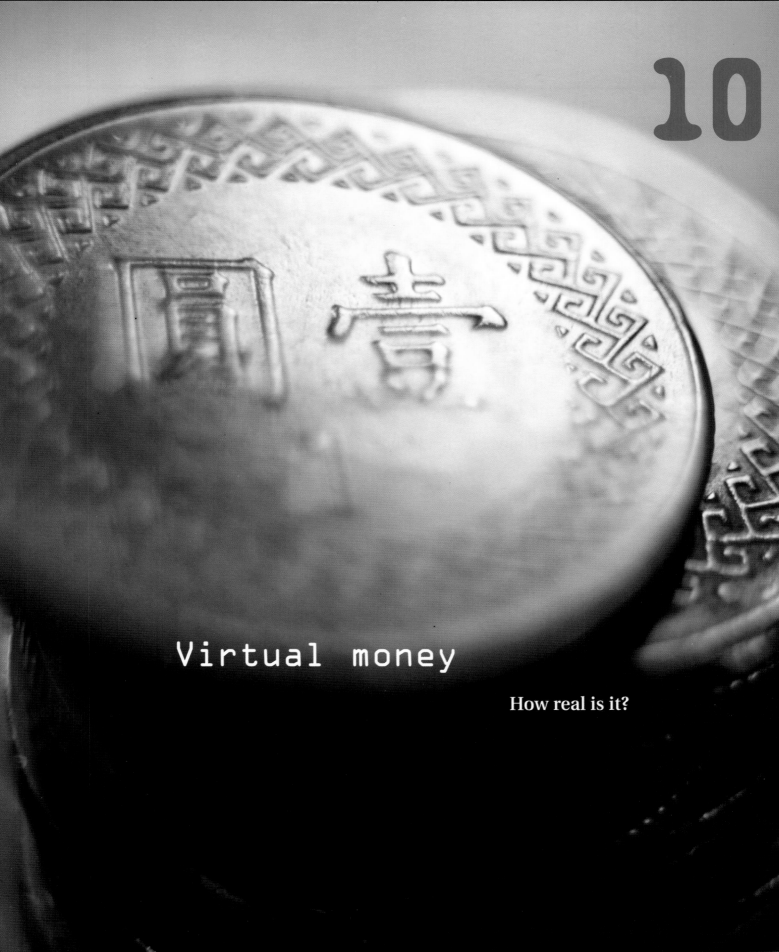

Virtual money

How real is it?

Remember Madam X? She was the woman who turned up at the Kennedy School of Government in Cambridge, Massachusetts to attempt to lay down the law on the Internet in China. We met her in Chapter Eight. You will recall that when a man in the audience asked her when China would let its people enjoy the evils of credit, there were chuckles in the audience but stony faces up front. Frankly, I don't think Madam X even heard it. If she did she probably would have thought it nonsensical. Credit? Why is credit so important? Especially for a country that boasts the highest per capita savings rate in the world?

*Neither a borrower nor a lender be, For loan oft loses both itself and friend, And borrowing dulls the edge of husbandry.**

—Hamlet, Act I, Scene III
Polonius to his son Laertes

* thrift

The question of credit is critical to the continuing development of the Internet in China—and everywhere else. Today in China, payment systems include postal orders, direct deposits into the e-tailer's bank account, cash on delivery and the use of debit or credit cards. In most of the rest of the wired world, credit cards are the standard source of payment. In North America, the convenience of shopping on the Web would be lost if we were forced to pay for our purchases with postal orders or deposits into someone else's bank account. We just wouldn't do it. eBay.com and Amazon.com wouldn't and couldn't exist.

Why are we so comfortable with credit and China so cautious? Perhaps the man in the audience shouldn't be so smug. I don't think people in the West are all that comfortable with the levels of debt our fellow citizens carry. I think we try not to think about it too much. All that credit has been extended on the assumption that prices and values will continue to rise—forever.

So what if I have a 25-year mortgage on my house? So what if it costs me half my salary? The interest rate on the mortgage is less than the appreciation rate of the house. I can sell it off when I retire and live off the interest. Yes, assuming it will continue to appreciate in value and interest rates remain stable. But...

www.statcan.ca

Unravelling the Golden Thread

www.mckinsey.com

In the West, we readily accept the notion of credit. It reinforces our optimism and our belief that even better days lie ahead. This may be naive or just plain silly. Its origins are in part historical. Most of us came to North America as immigrants. Our families chose to come to a new continent, in the belief it would provide a better life. Many also wanted to be free of the history of the countries we left behind—and all that that implied. We believe in a

FIGURE 10.1

SOCIAL AND ECONOMIC INDICATORS (US$) FOR CHINA

Overall (1998)	Rank in world
Population: 1.248billion	1
Territory: 9,596,960 sq. km.	3
GDP: 961bn	7
Exports: 183.8bn	9
Imports: 140.2bn	11
Total Trade: 323.9bn	11
Foreign Exchange Reserves: 145.0bn	2
Per Capita GDP: 774	81

Corporate (1997)

Number of corporations with annual sales >1bn: 79

Individual (1997)

Annual savings rate: 40%
Average savings per household: $1,800
Home ownership: 33%
Household car ownership: 3%

Source: McKinsey

better future because it would be a future we created, not one we inherited. Such optimism was essential for our founding fathers; without it their many sacrifices and hardships would have been impossible to endure.

Such historical references may explain the North American love of credit—or at least our comfort with it. But why is China so reticent to indulge? The Internet in China will continue to grow only if systems of payment can be devised that are efficient, easy and secure. Systems like all-purpose credit cards.

www.moftec.gov.cn

Chinese from Guangdong Province have been immigrating to the west coast of North America since the latter part of the 19th century. At the time, there was little work for them in southern China. Famine and political instability had ravaged the region.

California here I come

There were jobs in North America—in the gold mines of California and on the railroads in Canada. Thousands of men immigrated to Vancouver in search of work[1]. Conditions were severe and the work punishing and dangerous. Some claim that one Chinese labourer died for every mile of railroad built. When construction on the line finished in 1885 many returned to their villages in China. Those that stayed in Canada maintained a strong spiritual and emotional connection with their motherland.

One of these men managed to find work picking rags in Vancouver. He earned barely enough to survive—but certainly more than he could ever make in China. At some point, he returned to his home village in China and married. It was a traditional, arranged marriage. Shortly after the ceremony he returned to Vancouver. He sent money back to his wife regularly and returned to see her every few years. Ultimately, five children were born to this couple.

It will be all very well to exclude Chinese labour, when we can replace it with white labour, but until that is done, it is better to have Chinese labour than no labour at all.

—*Prime Minister John A. Macdonald, House of Commons Debates, Canada 1883.*

[1] *In 1881, there were 4,383 Chinese in Canada. In 1891, the number had risen to 9,126. By 1901, the total number of Chinese in Canada was 17,314. According to a recent census(1996), there were 860,000 Chinese in Canada.*

This was not an uncommon scenario. Canada had a Chinese Immigration Act in place between 1923 and 1947. Men who had come to work on the railroad often returned home to find wives and start families. The exclusion act allowed them to stay and work in Canada but did not allow them to bring over their wives and children. Finally, in 1948, this man brought his wife and five children to live with him in Vancouver.

It wasn't chicken-feed

There were four boys and one girl. The four boys were particularly industrious. In the 1950s, they opened a chicken shop in downtown Vancouver. The brothers kept live chickens on the premises. Customers were free to choose a chicken to suit their needs. The brothers would then kill it, pluck it and butcher it. The customer would return twenty minutes later to pick up the freshly butchered chicken. The brothers did well. The store prospered. Eventually, the brothers were able to buy the property.

Times changed. The city decided that it wasn't very healthy for the brothers to be selling chickens from the same location where they'd been butchered. They were given an ultimatum. Move the butchering elsewhere or close up the shop. The brothers decided to set up a chicken processing plant. In time,

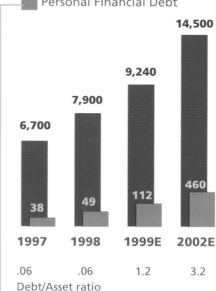

Personal Debt vs. Assets China (RMB Billions)

■ Personal Financial Assets
■ Personal Financial Debt

14,500

9,240

7,900

6,700

38   49   112   460

1997   1998   1999E   2002E

.06   .06   1.2   3.2
Debt/Asset ratio

Personal debt as a percentage of assets in the U.S. is 36%, ('97)

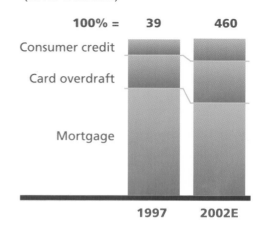

Breakdown of debt in China (RMB Billions)

100% =   39   460

Consumer credit

Card overdraft

Mortgage

1997   2002E

Source: McKinsey—statistical analysis

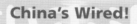

www.hastingspark.com

www.bankrate.com

FIGURE 10.3

it became one of Vancouver's most successful meat processing plants. The brothers became very wealthy.

The brothers grew old. They worked less and enjoyed life. One day, one of the brothers was leaving the race track when he was struck and killed by a drunk driver. He was sixty-five. He left a widow and three children. Fortunately, the drunk driver had insurance. The family of the dead brother took the drunk driver to court. They wanted compensation.

In North America, it's not uncommon to sue someone for lost wages. Nor is it uncommon to sue for the financial support of a widow and her children. In this case, the deceased was sixty-five and very wealthy. His children were grown and had families of their own. What did they want compensation for, emotional distress?

The family argued that the untimely death of the father reduced the amount of inheritance his estate would eventually be passing along to his children. They based their claim on the notion of the Golden Thread. In China, people save money for their estate. They put money aside to be sure that it is passed down to their children or heirs. It is cultural more than it is economic.

The Golden Thread is the economic lifeline that ties one generation to the next. Each generation is only a custodian of the family's wealth. Each generation is expected to add to the inheritance. The money is only touched if the family's very existence is threatened.

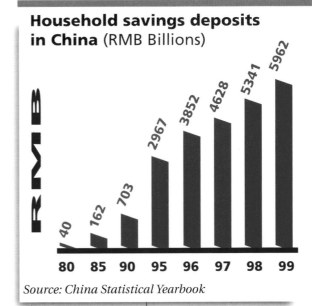

Household savings deposits in China (RMB Billions)

RMB

| 80 | 85 | 90 | 95 | 96 | 97 | 98 | 99 |

40 162 703 2967 3852 4628 5341 5962

Source: China Statistical Yearbook

In court, expert witnesses confirmed the existence of the Golden Thread and its importance in the life of the Chinese family. It was accepted as fact. Ultimately, the courtroom battle was not over the existence of the Golden Thread, but about the amount of the award.

Money has a different value in China, and is seen in a different light.

Personal money management since 1978

Until 1978, most citizens relied upon the State to provide the necessities of life. The State provided food, shelter, education and employment for life. Deng's reforms of 1978 changed all that and began to shift responsibility for individual welfare back onto the shoulders of the individual. How does this affect saving and spending habits?

Approximately 85 per cent of all families in China choose bank deposits as a means of saving money. At the beginning of the economic reforms in 1978, total deposits were RMB21 billion. By 1986, total deposits had reached RMB223.7 billion. And by 1996, the figure had reached an astonishing RMB3,500 billion (US$420 billion). Urban residents had the highest rate of savings with each resident holding an average of RMB10,000 (US$1,200).

 www.site-by-site.com

In the early days, there were few options for those hoping to generate wealth through investment. Even if they had the means, China's saving public had few options but bank deposits. When the Shenzhen stock market opened in July 1991, over 1.5 million people stepped forward to put cash into stocks. A 1996 survey showed that at least one in ten residents of Guangzhou invested in the market.

By 1994, the total trading volume of A shares on the Shenzhen and Shanghai exchanges was approximately US$95 billion. Most of the investors were local Chinese. One reason for the dramatic growth of activity on the exchange was certainly the lack of investment alternatives.

The development of security firms followed the development of the stock markets. At the end of 1993, there were already 87 security firms in operation, with 400 non-specialized financial institutions engaged in securities trading. The number of local branches of

 www.dsl-intl.com

security companies throughout China grew to 3,000. Chinese investors could do their trading through local offices, or through two nation-wide centralized electronic systems.

By 1996, there were approximately 575,000 bank branches or other credit outlets located throughout China. Nevertheless real investment opportunities continued to remain

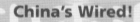

limited. At this time, the most attractive investment for China's growing rich were government bonds. The Chinese government has sold approximately RMB500 billion (US$60 billion) worth of government bonds since 1981.

Insurance becomes a must

And what about all those single children whose parents and grandparents continue to cover their living expenses? What are they doing with their money? Do they need credit? And if so, for what? A survey conducted in Shanghai in 1995 showed that approximately 20 per cent of the young people between 18 and 28 worked for foreign companies. Their average wage was approximately RMB 1,085. Their average savings per month were an astonishing RMB710 or 65 per cent of their salary. Of these savings, an average of 44 per cent was directed into some form of savings or investment vehicle.

What were these young people saving all this money for? Certainly not for the same reasons as their parents saved money.

Insurance in China grew in direct proportion to the shift away from cradle-to-grave State support. Chinese consumers began to realize if they wanted better health care they'd have to pay for it themselves. By 1995, the insurance business in China was dominated by two domestic firms. The People's Insurance Company collected premiums totaling RMB 47.6 billion, representing 79.12 per cent of the total insurance market. The Pacific Insurance Company collected RMB 6.6 billion representing approximately 11 per cent of the market. In 1995, these two firms controlled over 90 per cent of China's insurance market.

One of the most popular insurance policies in China in the early 1990s was called "The Child's Life Long Happiness

www.hi2000.net

FIGURE 10.4

AVERAGE EXCHANGE RATE OF RMB TO THE U.S. DOLLAR

Year	Rate
1998	8.27
1997	8.28
1996	8.31
1995	8.35
1994	8.61
1993	5.76
1992	5.51
1991	5.52
1990	4.78
1985	2.93
1981	1.70

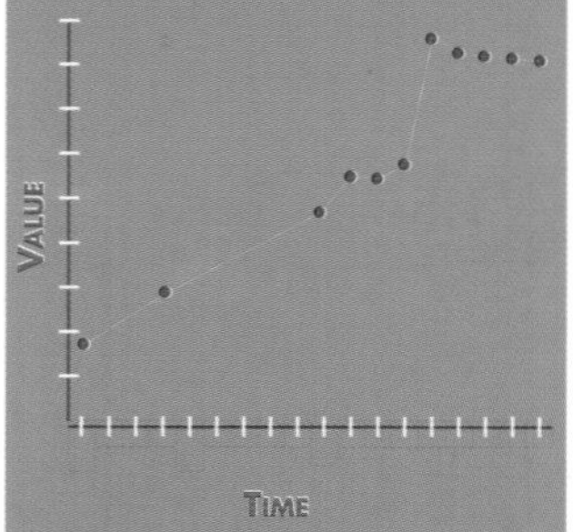

Insurance." Essentially, the policy offered an income supplement to the child. Parents, or grandparents would pay RMB360 each year until the child was 14. From the age of 15 until the age of 65 the child can draw from a total of RMB170,000. This policy was tremendously successful in the early 1990s representing almost 80 per cent of all insurance policies sold.

Today, there are approximately 125 million people in China over the age of 60. One of the most successful policies introduced in the last few years is a road safety policy for seniors. Increased traffic has led to an increase in the number of seniors killed in road accidents. In 1995 alone, 4,741 seniors over 60 were killed while walking, and 2,146 were killed while riding their bicycles. By December 1996, the Pacific Insurance Company's policy for road safety was available in 88 cities. Consumers could buy up to twenty units. A single unit cost RMB10 which provided total compensation of RMB3,500 (US$421).

By 1996, approximately 87 million urban employees had joined some sort of pension plan. This number accounted for approximately 75 per cent of all urban employees. Rural residents are much less likely to join pension plans. In 1997, only 20 per cent of all rural employees participated in such plans.

Unemployment insurance is also a growing concern—and market—especially with the continuing drive to close down inefficient State-Owned Enterprises. By 1996, 80 million employees from 530,000 State-Owned Enterprises had joined some form of unemployment insurance plan.

 www.sinofile.com/insurance

International insurance companies are anxious to have access to China's consumer base for both insurance and investment purposes. By 1997, over 150 international

NOTE

Renminbi (RMB)—the name means "people's money"—is the currency which is issued by the People's Bank of China. The standard units of RMB are the Yuan, Jiao, and Fen. Renminbi is available in one, two, five, ten, fifty and hundred Yuan denominations. One Yuan equals ten Jiao and one Jiao equals ten Fen.

Yuan, Jiao and Fen are all issued as bills and coins. The terms "RMB" and "Yuan" are equal and interchangeable, so, while there is no bill called the RMB, it is customary to refer to RMB10, etc.

insurance companies had set up representative offices in China. AXA/National Mutual Corporation has also established an investment fund. The company planned to raise a total of US$500 million, 70 per cent of which would be invested in China's high-tech industries.

Financial Institutions— foreign and local

How are foreign banks doing in China? Presently, foreign banks are not allowed to do any consumer banking. They can only drool over China's per capita savings rate of 40 per cent of gross income annually.

Standard Chartered Bank opened its first branch in China in Shanghai in 1858.[1] It has remained open and active in China ever since. Today, Standard Chartered has eight branches, one sub-branch and eight representative offices in fifteen cities throughout China.

Very few foreign banks operated in China before the founding of the People's Republic in 1949. By this time, Standard Chartered's presence was reduced to its original branch in Shanghai. The bank was not allowed to conduct business with the local population. The only business open to them was business related to trade.

www.bank-of-china.com

www.standardchartered.com

Some trade-related business was passed to Standard Chartered by the Bank of China. At that time in China, there were only two Chinese banks in operation. The Bank of China handled all international business, and the People's Bank of China handled all domestic business.

There was very little for foreign banks to do until Deng's reforms of 1978. These included the

[1] *Standard Chartered Bank was recently voted the "Best Foreign Commercial Bank in China" by Finance Asia in both their 1999 and 2000 awards for achievement.*

FIGURE 10.5

CHART OF FOREIGN BANKS.

Number of Foreign Banks: Approximately 266

Number of Branches: Approximately 155

Number of Representative Offices: Approximately 277

Total Assets: US$31.4bn (Sept. 99)

Outstanding Loans: US$22.6bn (Sept. 99)

Total Liabilities: US$28.6bn (Sept. 99)

Source: Standard Chartered Bank

construction of a number of power stations, steel processing plants and various other heavy industry projects. China invited the world's great engineering firms to step in and roll up their sleeves. This foreign influx of both human capital and foreign cash brought badly needed business to Standard Chartered's operations.

In the early days China paid for much of this development with letters of credit. There was a great reluctance to borrow money to fund development. Slowly, it became apparent that China would need all the facilities foreign banking and foreign banking technology could supply. Three foreign banks were subsequently invited to set up representative offices in China—Midland Bank, Export Import Bank of Japan and First Chicago.

In time, other countries began to apply pressure on China to allow their banks to open representative offices in China. These early banks operated exclusively as liaison offices rather than lending or banking institutions. Finally, China signed agreements with foreign governments over export credits. This allowed many of the early projects that had been cancelled or postponed for lack of financing to go forward. This was tremendous news for the foreign banks. Whatever credit they extended would be guaranteed by their governments back home.

Export credit and the rebirth of banking

Export credit is largely responsible for the rebirth of banking in modern China. The Daya Bay nuclear power development in Guangdong Province was one of the key projects financed by export credits. The banks waived their customary fees and only charged seven-eighths of one per cent interest on the twenty-year loan. Nevertheless, it was an extremely profitable and 'comfortable' business. Under normal circumstances, banks must allocate reserves

---

FIGURE 10.6

FOREIGN BANKS, SCOPE OF OPERATIONS:

- Only allowed to operate in 24 designated cities.
- Foreign exchange transactions for Foreign-Invested Enterprises (FIEs).
- Trade Finance, loan guarantees and bill discounting.
- Foreign Trade accounts, remittances and foreign shares and bonds.
- Advisory services on doing business in China and introductions.
- Project finance advisory for both Chinese and foreign sponsors.
- Hard-currency credit card transactions agent.
- Certain share underwriting, stock custody, and share flotation assistance for foreign purchases.
- Syndicated hard-currency loans.
- Foreign currency loan and foreign exchange exposure hedging.
- Target Chinese clients which need foreign exchange.
- Safety deposit boxes.
- Credit investigation and consultancy.

Lit Search, EIU, McKinsey Report

against such a loan. As the loan was ultimately guaranteed by the bank's own home government, no such allocations were necessary. The lending bank or banks were free to use those funds for other purposes.

Expanding a foreign bank's operations in China is as complicated as conducting any other business. Banks must first open a Representative Office. They can do no commercial business from a Representative Office, they can only 'liaise.' After a period of time, the bank may be given permission to open a branch. This branch can only conduct certain types of commercial business. And there is a geographic restriction as to where the branch can enter into business. A branch in one province cannot conduct business in another province.

Foreign banks also have restrictions against doing business with local consumers. Consequently, every month, Standard Chartered Bank is obliged to transfer a considerable sum of money to a local bank to pay its local employees. Though they work at Standard Chartered Bank, citizens of the P.R.C. can only bank and draw their salaries from local banks.

www.hangseng.com

Foreign banks are also restricted from doing business with Chinese businesses in RMB. Foreign banks can, with permission, loan U.S. dollars to Chinese businesses.

The WTO and banking

The WTO is critical for the development of foreign banking in China. It's the payoff for all the lean years. Traditionally, banks earn revenue from three distinct areas: treasury, consumer banking and corporate and institutional banking. Presently in China, foreign banks are only able to make money from corporate and institutional banking. WTO begins to change all of that.

Two years after China's accession into the WTO, foreign banks will be permitted to do U.S. dollar business with all

NOTE

Banks granted RMB licenses:

19 Foreign bank branches have been granted 24 licenses to conduct business in branches of banks in Pudong & Shenzhen including:

Standard Chartered Bank*

HSBC*

Citibank*

Tokyo & Mitsubishi Bank*

Industrial Bank of Japan

Dai-Ichi Kangyo

International Bank of Paris and Shanghai

Sanwa Bank

Banque Indosuez

BofA*

Bank of East Asia

Credit Suisse First Boston

Development Bank of Singapore

Overseas-Chinese Banking Corporation

Sakura Bank

Sumitomo Bank

Nanyang Commercial Bank

ABN AMRO

Dresdner

Have Shenzhen & Pudong licenses.

Chinese businesses without seeking special permission. Three years after accession, foreign banks will be able to do RMB business with Chinese companies in the same way. And after five years, foreign banks will finally be able to conduct business with Chinese citizens.

The WTO will allow foreign banks to begin to do business and make money as they do everywhere else in the world. But even as things stand, a bank such as Standard Chartered has much to gain for itself and its branches all over the world by remaining in China.

Standard Chartered has significant long-term relationships with many Fortune 500 companies operating in China. These relationships are not necessarily based on being the banker to these companies in their home countries. Standard Chartered has deep relationships with government and industry throughout China—relationships built up over many decades of uninterrupted presence. Many Fortune 500 companies are drawn to the bank because of the tremendous value of those relationships. Inevitably, assistance offered to these companies in China leads them to seek out Standard Chartered Bank in other parts of the world where business conditions are not so restricted. It's the original Internet. An interconnected web of contacts and connections that helps the world turn.

While Standard Chartered is the largest foreign bank in China, and has offices in fifteen cities, the four largest Chinese banks have 140,000 branches among them. China's two largest banks have over 1.1 million employees. The WTO will help level the playing field for foreign banks. Gaining market share is another issue entirely.

Some argue that the Internet and Internet banking will help foreign banks gain market share. Foreign banks could never

Every cloud has a silver lining, but sometimes it's a little difficult to get it to the mint.
—*Don Marquis, Certain Maxims of archie*

compete physically with local banks. They could, however, compete on an almost equal footing in virtual banking.

A bank on the Web

By the time Standard Chartered Bank is allowed to conduct consumer banking on the Web, it will be a very crowded field indeed. China Merchants Bank has recently

FIGURE **10.7**

Standard Chartered's Web site.

launched a beautifully-designed site aimed to take advantage of all the opportunities the Internet offers for the banking industry.

China Merchants Bank was founded in Shenzhen on April 8, 1987, with the help of the People's Bank of China. China Merchants Bank was also one of the first banks in China to issue shares, which are now owned by a number of large commercial entities. The bank has expanded rapidly since 1987 and now has a total of 190 branches throughout China.

www.cmbchina.com

This institution began offering banking services over the Internet in 1998. Cmbchina.com is a richly-designed and detailed site. The front page has a section for financial news—current articles on business and finance from all of China's leading newspapers. Along the bottom of the site there are three small windows. Two of these carry the current status of the Shanghai and Shenzhen stock exchanges. The third holds a rolling display for currency conversion. U.S. dollar to RMB is posted, followed by British pound to RMB, Canadian dollar to RMB etc—a rare and extremely helpful feature for foreign businesses.

There are tabs along the top of the site for home, e-commerce, personal banking, commercial banking, payment systems and stocks. The e-commerce page was not yet operational when I visited it in early June 2000. There was, however, a notice explaining how the site would work. China Merchants Bank intends to bring together all the best e-commerce sites available—a portal of sites endorsed by China Merchants Bank. There will be sites selling electronic goods, hardware, software and books—among other items. The bank will process all payments for goods sold through their site. Purchases can be made with China Merchants Bank payment cards. Very clever. And, I'm sure, lucrative.

The personal banking page offers a mobile phone banking service. Customers can pay bills and verify account balances using their cellular phones. These services are now available to customers in Beijing, Shanghai, Chongqing, Hangzhou, Nanjing, Shenzhen, Wuhan and other major cities throughout

FIGURE 10.8

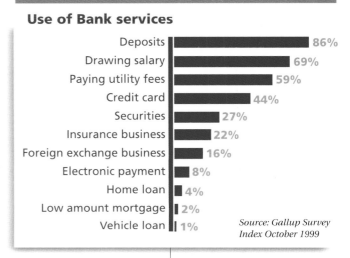

Use of Bank services

Deposits	86%
Drawing salary	69%
Paying utility fees	59%
Credit card	44%
Securities	27%
Insurance business	22%
Foreign exchange business	16%
Electronic payment	8%
Home loan	4%
Low amount mortgage	2%
Vehicle loan	1%

Source: Gallup Survey Index October 1999

FIGURE 10.9

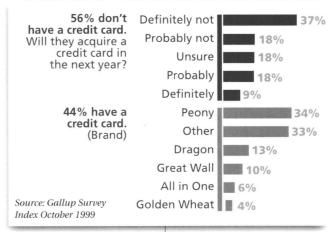

Credit cards—the haves and the have nots

56% don't have a credit card. Will they acquire a credit card in the next year?

Definitely not	37%
Probably not	18%
Unsure	18%
Probably	18%
Definitely	9%

44% have a credit card. (Brand)

Peony	34%
Other	33%
Dragon	13%
Great Wall	10%
All in One	6%
Golden Wheat	4%

Source: Gallup Survey Index October 1999

China. Customers can also open accounts with the mobile phone service and buy and sell stocks.

Corporate banking offers similar benefits. The page invites enterprises to go online. They're invited to contact the bank for more details. The payment systems page also invites enquiries. Customers can arrange to set up online payment facilities. The final tab is for online stock purchases. Customers who sign up for personal banking can also open accounts with the bank from which they can buy and sell stocks. How sophisticated is this? About as cutting edge as any bank anywhere.

Various electronic products to assist bill payment and collection are bound to be added to the products China Merchants Bank is offering. Electronic Bill Payment and Presentment systems (EBPPs) are only just emerging in North America. These systems offer tremendous savings in time to consumers, and savings in customer service related costs to businesses.

The most sophisticated systems will allow consumers to call up their credit card account and click on any transaction to get a complete accounting of where, when and with whom any transaction was conducted. Such a system offers tremendous convenience to the consumer, and saves credit card companies the huge costs included in maintaining call centres.

An emerging credit culture

The younger generation in China—those under 35—do not feel quite as conflicted about borrowing money as older generations. The older generation is conservative in its spending and saving habits. They tend to see borrowing as something dishonourable, and try at all costs to avoid borrowing or lending between relatives or friends.

Like consumers everywhere, Chinese consumers spending

Annual income twenty pounds, annual expenditure nineteen nineteen six, result happiness. Annual income twenty pounds, annual expenditure twenty pounds ought and six, result misery.
—Charles Dickens, David Copperfield.

habits fall into four distinct categories: emergency, short term, long term and investment. Emergency spending includes health needs or liability from an accident. Short term spending is money allocated for retail purchases such as food, clothing and entertainment. Long term spending could be a mortgage payment or savings set aside for the purchase of a house. And investment money is not to be touched—it's money that could be passed along as an inheritance.

In China today, most short term spending is done with cash or debit cards. The government is trying to encourage more consumer spending as well as some borrowing. (In May 2000, the government gave everyone a one-week paid holiday in the hopes that it would stimulate consumer spending. It worked. Consumer spending increased dramatically.) Housing loans and automobile loans have been introduced on a small scale. Consumers can also borrow small amounts using their savings deposits or government bonds as collateral. The government believes consumer spending will stimulate the general economy. Allowing people credit facilities is seen as an additional enticement to spend.

In 1997 in China, average personal debt as a percentage of assets was 0.6 per cent. In the United States, average personal debt as a percentage of assets was 36 per cent. China's banks are as risk-averse as China's consumers are debt-reticent. The debit card is the result. To acquire a debit card, the cardholder must make a deposit into a secured deposit account. Generally, consumers put a minimum of RMB10,000 into the secured deposit, which earns some interest. Using the card also incurs cost. One doesn't quite cancel out the other. Nevertheless, convenience is compensation enough.

In the early days, debit cards from one bank were not

www.shu.edu.cn

TYPES OF CARDS AVAILABLE:

Definition

ATM card: Can only do deposit/withdrawal with ATM, no purchase function.

Debit card: Purchase must be processed using designated POS, no overdraft permission.

Debit/Overdraft card: With provision for overdraft up to 60 days. The limit varies from RMB1,000~10,000.

Fund Transfer card: Can only be used for transferring money between accounts.

Other cards available: Can use to pay transportation fee, toll fee, gas fee, dinner fee, etc.

Credit card: There are fewer than 100,000 true domestic credit cards in circulation.

accepted by other banks. Merchants had to acquire separate terminals for each bank's card. Obviously, this was cumbersome for merchants and confusing for cardholders. The cost to each bank to support the system was also very high. Today, there are over twelve local networks in the major coastal cities. Within those cities, terminals can be shared. Nevertheless, there are still cards that can only be used in certain areas.

Today, there are fewer than 100,000 true domestic credit cards in China. Most payment cards fall under the category of a debit card. Other cards available include ATM cards, which can only do deposits or withdrawals and have no purchase function; fund transfer cards, which can only be used for transferring money between accounts; and various cards used for transportation, gas and dining etc.

Money: The Poor Man's Credit Card.
— *Marshall McLuhan*

High interest rates charged on most cards are also hindering growth. The cardholder is expected to pay an annual interest rate of 55 per cent if payment is made within 15 days. The interest rate increases to 110 per cent if the card holder pays within 30 days. Payments made after 30 days are charged at an annual rate of 165 per cent.

A credit courtship

As a result, in 1997, only 3 per cent of consumer payments were made with payment cards. Nevertheless, the trend toward payment cards of some form is growing. In 1997, there were approximately 100 million debit or payment cards in use in China. The government hopes to see approximately 200 million bank cards in operation by 2003. Of the 100 million in use in 1997, 30 million were Visa cards, 20 million were other international payment cards and 50 million were domestic debit cards.

Debit cards also give banks an opportunity to oversee their clients' spending habits. Such information will make it easier for the banks to qualify those applying for true credit cards. The credit culture is a slowly developing courtship between consumers and banks. It's a push-pull relationship. How comfortable the banks feel giving, and how deeply the consumer wishes to plunge.

Foreign credit card companies recognize the huge opportunity a market like China presents. But the greatest opportunities and advantages for the credit card industry won't be realized until the RMB becomes freely convertible. Presently, credit cards issued in China can only be used in China.

The government is pushing the use of debit cards for a number of reasons. First, because cash is expensive to print, circulate and maintain. Counterfeiting is also a growing problem. Second, debit cards or cards of any kind allow the government and the lending institutions to gather a lot of information on their clients and their clients' spending habits. Finally, cards can do things cash can't. Visa International is developing a chip card that would carry personal information like driver information. The cardholder could pay tolls, fines or fees automatically from the card account.

www.safe.gov.cn

Payment cards are becoming more and more a part of everyday life in China. Recently, China Construction Bank issued cards to every government worker in Shanghai with a housing fund. Cardholders can use the card to withdraw cash from an ATM, check their housing fund balance, as well as use the card to make retail purchases.

Will China's cultural reluctance to enter into debt hinder the growth of the Internet? No. But distrust of—and unfamiliarity with—electronic payment systems hinders their widespread use—especially over the Net. Current trends suggest this will change.

The inherent vice of capitalism is the unequal sharing of blessings; the inherent virtue of socialism is the equal sharing of miseries.

—*Winston Churchill*

Will the lack of electronic payment systems hinder the development of the Internet in China? No. From my perspective, they're developing as rapidly as the Internet. Check out China Merchants Bank. Concern over the security of the system remains, however—as it does everywhere. But the lack of electronic payment systems as we know them in the West is probably less of a hindrance to the development of the Internet in China than the lack of fast, effective and cheap delivery services. Once again, the Internet leaps over the shortfalls of traditional infrastructures. ➡

Your notes

go to...

For additional information and updates to charts and graphs, visit: **www.flyingarmchair.com** *the* China's Wired! *resource site.*

Launching an Internet company

The seven steps to an IPO

NOTE

Chapter Eleven of the U.S. Bankruptcy Reform Act allows debtors to seek protection from creditors. It means "I know I'm in trouble just give me a chance to sort things out." It stops creditors from pulling the plug—for a while. Hopefully, it buys the company time to resolve its economic crisis, find additional financing, or negotiate a sale or merger.

At the end of the Second World War North America entered a period of rapid economic expansion. Cities grew and industries flourished.

www.ussteel.com

A new sheet metal steel mill was being built outside of Pittsburgh. They were behind schedule. The chief engineer decided he'd probably get more work done if he worked at home. He could work through the day and into the night without distraction. The engineer's wife was delighted. She'd know where he was and could make sure he remembered to eat his meals. Everything went very well during the first week.

Every day, the engineer's wife would bring his lunch on a tray to his study. One day in the second week she looked over his shoulder and asked him what he was doing. The engineer exploded in rage. His wife shrugged and left the room. It wasn't that important to her that she know what he was doing. She was curious, that's all.

That night, when she brought him his dinner, the engineer apologized. He said he was struggling with a very difficult problem and was sorry he'd snapped. The engineer's wife said it wasn't very important, she was just curious as to what he was doing.

The engineer rolled open the blueprints of the new steel mill. The mill was composed of two sections. A refining section and a section where molten steel is rolled into sheets. The engineer's job was to find the most efficient location for the huge machines that rolled the molten steel into sheets.

The engineer's wife asked him how the machines worked. He explained that the machines were composed of huge rollers. A bar of molten steel entered the rollers at one end and came out as a flat sheet at the other. The engineer's wife asked why there were three machines. He explained that this particular mill was going to produce three thicknesses of steel sheet: 1", 1/2" and 1/4."

The engineer's wife thought quietly for a moment and then said that they really didn't need three machines, only one. The engineer asked his wife to explain. "All you need is the 1" press. Roll the steel out in 1" sheets, then put one 1" sheet on top of another and put them through the press again. You'll get two 1/2" sheets. Repeat the process with four 1/2" sheets and you'll get your 1/4" sheets."

In a few seconds—a brainwave or an epiphany—the engineer's wife solved her husband's problem and saved his employer millions of dollars. Was she a genius? No, but she knew the secret of fine pastry. Roll out the pastry on a flat surface, fold it over on itself and roll it out again. Repeat this process until the dough is composed of a multitude of fine layers.

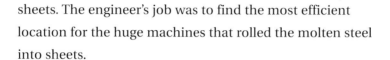

www.ebay.com

The engineer's wife applied her knowledge and experience to her husband's needs. Pierre Omidyar did much the same thing when he applied his knowledge and experience to his wife's needs and created eBay.com. They came up with an idea. And they were ideas that saved time, energy, space and money. Fortunately, they were also developed at the right place at the right time and in front of the right audience. The ideas got to market without even trying.

> *Bankruptcy is when you put your money in your hip pocket and let your creditors take your coat.*
>
> —Bob Edwards, Calgary Eye Opener

Unfortunately, most ideas develop in something of a wilderness. They appear unexpectedly in the minds of bored students, day-dreaming postmen and children who could care less anyway. They operate on their own time table. And their value is not usually a reflection of the time or energy spent creating them.

How do you grow an idea into a business? The first step is to be able to explain it. Could you explain the idea expressed by the engineer's wife? Or the idea behind eBay? Could you do it in three minutes or less? You'd certainly have to if you wanted anyone to invest in it.

There are several good reasons for being able to explain your idea in three minutes or less. First, because that is all the time you'll get to interest an investor. Second, explaining your idea to others refines the idea itself. Oscar Wilde said, "I never know what I'm thinking until I hear myself say it."

Creativity is a high-risk enterprise. Chances are you're going to fail more times than you succeed. You might have a good idea but have no access to the seed money needed to take it those first fragile steps. Or you could have all the money in the world but be stuck with stubborn, narrow minded partners. Or everything could be perfect and the market turns on you. We learn nothing from success—and everything from failure. Rule number one: Never give up.

The first step is creating an original idea. The second step is explaining that idea to others in three minutes or less. The third step is writing it down.

Writing an idea down is harder than explaining it verbally. Written language is an entirely different medium. In some respects, words are very limited. They do not wear the latest fashions, have an expressive or seductive voice,

What we are aiming at, in the end, a year or so down the road, is the capitalist's dream. We want to be bought out by a huge American firm that will give us twice what our shares are worth and hire us back to run our company under generous management contracts.

—*Walter Stewart, The Golden Fleece, 1992*

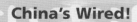

intense eyes, or a personal relationship with the person who reads them. They don't care if you succeed or fail. They have no feelings or conscience. They are just words.

Writing isn't necessarily easier or safer than speaking. The same general rules apply. You must be concise and clear. Rule number two: You want people to understand before they lose interest.

Writing down your idea has risks. It will be the first time the idea truly leaves your possession. Someone might steal it from you. How can you protect yourself? If you have the funds, get a lawyer. If you don't, you want to be sure that you can prove you owned the idea at a specific point in time. The simplest way to do this, as we saw in Chapter Four, is to mail yourself the idea by registered post. When the envelope arrives, don't open it. The post office stamps and seals will show when the envelope containing the idea first came into your possession. In the West, it's called a poor man's copyright. Will this guarantee that nobody steals your idea? No. Nothing can do that.

These are the first three steps you take if you're starting a business from an idea—something that came into your mind in a flash. But e-commerce can develop in other ways. Zhaopin was a discovery. They kept their eyes glued to the screen until one day it all came into focus. aba.com evolved. They probably didn't need these first three steps. Their e-volution happened. Nevertheless, they probably articulated their e-volution in some sort of executive summary.

An executive summary is very important and very serious. If you don't get it right you won't raise the money you need to build your business. Without money, all you've got is ambition. And ambition won't pay the rent.

Raising money is a soul-destroying experience. I know

www.new.usps.com

www.chinapost.com.cn

www.canadapost.ca

ELEVEN QUESTIONS:

Ask yourself:

1. Is my idea unique?

2. Why is my product better?

3. How will it make money?

4. Who is my customer?

5. Who is the competition?

6. What is my advantage over the competition?

7. How will it change the world?

8. Is it scalable?

9. Will every customer become a promoter of your product or service? (Using hotmail.com delivers a hotmail.com promotion with each and every e-mail you send.)

10. How much money do you really need to get started?

11. What's in it for you?

because I've tried. You stand in front of three or four bored men in suits and try and convince them to give you some money. You ask them to believe in you—that it'll all work out and everyone will end up rich. The problem is that they've heard it all before. And maybe they're having a bad day. Or maybe you're pitching something they don't know anything about and don't care. The point is, it's a horrible, harrowing and humiliating experience. (And you thought all you needed was a great idea?)

An executive summary adds detail to the description of your idea. It answers a series of basic business questions. First, it begins to put your idea into a business context. It describes how your idea or innovation can become a profitable business. And of course, that's what it's all about—profit and money. You create an executive summary because you're trying to raise some money.

An executive summary doesn't have to be very long. It can range from a single page, to three or four pages. You begin by offering an overview of your idea or business and its industry sector. The executive summary can describe a start-up situation or be shaped around an existing business. If it's a start-up, you describe the idea, discuss the market opportunities and explain how much money you need and why. If it's an existing business you explain how the money you're trying to raise will improve the existing business' market advantage.

The Internet is probably the greatest single resource available for preparing a good executive summary or business plan. There are now dozens of sites like vfinance.com and **garage.com**[1] that allow you to download templates for executive summaries and business plans. They're also a potential audience for your finished product.

[1] *Individual Member Investors of garage.com:*

Ben Rosen, *Chairman of Compaq Computer Corporation*

Chong-Moon Lee, *Founder of Diamond Multimedia Systems*

George Gilder, *President, Gilder Technology Group*

Sandy Robertson, *Founder and former CEO of investment bank Robertson Stephens.*

The fifth step on the road to your Nasdaq IPO is the business plan. If you have little or no formal business training or experience, the preparation of a business plan can be a daunting task. Some entrepreneurs are lucky enough to be able to raise funds without the support of a thirty or forty page business plan. The venture capital executives at the Harvard conference claimed that their decisions were usually based on the idea, the commitment of the person or people behind the idea and the team that had been assembled to bring the business to life. So, why go to all the bother of writing a formal business plan? Again, the first reason is that it will help refine your idea. It might also uncover unexpected problems or opportunities.

A three-minute pitch and an executive summary focus on the unique advantage of your idea or innovation right now. What my idea means today. A business plan adds flesh to the idea and projects it into the future. How the business will unfold over the next three, six or eighteen months. Since the future is nothing if not unpredictable, the business plan has to be supported by as much solid data as possible. You have to assemble data on competitors, market growth, demographics and general economic conditions. You have to create a historical context in which to place your new business. Your information should go back three or four years and project forward two or three years. A business plan makes an idea as real as it will ever be before your staff start punching the clock.

The sixth step is an option. Some may want to take their ideas to e-commerce **incubators**[2] or accelerators, while others may prefer to go strait to investors. The choice is yours.

The rapid evolution of the Internet and e-commerce has created a new kind of business called an incubator or

[1] www.tie.org.com

[1] *TiE.org*

TiE is a similar assembly of individuals sharing mutual interests. The Indus Entrepreneurs or TiE was founded in 1993. TiE began as a network of Silicon Valley entrepreneurs with Indian background. Today, there are eight chapters in the United States and one in Canada.

[2] *Incubators were created to fund start-ups, but they are swiftly becoming a different beast-one that suggests how businesses will be organized, structured, and operated in the early decades of the 21st century.*

They start with a single mission: to incubate Internet companies, accelerate them to market, and prepare them for lightning-speed IPOs. The theory behind the traditional incubator was that with private equity flowing like wine, it was time—not money—that was the critical resource. It made sense to finance a collection of startups, offer them management advice and prepackage their business needs.

Peter D. Henig, Red Herring.

accelerator. Some might argue that they're really only the research and development departments of an industry that has grown so fast it's had no time to include research and development departments in its corporate structures. This seems increasingly apparent as almost every major Internet portal, or e-business conglomerate includes an incubator or accelerator among its cluster of inter-related e-businesses. chinadotcom has Jumpstart.com, Sunevision has Incubasia and CyberIncubator. And many hold minority interests in other Internet incubators. PCCW holds shares in Boston's CMGI and chinadotcom has a small interest in Toronto-based NRG.

Why is everybody in everybody else's pocket? They're hedging their bets. They all want a piece of the next big thing. All it takes is a great idea. Remember eBay? Remember, the price of entry into this economic revolution is a good idea and the discipline and determination to bring it to market.

Essentially, incubators offer entrepreneurs all the resources necessary to build their idea into a business. Some incubators offer office space and support staff. Some run boot camps. Both cost money (on top of the piece of your business they'll take for helping you through the process). The most valuable resources an incubator offers are the experience of its core executives and their contacts within the community. They've been through it all before. They know the pitfalls and can identify the dangers. Often, incubators also have a close association with a group of venture capital investors. When you're ready, they're ready.

Now that you have a strong executive summary—or a solid business plan—you're ready to go out and pitch. First, prepare for rejection. Second, know your audience. Most venture capital companies specialize in certain fields or industry sectors. If your business is B2B make sure your

www.jumpstart.com

www.thenrggroup.com

NOTE

Network your ideas:

First Tuesdays was founded in London, England in 1998. It began when a group of entrepreneurs began to meet at a local pub at the same time on the first Tuesday of every month. Soon, the entrepreneurs were joined by investors and others interested in profiting from new Net opportunities.

The first Tuesday concept has spread to over 40 cities around the world including Munich, Paris and Buenos Aires. Entrepreneurs are identified by wearing green dots. Venture capitalists wear red dots and professional service providers such as accountants and lawyers wear yellow dots.

The events are usually underwritten by corporate sponsors. Pre-registration is often a requirement. First Tuesdays has become a truly global portal for e-business start-ups.

audience knows the sector and is interested.

It may happen that your first investors are not professional investors. They could be family, friends or acquaintances. They might even include one of your partners. These 'angel' investors can come with complicated expectations. Ultimately, their influence may be much greater than the size of their investment. Be careful.

The seventh step is negotiating the deal. An angel investor or a venture capital company likes your pitch or business plan and want to invest. What next? First, hire a lawyer.

This is where you start to see your idea slipping away from you. This is both a good thing and a bad thing. It's a good thing because it means people are investing in your idea. It should confirm the value of your idea and set the wheels in motion. It also means other people now want the idea to work as badly as you do. Responsibility is shared. The bad part is that you're now on the slippery slope toward becoming a minority shareholder. Me, a minority shareholder? But it's my idea!

Those sentiments, and a couple of bucks will still get you a double mocha latte at your local Starbucks. But not much more. Unfortunately, you have to give up something in order to get somebody to give you some money. Let's say your first investor is a rich uncle. First, Uncle X didn't get rich by being stupid. He's going to want a fair piece of the action for his money. How much do you give up? How much do you need? Let's say you need US$100,000. It's not enough to get the business up and running but it's enough to get some professional help to finish your business plan, pay your lawyers, do some preliminary marketing and perhaps even secure a tentative commitment to purchase your product or services. All very important as they make it

Garage.com venture capital firms:

Advanced Technology Ventures

AT&T Ventures

Battery Ventures

Bedrock Capital Partners

Burrill & Company

Calvert Social Venture Partners

CCMG Inc.

Chase Capital Partners

Draper Fisher Jurvetson

El Dorado Ventures

Flatiron Partners

H&Q Venture Associates

Internet Capital Group

Kettle Partners

Mayfield Fund

Media Technology Ventures

Mentor Venture Partners

Montreux Equity Partners

NIF Ventures

Pacific Century Group Ventures

Redleaf Venture Management

Red Rock Ventures

Rosewood Capital

St. Paul Venture Capital

Sierra Ventures

Telos Venture Partners

Trident Capital

US Venture Partners

Vanguard Venture Partners

Voyager Capital

The Walden Group

easier to raise the next round of money.

So, how much do you give Uncle X for his US$100,000? Traditionally, a company's value is determined by a multiple of its annual profits. But you have no profit—only an idea and an inkling of its potential. Offer him 5%. He'll ask for 15%. Settle at 10%. So, what does that mean? First, it means you've got your seed money. It also means you now control only 90% of your company. And you've got a shareholder who might need some hand holding. Still...

The good part is that it gives the company a starting value. If Uncle X gave you US$100,000 for 10% of your company, then your company is worth 10 x US$100,000 or US$1 million. Congratulations, you now have a 'paper' worth of US$900,000. That, and a couple of bucks, will still only get you a double mocha latte at your local Starbucks.

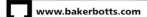
www.heenanblaikie.com

The big boys won't be nearly as kind, or generous, or easy as Uncle X. They'll also be more concerned about getting their money out. They don't invest for the long term. They put their money in at the beginning, when the risk is highest, and cash out on the first big upswing—usually the IPO. They don't care about you, your dream, or dear old Uncle X. They want to make money—as much as they can— as fast as they can. And they'll do whatever they have to do to get the best deal possible. This is where the term 'blood on the floor' comes from. And 'pound of flesh.' And 'isn't there a law against this?'

www.vcclawservices.com

Venture capital investors are prepared to take much greater risks than banks. They also expect much greater rewards. The common rule seems to be that they only invest in something if they think they can make five times their investment. Obviously, they don't win every time. Nobody does. Sometimes, they're lucky to get their original investment back.

Wall Street, in these matters, is like a lovely and accomplished woman who must wear black cotton stockings, heavy woolen underwear and parade her knowledge as a cook because, unhappily, her supreme accomplishment is as a harlot.

—*John Kenneth Galbraith, 1955*

Sometimes they lose everything. But their law of averages says they'll be right often enough to make some serious money.

A venture capital investor has to really believe in you and your idea to conclude that they'll make five times their money. Which puts even more pressure on you because you're the only one who can make them believe. This is what these people do best in the whole world. And sometimes, a three-minute pitch is all it takes to convince them. How? Experience, instinct and a profound understanding of the industry and sector in which they operate.

So, let's say your pitch worked and Venture Capital Co. X wants to invest US$2 million in your company. What next? Well, you probably won't have time to ask what's next. That's when you turn it over to your lawyers. You may not even want to be in the room when they discuss you and your idea. Remember, this is a negotiation. I want what you have but I don't want to pay too much for it. I want what you have but I'm going to start reducing it to an ill-conceived folly just so I don't have to pay you what it's worth. This is when you really start to see your precious idea slipping away from you.

Uncle X bought 10% of your company for US$100,000. Venture Capital Co. X wants 25% of your company for US$2 million. The new investment values your company at US$8 million. Uncle X is going to be very happy because his $100,000 investment is now worth US$800,000—on paper. But you've given up 35% of your company. And you're going to give up even more. Why? Because you'll probably have to raise a second round of financing before you go to an IPO. And you'll probably have to offer shares as part of an employment package to entice the most qualified senior management to join you. (It never seems to end, does it?)

To spekilate in Wall Street when you are no longer an insider is like buying cows by candle light.
—*Daniel Drew, 1877. N.B., Drew was a great speculator, not a great speller.*

If you're lucky, your venture capital investors will leave you alone to build your business. Of course, they'll be ready to step in and help if you need them or get into trouble. They have an investment to protect. Some venture capital investors don't wait to be asked. A condition of their investment—no matter how large—may be the right to run the show. This is where you need the advice of people with experience. There's such a thing as stupid money. Money attached to an investor who thinks he knows how to run a business. Some do, but running a business isn't their area of expertise, investing is.

So, let's say your idea has turned into a business that's been in operation now for eighteen months and you've just closed the deal on that third round of financing for US$20 million. The good part? You're well on your way to that IPO. And it finally looks as if that little idea wasn't so bad after all. The bad part? That last round of financing cost you 40% of your company and control. You're now a minority shareholder with only 25%. The good part? The last round of financing valued your company at US$50 million. Your share is now worth US$12.5 million—on paper. Uncle X is ecstatic—or dead from shock—as his measly investment of US$100,000 is now worth US$5 million. Doesn't seem fair, does it?

Eighteen months ago all you wanted to do was raise a few dollars and try and see if you could make your little idea work. Well, now you know it works. And you're only months away from that magical IPO. And it's only taken 20-hour days and seven-day weeks. Cost you family, friends and health. And probably taken a few years off your life—and 70% of the business. Having fun yet?

And what about that IPO? Do you really need to raise another fifty or sixty million dollars? By the time your

SEVEN STEPS TO AN IPO.

1. Create the idea.

2. Write it down.

3. Protect the idea.

4. Prepare the executive summary.

5. Set out the business plan.

6. Line up an incubator (or not).

7. Negotiate the deal.

company reaches the point of launching an IPO it probably won't feel much like your company any more. This whole process of growing a company ends up diminishing your influence in or on that company. At some point—or many points—along this route you should find a quiet corner and sit down and ask yourself why you're doing this. Many entrepreneurs have the wisdom to step to the side and focus on what they do best. Jerry Yang might have been one of the key founders of Yahoo but he doesn't run it. And not every company needs to go all the way to an IPO. You can make just as much money remaining a private entity.

The farther you go down this route and the more people you involve the more complicated it all becomes. The IPO may be the pot of gold at the end of the rainbow. It also presents some of the most complicated legal and administrative problems.

Sina.com achieved something of a miracle with its April debut on the Nasdaq. First, its share price rose on its first day of trading—at a time when technology stocks generally and dot coms particularly were fading dramatically. Second, Sina.com had restructured itself to satisfy Beijing's restrictions against foreign control of Web-based businesses. Control of its content-related businesses was spun off into wholly Chinese owned commercial entities. So what are you buying when you buy Sina.com? Hope. Hope that those last-minute restructurings are cosmetic, and temporary.

My purpose here has been to give a general overview—and present a general impression—of the steps an entrepreneur may have to take to build his or her company in the new digital age. None of this is written in stone. Every company's history will be different. The point is to show how complicated and difficult the process is. And prove

> *As long as everybody takes a whipping like little ladies and gentlemen, the company emerges from bankruptcy and survives as an on-going business.*
>
> —Stratford P. Sherman, 1991.

that the Nasdaq listings of chinadotcom and Sina.com are nothing short of miraculous. It requires more than a bright idea and discipline. It requires almost equal measures of business skills and people skills. And it requires luck. Most importantly, it requires an open mind. Conditions are changing rapidly. Laws are being written and re-written. Rules are changing. What was true for today won't be true tomorrow.

www.qis.net/chinalaw

How do you set up and run a business when the laws for that business have not yet been written—or are changing from one day to the next? The short answer is that you do what you think is morally correct, or what you believe the law intends.

www.beijing-jeep.com

If laws were absolute, there would be no justice.

Fortunately, laws are not absolute. They're enforced by human beings. The mercy killing of one terminally-ill spouse by the other can make us forgive something that the law says should be punished by death. And the same crime tried in different jurisdictions of the same country can result in entirely different outcomes. Laws are not absolute, nor is justice guaranteed.

It's not that you need them to say yes, you just don't want them to say no.

China's changing legal environment is a lot like Beijing traffic. Beijing drivers are aggressive and determined. Sometimes, it feels as if you're in the middle of a very dangerous game of chicken. Cab drivers make left-hand turns into a river of oncoming traffic. Somehow, they make it through. Somehow, at the last possible moment, one of the drivers concedes—but concedes in a way that leaves the other unoffended.

In time, the laws will come and they will be enforced. In the

This is a translation of a street sign in Xiamen, outlining the Ten Rules of urban conduct.

1. No Littering

2 No Spitting on the Ground

3 No Damaging Plants and Trees

4 No Destroying Public Property

5 No Running Red Lights

6 No Forcing One's Way into Public Transport Queues

7 No Foul Language

8 No Smoking in Public Places

9 No Disturbing the Peace

10 No Graffiti or Posters

interim, if you're starting an Internet business in China you need to find a lawyer who understands the Internet and the laws governing the Internet in China. It's also important that your lawyer understand international law. Your server may be in Shanghai, but your audience is everywhere. And you're responsible for what the audience sees—or does—via your Web site.

The Internet will introduce some entrepreneurs to legal issues they might never have confronted in more traditional businesses. These legal issues fall under the category of intellectual property. A patent, a trade mark, copyright, **cybersquatting**[1] and domain names are all about intellectual property.

www.uspto.gov

Intellectual property is the product of the mind. It can be an idea, an invention, a poem, a trademark or a design. Many in China find the notion of intellectual property difficult to understand. An idea has no physical substance—how can anyone own it? Some of this is because intellectual property has only become relevant recently, some of it is cultural.

www.cipo.gc.cn

www.cpo.cn.net

Attitudes will change slowly in China. Soon, someone in China will develop a new accounting software, or a new search engine. The inventor will appear on television and become a national celebrity. His or her new-found wealth will quickly erase any doubts about the value of an idea in China. Everyone will want to get in on the act. China's patent offices will be overwhelmed.

www.cntrademark.com

There's also a cultural reluctance to ascribe value to something as ephemeral as an idea, or a name. In the West, contracts are constructed to try and cover every possible eventuality. They try to be all-inclusive. Each party's responsibilities are outlined in great detail.

[1] *Julia Roberts has won her case at an international arbitration panel to control her Internet domain name— www.juliaroberts.com*

Roberts filed a complaint with World Intellectual Property Organization (WIPO) in March. A Princeton, N.J. resident had registered the site and had tried unsuccessfully to sell it on eBay.

The ruling by WIPO stated that the individual had used the domain name in bad faith.

WIPO said that this dispute was longer than normal and usually takes less than 60 days to render a decision and settlement.

Costs for filing a complaint vary but at about US$3,000, it is far less than launching a lawsuit.

And if we sign the contract, we agree to be held to all its terms, conditions and timetables. The negotiations are over and we're expected to get down to work. If we fail to satisfy the terms and conditions set down, the other party can take us to court and sue us for damages. It's all very linear and logical. Black and white.

In China, a contract is seen as a starting point, not an end point. It is seen more as a testament to the existence of a relationship, than a list of duties to be executed. The working relationship is expected to grow and change—to try and fix it in time makes little sense.

In the West, copying something has a negative connotation. It suggests you lack originality and so stole something from someone else. In China, copying something, or reproducing it, has extremely positive connotations. Many spend years— if not lifetimes—copying the calligraphy of ancient masters. The art of calligraphy is an immensely rich and complicated art as it involves both language and painting. Most believe the subtle movements of the brush strokes convey the inner personal qualities of the painter. To copy these works is to try and approach these qualities yourself.

Many of China's museums hold what appear to be impeccably preserved painted ceramic vases. Many of these vases were found broken or damaged but have been completely restored by museum staff. And often, no notice is posted to tell the museum visitor which vases have been restored. The restored and the intact are seen as having the same value.

In the West, museum staff might assemble a broken vase in order to restore its original shape, but they would never try to conceal its damage. The vase would appear with pieces missing. And any material they might add to the body is always of a different colour and texture than the original

> *Bankruptcy is essentially the way you divide up the pie, when there isn't enough pie to go around.*
> —*Gordon Marantz, 1993.*

vase. We try to preserve things in their 'original' state—as we found them, not as they were. In China, repair is renewal, not disguise.

These subtle cultural notions impact not only issues of law but all manner of exchange between China and the West. The Internet will accelerate collisions of cultural convergence—for both Chinese e-businesses, and businesses in the West. New laws will help. Patience and tolerance go a lot farther—and are a whole lot cheaper.

Now for the good news...

The Internet has grown as fast and as large as it has because it was developed as a free and open system. The more it penetrates our lives and the more commerce it carries the more likely it seems that it will be taxed. After all, why should a bricks and mortar retail store pay tax when a virtual B2C doesn't? Something's gotta give.

www.house.gov/chriscox/nettax

The United States Congress passed the Internet Tax Freedom Act in 1998. The act placed a moratorium on Internet taxes until 2001. Some law makers are beginning to suggest that taxation begin with a flat 5% tax on all Internet retail sales. But how do you collect it, re-distribute it and reinforce it?

How do you enforce a tax code that is geographically-based? The Internet exists in the ether. Where did the transaction take place and who deserves what and where? Does the consumer or end-user determine where the collected tax goes? Of course, that assumes that all or most transactions will take place within the borders of one country. What if most of your clients are overseas? The Internet is changing. No one knows how global it will really become.

What about taxing at the point of sale? Well, what if I bought something from a site that I had accessed through a

Tears and taxes are the price of liberty. The pockets that pay are more blessed than the eyes that weep.

—John "Blackjack" Robinson

link on another site? Say I went to Amazon.com and clicked through eBay's banner ad to make the purchase there? Was Amazon.com the the point of sale, or eBay? And what if Amazon.com receives a commission from eBay for the sale?

And which country is going to start taxing first? The United States? Won't everyone just move offshore? After all, it really doesn't matter where your server is, does it? And won't the United States start losing its competitive edge if it starts taxing the Internet before everyone else?

It seems inevitable that some form of taxation will soon appear on the Internet. What, when and where is anybody's guess. Will it succeed? It'll be fun to watch them try. ➡

go to...

For additional information and updates to charts and graphs, visit: **www.flyingarmchair.com** *the* China s Wired! *resource site.*

12

The Sum of its parts

The Eight Immortals and the Internet

We have come to the point where, in every instruction manual and how-to book, the author summarizes the main themes of the work that has gone before, and draws lessons from it for our edification, enlightenment, and, we hope, profit. Well, this is a book about China, a nation unlike any other, about the Internet, an array of burgeoning intelligence, practical purposes and barely-controlled chaos unlike any other, so we must approach our present task through a medium that seems to suit the context.

We need a device that will help the reader to come to grips with a mass of information within the parameters of the particular civilization that is under study here. The Internet is new, very new; China is old, very old, and the two together make a heady mixture indeed.

As we have seen, there are elements of this new technology that ring much the same in China as elsewhere in the world—the mechanics are the same in Beijing as in Boston. You plug it in, turn it on, and tap into the universe.

However, as we have also seen, there are elements that ring, in China, on a different note. As we saw in Chapter Ten, the

NOTE

The Eight Immortals are:

He Xian Gu, a girl who carries a magic blossom.

Zhong Li Quan, a fat hermit who knows the secrets of longevity; he holds a feather fan with which he can revive the dead.

Li Tie Guai, who carries a smoking gourd and leans on a crutch; the smoke from his gourd frees the spirit from the body.

Cao Guo Jiu, who serves as the patron deity of actors; he is a courtier, and carries a writing tablet.

Lu Dong Bin, who carries a sword to rid the world of evil monsters.

Han Xiang Zi, the patron deity of musicians, who carries a lute, and can cause flowers to come into blossom.

Lan Cai He, who carries a basket of flowers, and contains both male and female characteristics.

Zhang Guo Lao, who rides a white donkey and beats a bamboo tube to announce his arrival. He is an elderly man, who can make himself invisible at will.

He Xian Gu

whole issue of financial credit is much more complex, much more difficult, in the People's Republic than in Pittsburg. In the same way, the attitude of the user, whether an individual flitting through Web pages in pursuit of idle curiosity, or a large corporation, pushing its wares, is different, springs from a different matrix, sounds at a different note. In the West, price is the dominating determinant in every commercial transaction; in China, it is nowhere near the top of the list.

Thinking this through one day back in Toronto, my mind turned to the Eight Immortals of Chinese myth. They make a fascinating crew. It occurred to me that these ancients carry the perfect metaphor, or series of metaphors, to reflect the reality of the Internet in China today.

In this chapter, therefore, we are going to meet the Immortals, use them to help explain, reinforce and consolidate some of the lessons of this book, and finish with a number of points—eight strikes me as a good number—that will help us absorb and use our new knowledge.

The Eight Immortals began life as ordinary human beings. They were granted everlasting life as a reward for honesty and good deeds. Their origins and their many adventures, are common subjects in Chinese painting and literature.

The Immortals are believed to have lived on an island east of China called Penglai Shan. According to myth, the ocean around their island paradise was 'weak' and could not support ships. Only the Immortals had the means to cross the water and visit the mortal world. The story of their voyage across the sea is one of the most popular themes in Chinese opera.

Each Immortal represents a different aspect of society.

Some sources describe each Immortal in very general terms. One represents youth, the others, old age, poverty, wealth, the populace, nobility and the male and female spirits. Other sources are more ambiguous or esoteric. Essentially, the Immortals' identity is shaped to fit the needs of the poet or painter. A poet might use Cao Guo Jiu in a poem about the power of the written word. A painter would have just as much right to portray Cao Guo Jiu as a dancer, or an actor in an elaborate costume.

He Xian Gu is one of only two female Immortals. She is generally portrayed as a young woman carrying a magic lotus blossom. She reminds us of the seemingly magical qualities of the Internet, which are, nonetheless, grounded in something as frail, evanescent and wondrous as a lotus blossom—the ether. The Internet is magical, but it's not magic. The Internet is the product of the human mind. It's about information. The Internet delivers, disseminates and distributes information instantly anywhere and everywhere. That is as true a fact in China as it is anywhere else.

Lessons of a lotus blossom

The Internet is made up of three core elements. First, there is the physical infrastructure to make it possible. Satellites, servers, cables and modems shunting information from one place to the next. The second element is the audience. Who are they? What do they want? How do they respond? How are they similar to other audiences? How are they different? Finally, there's content. What those cables carry and what that audience sees.

The Internet's physical structure—or lack of it—is critical for China's economic development. The Internet allows China to leapfrog over its lack of traditional infrastructures. Business can be conducted in virtual marketplaces or trading centres on a global basis. The Internet becomes the supply chain China does not have and can't afford to build.

Zhong Li Quan

The Internet will not stop growing in China. It's too late, the genie's out of the bottle. There was a period of time in the development of this phenomenon in China when pulling the plug was possible. New technologies, and the pervasiveness of the Internet, make pulling the plug less and less likely. Some say impossible.

Most Chinese Web sites now have 'mirror' sites located outside mainland China. Many are located in California, others in Hong Kong. If Beijing pulled the plug on their China operations, business would continue uninterrupted. These 'mirror' sites are not necessarily set up in anticipation of official censure. They're about efficiency. A site located in California will have all the benefits of a North American served site—most importantly, speed. If you're trying to do business in a global environment you've got to meet global standards. No business will survive very long if it takes five minutes to download its front page.

One of the reasons why it's almost impossible for China to pull the plug on the Internet is because no one knows exactly whose plug they'd be pulling. Everybody and every government agency seems to be involved in some entrepreneurial capacity or another. Government agencies own pieces of Sohu.com, Sina.com and chinadotcom. chinanow.com was financed in part by two government venture funds, Shanghai Industrial and Shanghai New Margin. Whose plug are you pulling and what are the economic and political implications of pulling it?

This means that the Internet must be accommodated. Government, industry and the consumer must respect each other's needs and work within each other's expectations and aspirations. To continue to move forward, all parties must accommodate. This dynamic is changing China's society—as it is changing societies everywhere.

The 'fan' is king

I chose Zhong Li Quan to represent Internet users, because he is considered the chief of the Immortals and holds the secret to longevity. In the same way, the audience is the most important element of the Internet, and the key to its life span. Zhong Li Quan is usually depicted in paintings as a fat man with a big, exposed belly. He carries a feather fan with which he can revive the dead.

As a student, I was taught that three people were responsible for the shape and direction of 20th century visual art. Rodin, for introducing the forces of nature. Gauguin, for introducing the visual style and structure of 'primitive' art. And Mr. X. Mr. X was a lover of art and a collector of ideas. Mr. X was the spoon that stirred the pot.

At the end of the 19th century, Europe was considered the cultural centre of the world. Nothing else and nowhere else really mattered. Paris, Rome, London and Berlin were the incubators of the culture of the times. By and large, these great cities operated in arrogant isolation—each believing themselves slightly more superior than the next.

In 1900, long distance communication between individuals was inefficient, expensive and slow. News from one great city could take weeks to reach another. And when it did, it wasn't always entirely accurate.

Mr. X travelled throughout Europe visiting the studios of the continent's most influential and innovative artists. He told every artist what the others were doing. Sometimes, he even carried paintings from an artist's studio in Rome, to another studio in Lisbon. He showed what others had accomplished, and explained how they achieved what they did.

Mr. X did for 20th century art what the Internet is doing for China and the rest of the world. He connected all the interested parties with all the interesting ideas. Mr. X stimulated innovation and accelerated change. Artistic innovation reached a critical mass. And in 1908, Picasso's cubist masterpiece, *The Women of Avignon*, shattered the prevailing tyranny of Renaissance perspective. The visual world has not been the same since.

China's Internet audience is as hungry for information and ideas as the artists Mr. X visited. The temper of the times is similar and the audience equally astute. Why? Because it's 'message time.' Because the Internet brings to China a dream we in the West take for granted. The possibility of personal riches, and the freedom of self-determination. Be your own boss. Write your own ticket. All you need is an idea. And in the blink of an eye—or the wave of a feather fan—destiny is yours to determine.

Technology's magic smoke

I have chosen Li Tie Guai to represent the technological infrastructure that drives the World Wide Web, the symbol, if you like, of magic smoke. Li Tie Guai often left his body and wandered the land as a spirit. One day, some travellers discovered his spiritless body and assumed that he was dead. Out of respect, the strangers cremated the body. When Li Tie Guai returned from his travels he was forced to find a new body to inhabit. The first body he came upon was that of a lame beggar.

Li Tie Guai is usually depicted as a lame beggar leaning on a crutch carrying a smoking gourd. The smoke from the gourd has the power to free the spirit from the body, just as technology frees knowledge to flit about the globe.

Technology changes the way we live more than the way we think or feel.

In the old days, newspaper journalists were taught to write according to an inverted pyramid. Put all the most important

Li Tie Guai

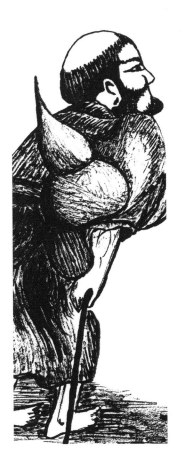

Li Tie Guai

information in the top few paragraphs and trail off toward the bottom. The last few paragraphs had to be expendable without hurting the article's meaning. Why? Newspapers were set in molten lead type. Editing was done by dropping the lead type out from the bottom up to fit the page.

Do writers still follow the model of the inverted pyramid? Yes, but not as strictly and not exactly for the same reasons. You still have to grab the reader's attention and answer all the basic questions before they get bored and wander off. Technology didn't create the form, it grew from it.

There is greater symbiosis between humans and technology than we care to admit. Certainly, the Internet seems greater than us. A superior, over-arching consciousness enveloping the globe. Its capacity seems super-human. But it's a product of the human mind. It's faster and can do a lot of neat tricks, but it's not smarter.

Search engines are coming closer and closer to imbuing the Internet with consciousness. Or transforming it into a thinking space instead of processing space.

Most search engines work by matching words from your request to the same words on another Web site. A content match. But a search engine can only search sites it has indexed. Inktomi, the largest search engine, has only indexed half of the Web. If what you want isn't indexed, it won't find it.

Today, there are approximately twenty-four major search engines operating on the Web. Most of these organize Web sites alphabetically and by content. Nevertheless, if they don't have what you're looking for in their indexes they won't find it.

Some search engines are better than others. The more detail entered into the index, the better the search and the

www.maplesquare.com

www.canada.com

www.toile.qc.ca

finer the results. Yahoo.com and Business.com employ editors and librarians to classify and catalogue Web sites for their search engines.

If you want your Web site listed on some search engines you must submit a detailed description of your site. Some search engines charge a fee for this.

All these search engines depend on deductive reasoning. They're how we think—sort of. Unfortunately, they're not particularly efficient. They don't discern meaning from content. What means one thing for one person or group of people doesn't necessarily mean the same thing for another. A theatrical 'bomb' in London is a huge hit, a 'bomb' in New York is a disaster. They're also inefficient because someone can always find a way to sabotage the process for selfish reasons.

If a search engine is following a specific word, it will put the site with the most mentions of that word at the top of the list. Some sites gain unfair advantage by filling the background of every page with that leading word. The word isn't visible to the viewer because it's printed in the same colour as the background.

Google is a new kind of search engine. Google isn't as interested in what's on the page as much as by what's attached to it. The more hyper-links linking a Web page to others, the more value ascribed to the site. The hyperlinks define a community as one site attaches to others out of shared interests and perceived benefits. Here, membership in a community is given a value. The more links you have attached to your site, the more valuable you are.

Google isn't infallible. It assumes that links exist for a purpose. Linking your site to many others for no other purpose than having a lot of links would distort its results

www.khoj.com

www.jadoo.com

www.surfindia.com

www.japan.infoseek.com

www.submit.ne.jp

SIGN OF THE TIMES

You could be a winner! no purchase necessary. Details inside.

Notice on snack food packet.

and elevate your rating.

Today, there are more than a billion pages on the World Wide Web linked together by some seven billion hyperlinks. Every day a million new pages are added to the Web. The bigger the Web becomes, the more important it will be to have a search engine or engines that can sift through this vast sea of information.

Every new engine adds depth and breadth to the search for information. New developments make it a finer tool. How? By thinking as we think and analyzing as we analyze. The closer they come to replicating our thought the more helpful—and powerful—they become.

What does all this mean for China? English is still the dominant language of the Web. Search engines are built around the English language and the Roman alphabet. Language is culture. The English language cannot serve China's needs—if anything, it may hinder them. The Chinese language is pictographic and allusive. Does this make it easier to design a search engine or more difficult?

China's consumers take to new technologies faster than consumers anywhere else. They insist on it. Wireless technologies like WAP and Blue Tooth will make the Internet more accessible, cheaper and easier to use. But the most important technological innovation—or infrastructure shift—will occur when China begins to develop powerful Chinese language search engines. This will be the great liberation—and a much more profound stimulus for growth—than any wireless technology.

Cao Guo Jiu is a courtier who carries a writing tablet. He is recognized as the patron deity of actors, but I have chosen him to represent Content on the Internet, because his writing tablet signifies the key importance of words,

www.Kor-seek.com

www.wakano.com

www.cari.com

substance, content, call it what you will, in this process.

The Chinese are deeply concerned about content on the Internet. They do not want to see the Internet become a medium for protest or dissent. This sensitivity is not likely to change. The definition of content will—however—remain fluid.

Golf is extremely popular in China. Arnold Palmer and Jumbo Ozaki have designed new golf courses in the P.R.C. But it's very difficult to get a license to build a golf course in China. Nevertheless, there are new golf courses everywhere. How did they get around the licensing issue? They're called 'green' courses. You don't need a license to build a green course in China. Change the name, and change the content; thus barriers are broken.

Presently, there are restrictions against Web sites generating original content. China wants them to carry only officially-sanctioned information and news. Nevertheless, many Web sites carry original writing generated by in-house writers and editors. How do they get around the restrictions? The profile of a businessman is 'human interest,' not news. An article about a restaurant or an exhibition of paintings is 'entertainment,' not news.

In the early days, many Web sites held 'raw' information. They were directories—a yellow pages of listings. But why should I come to your site for something I can get somewhere else? Slowly, content began to be perceived as important. Slower still has emerged the unique nature of Web content.

The Internet is a mass medium. But it is a mass medium like no other. Television broadcasts. Its audience can turn it on or turn it off, but plays no role in the shape, direction or nature of the broadcast. Television viewers are passive. The

Cao Guo Jiu

www.chinapages.com

Internet speaks to millions but treats each one as an individual. The Internet doesn't broadcast, it offers. It holds something out—an invitation to participate.

Content needs to be created. Content is always created in the dark—you don't know if you've got it right until an audience has seen it. ("I don't know what I'm thinking until I hear myself say it.") Content for the Internet is different than content for any other mass medium. Internet audiences are interactive, not passive. The audience may be tens of millions, but the response is individual and unique.

How does that change content? It must be specific to my needs and rich enough to answer my whims. Yaolan aims to fill its data bases with every conceivable answer any visitor might ask. They'll keep their audience only as long as they keep providing information that's relevant. Answer the questions with better answers than expected. The Internet expects more content from its content.

Lu Dong Bin carries a magical sword with which he slays dragons and evil monsters, so I chose him to represent the law as it applies to the Internet.

The long sword of the law

www.goyoyo.com

Law reflects the values of the society. As a society changes, new laws are required. China—like all nations—is in the process of writing its laws for the Internet. But the Internet is only one aspect of China's new society. The economic reforms of 1978 have led to a gradual but inevitable reassessment of such notions as private property and pride of ownership. These notions will also reshape China's laws. Nothing happens in a vacuum. Shifting one law, casts a new light on another.

When I was in Shanghai doing research for this book I found the house where my mother was born in 1926. My grandparents lived in the house until they left China just before the Second World War.

I've carried a photograph of my mother's house in my wallet for a number of years. From the outside, very little seems to have changed. The residents of the house noticed me taking pictures and invited me in. Today, four families live in the house. In 1930, there was only my mother, my aunt and my grandparents—and a staff of six.

The home has been divided up to accommodate the four families. Each family has a legal right to inhabit their particular space. If I wanted to purchase or reclaim the house, or the government wanted to demolish it to make room for a highway, each family would have to be relocated in comparable accommodation. Today, that would mean I'd have to buy four condominiums for the four families—and four condominiums they would approve of. Then, and only then, could I move them out together.

I was introduced to each family and shown from one living space to the next and from one floor to the other. I couldn't tell where one family's private space began or another's ended. The house hadn't been renovated into four separate living quarters. It seemed to me as if they'd all just moved in.

Each family's private space was clean and ordered. But the shared or communal spaces—the stairs or hallways—were in bad condition. They were also piled high with boxes of household goods. It didn't look as if anything had been done to repair or improve the house since my grandparents' time.

Did the sad state of repair mean these people were lazy? Did it mean they were dirty or slovenly or didn't value private property? If that were true, their personal spaces would also reflect such an attitude, and they didn't. There

Lu Dong Bin

www.chinaburst.com

www.yahoo.com.cn

was much pride of ownership of the places they knew to be their own.

Why care about something that is not yours? What is the value in spending time, effort and money on something that belongs to the State? Surely, that is the responsibility of the State?

Concepts of private property and personal responsibility are undergoing slow but dramatic changes in China today. One day, these people will be offered accommodation in new high-rise condominiums. They—like millions of Chinese—will become home 'owners.' They will not only have the right to inhabit these dwellings, they will 'own' them. Ownership becomes a right. Ownership comes with privileges and responsibilities. Ownership takes on a new and higher value in society. Laws will change to reflect that fact.

'You don't need them to say yes, you just don't want them to say no' is a short-term strategy for survival in a country where laws are in flux. But it's dancing between the rain drops. No matter how fast you dance, you're going to get wet. The proper course is patience. The laws are changing. They're being shaped from the outside by ideas like intellectual property. And moved from the inside by such fundamental notions as private property and individual responsibility.

I have chosen Han Xiang Zi to remind us that business in China is not at all like in the West, whether it is a matter of cutting a deal on the Internet or starting up a new manufacturing concern. The music of management is in a different key, as is the music of bargaining. That is why I am drawn to Han Xiang Zi; because this Immortal carries a magic flute, which can make flowers bloom. Or contracts.

The magic flute

Many Western businessmen and women are very skeptical about doing business in China. Some, because they have lost money in China, some because they have heard too many horror stories. Is their decision based on concern over rule of law, politics, or the business environment that exists in China today? Will the WTO make a difference?

One of the best stories I've heard about business in China concerned the exploits of a hot-shot senior executive of a large multinational sent to China to "Clean up the mess and get the deal done!" The company had been involved in long and arduous negotiations with a local supplier. Talks had been going on for eight months without significant progress. The parent company had lost confidence in the ability of their local expat manager to conclude the deal.

So the big boys back home sent in Mr. Hot-shot. The first thing he did when he arrived was to set an ultimatum. He told the local supplier he only had a limited amount of time in which to conclude contract negotiations. He had two weeks now in which he planned to get the lay of the land and come to know and understand the supplier's reservations. He would then take these findings back to the executives at the parent company. After due consideration he would return and present the company's final offer. If they couldn't sign the deal before he was scheduled to return they'd have no deal. Those were his terms. Take them or leave them, but that's where he stood.

The Chinese supplier seemed almost chastened by this new tactic. They agreed to do their best to reach a mutually beneficial conclusion. Negotiations seemed to go well in the first week. Tensions rose in the second week. Before he got on the plane to go home Mr. Hot-shot told the local expat that he thought they'd be able to do business with these people after all. He could see it

www.webcrawler.com

Han Xiang Zi

turning in their favour.

Mr. Hot-shot returned a few weeks later. He brought with him additional concessions from the executives back home. Nevertheless, negotiations dragged on. Mr. Hot-shot reminded the local supplier that they had to sign this contract before he left or the deal was off. The local supplier nodded gravely and agreed to try harder.

Finally, on the day before Mr. Hot-shot's departure, all parties came to agreement. They broke out the champagne. Everyone was happy and relieved. The local supplier told Mr. Hotshot that they'd never dealt with such a tough negotiator. All praised him. He was a hero. He invited everyone out to a celebratory feast.

That night, before going to bed, Mr. Hot-shot called the parent company overseas to tell them the good news. They had a deal. He'd be signing the contract in the morning. His boss praised him, his colleagues envied him. He slept well.

The next morning, he checked out of the hotel. His plane was leaving in the early afternoon. He'd take his bags with him to the signing. He knew something was wrong the minute he walked in the room where this was to take place. They were all too quiet. The expat manager explained that the local supplier had a new list of demands. They wouldn't sign the contract without them. Mr. Hot-shot was dumfounded. He'd been out-manoeuvered.

Mr. Hot-shot had two choices. Lose face here, or lose face back home. He'd already told his boss it was a done deal. He didn't tell him what the deal was—only that he had one. He studied the list of demands. He signed the contract.

Will business between the West and China get easier after China's accession to the WTO? No. But business might be more about business, and less about politics.

You know I was never very good with money, I never really understood it; till I went to France...The French print their money on a very fine paper; it's brittle, almost transparent. When you hold it, when you count it out, it's not like money, it's like dry leaves. So you're careful with it because you think if I'm not, if I don't handle it carefully, with respect, it will crumble to dust...The fragility reminded me, each time I handled it, that money was something real; it was a part of the person who had given it to me: the part they had sacrificed to earn it...

—*Precipice, Act Two*

The lovely, frail flower of cultural convergence

Lan Cai He is the other female Immortal. She embodies both male and female characteristics and carries a basket of flowers. He/she is surely the apt symbol of the cultural convergence that is both promised and threatened by the advent, or onslaught, of the new technology on an ancient and honoured civilization. The fact that Lan Cai He is usually depicted carrying flowers strikes me as particularly apt, since these represent both optimism and frailty, two characteristics that have been associated with the Internet from Day One. Generally, cultural convergence leads to confusion or misunderstanding. Studying history and culture helps us to understand the point of view of others. It helps us understand one another, but it doesn't always help us to bridge the gulf between us.

Eric Rosenblum is the COO of ChinaNow.com. It's his job to make everything work well together and in the same direction. The other two founders of ChinaNow are writers, publishers and restaurateurs. They're idea men. They think it up and then find someone like Eric to make it happen.

Eric speaks Chinese fluently and has a degree from Harvard. He told me he'd like to return some day to complete a PhD. He's also a careful observer of human nature. We talked a lot about issues of cultural convergence. When I met with Eric in Shanghai in February, ChinaNow had a staff of about 40. Eric had hired most of them, or at least played a major role in their hiring.

What were the strengths and weaknesses of the young people he hired? Most were college graduates in their early twenties. (No Madam Xs here.) He referred to his young employees affectionately as Web monkeys. They love the Internet. It's all they care about and the only place they want to be. Surfing from link to link like monkeys swinging from tree to tree.

Lan Cai He

Eric said that his staff is phenomenally dedicated and as sophisticated about the Internet as anyone anywhere. And they love to work. The problems arise when they're asked to flesh out an idea Eric has given them. Sometimes, Eric makes a rough sketch of how he wants a page to appear. He leaves the sketch with the designer as a reference. When he returns he finds that the designer has made the page look exactly like the sketch. He's copied it instead of using it as a point of departure.

Eric certainly wasn't the first to bring up this problem. And it isn't exclusive to the Internet. A friend of mine used to run a factory in Shanghai. He told me you couldn't just hand somebody a mop and tell them it was their responsibility to make sure the washroom was kept clean. He would have no point of reference. What does clean mean? Do I clean it every time someone uses it? Every hour? Or only when it starts to smell?

He told me that once he'd explained the parameters and walked them through it a few times, they'd get it. And they'd do a great job. Of course, cleaning a washroom is not about taking an imaginative leap. At least not in the way Eric was asking his employees to grow something from a sketch or an idea.

What is this imaginative reticence about? Is it fear that holds them back? Fear of failure, or fear of showing up the boss? Surely, it's not that they're incapable of imaginative thought. Will the Internet open their minds to possibility? Will it give them the confidence to make the imaginative leap? If it does, there's no telling what kind of amazing and beautiful world they might create. It's certainly one of the Internet's greatest challenges.

Zuang Guo Lao is an elderly man riding a donkey. He beats

a bamboo drum to announce his arrival. He has the power of invisibility.

The elements that define a community are invisible, and that is why, to represent this key element, I have turned to Zuang Guo Lao, the Immortal who is usually depicted as someone who has the ability to make himself invisible at will. (He is also shown as an elderly man riding a donkey and beating on a drum, but I don't think we'll follow the metaphor that far; it can only lead to trouble.) The invisible links that hold the community together begin with shared interests and mutual benefit. The strength of a community is proportional to the depth of its meaning to its members.

Community gives the Internet meaning and purpose. It is its greatest strength and holds its greatest potential. Internet communities are only restricted by the limits of the imagination.

James Joyce wrote that the measure of a work of art is from how deep a life it springs. I used to believe this. I used to think great art had to come from deep souls. As time went by, I met a few artists who'd made great art—or had come pretty close. They seemed to me to have pretty shallow souls. I also met some people with quite profound souls. Some were ordinary people, some artists. But none of them made art that was much good. So, I began to rethink Mr. Joyce's notion.

It seems to me that it has less to do with depth of soul and more to do with reach. If my soul isn't deep enough I'll lean over and reach into yours.

The Internet allows us into other people's lives in a way unlike anything ever before. It allows us into someone else's space—wherever that happens to be. China, South America, Australia—we are everywhere simultaneously.

Zhang Guo Lao

This offers rich experience—in the same way reach allows shallow people to make great art.

The Internet is an expanding universe—with all that that implies. As time and space become less relevant, personal identity becomes more important. Who am I? What do I want? Where do we go from here? Old questions for a new universe. New concepts for the wired world. ➡

EIGHT IMMORTAL LESSONS FROM THE INTERNET IN CHINA.

1. The Internet is magical, but it's not magic. The Internet is the product of the human mind. It's about information. The Internet delivers, disseminates and distributes information instantly anywhere and everywhere. That is as true a fact in China as it is anywhere else.

2. The audience is the single most important element of the Internet.

3. Technology changes the way we live more than the way we think or feel.

4. Content for the Internet is different than content for any other medium. Internet audiences are interactive, not passive. The audience may be tens of millions, but the response is individual and unique.

5. Law reflects the values of the society. China—like all nations—is in the process of writing its laws for the Internet. The economic reforms of 1978 have led to a gradual but inevitable reassessment of such notions as private property and pride of ownership. These notions will also reshape China's laws. Nothing happens in a vacuum. Shifting one law, casts a new light on another.

6. Business in China is not at all like business in the West. The music of management is in a different key, as is the music of bargaining.

7. The Internet heightens issues of cultural convergence. Generally, cultural convergence leads to confusion and misunderstanding. Studying history and culture helps us to understand the point of view of others. It helps us understand one another, but doesn't always help us bridge the gulf between us.

8. The strength of a community is proportional to the depth of its meaning to its members. Community gives the Internet meaning and purpose. It is its greatest strength and holds its greatest potential. Internet communities are only restricted by the limits of the imagination.

Your Notes

go to...

For additional information and updates to charts and graphs,
visit: **www.flyingarmchair.com**
the China s Wired! *resource site.*

Appendix

WEB SITES MENTIONED IN THIS BOOK— BY CHAPTER

Chapter One 1

www.china.com
www.cnnic.net
www.deadradio.com
www.hotmail.com
www.pbs.org/internet/
www.pcg-group.com
www.sina.com
www.tom.com
www.w3.org
www.yahoo.com

Chapter Two 2

www.china.org.cn
www.china-embassy.org
www.chinainvestguide.com
www.chinatradeworld.com
www.focus.com.cn
www.giftme.com
www.gov.cn
www.info.gov.hk
www.net.cn
www.peninsula.com
www.shac.gov.cn
www.shu.edu.cn
www.smprc.gov.cn
www.surfchina.com
www.tdc.org.hk
www.ubuytimeshare.com
www.xinhua.org
www.zjcninfo.net

Chapter Three 3

www.21cn.com
www.bupto.com
www.cei.gov.cn
www.cernet.edu.cn
www.chinatelecom.cninfo.net
www.cnc.ac.cn
www.confucius.com
www.expertcity.com
www.gd.com.cn
www.gdcb.gd.cn
www.gztelecom.com.cn
www.ihep.ac.cn
www.net.edu.cn
www.planet-payment.com
www.rdc.com.au

Chapter Four 4

www.altavista.com
www.chinanewsletter.com
www.chinaunicom.com
www.ckh.com.hk
www.cki.com.hk
www.cmgi.com
www.cwhkt.com
www.dictionary.com
www.east.net.cn
www.forbes.com
www.hkt.com
www.intel.com
www.legend.com
www.lewiscarroll.org
www.newscorp.com
www.sh.com
www.softbank.com
www.sztdb.gov.cn

www.timewarner.com
www.zgc.gov.cn
www.zhaopin.com

Chapter Five 5

www.163.com
www.cgc21.com
www.chinadaily.com.cn
www.corp.china.com
www.cwrank.com
www.cww.com
www.feer.com
www.hkgem.com
www.hongkong.com
www.idgchina.com
www.nasdaq.com
www.netease.com
www.portal.com
www.sohu.com
www.taiwan.com
www.wavdev.com
www.wharton.upenn.edu
www.yaolan.com
www.zhaodaola.com

Chapter Six 6

www.alibaba.com
www.ariba.com
www.bartoninc.com
www.chinae.com
www.chinasources.com
www.chinatradeworld.com
www.china-window.com
www.commerceone.com
www.dell.com

www.handheld.com
www.kelon.com
www.kfc.com
www.meetchina.com
www.sh.com/dish
www.shanghai.chinats.com
www.thecocacolacompany.com
www.tradex.com

Chapter Seven 7

www.8848.com
www.8848.net.cn
www.aba.com
www.amazon.com
www.babybag.com
www.babycare-direct.co.uk
www.babycenter.com
www.babyhood.com
www.babyplace.com
www.babysoon.com
www.babytrader.com
www.babyzone.com
www.barnesandnoble.com
www.beijing.gov.cn
www.bjbb.com
www.cgibinerols.com
www.dangdang.com
www.etoy.com
www.hbs.edu
www.ups.com
www.yoalan.com

Chapter Eight 8

cyber.law.harvard.edu
www.asia4sale.com

www.auctionauction.com
www.auctionguide.com
www.chinalabs.com
www.chinaren.com
www.christies.com
www.crystalventure.com
www.csfisc.com
www.diglark.com
www.eachnet.com
www.ebay.com
www.franklloydwright.com
www.goodwill.org
www.hot100.com.cn
www.idominc.com
www.ksg.harvard.edu
www.netalone.com
www.netcel360.com
www.outblaze.com
www.pacfusion.com
www.paulallen.com
www.pez.com
www.sothebys.com
www.tenderbuttons.com
www.tsinghua.edu.cn

Chapter Nine 9

www.121.com
www.abookloversshoppe.com
www.aisamix.com
www.arizona.edu
www.bcg.com
www.chimeb.edu.cn.org
www.chinabooks.com
www.chinanow.com
www.citysearch.com
www.cnmall.com
www.community.com

www.creativity.com
www.eduasian.com
www.excite.com/travel
www.fudan.edu.cn
www.iadvantage.net
www.igigroup.com
www.insurancestreet.com
www.matrix.com
www.mit.edu
www.netcafeguide.com
www.netcomsystems.com
www.nju.edu.cn
www.propertystreet.com
www.red-dots.com
www.shkp.com.hk
www.sparkice.com
www.sunevision.com
www.superhome.net
www.ucla.com
www.yuppy.com

Chapter Ten 10

www.bank-of-china.com
www.bankrate.com
www.ccbhk.com
www.cmbchina.com
www.csfb.com
www.discovervancouver.com
www.dsl-intl.com
www.hangseng.com
www.hastingspark.com
www.hi2000.net
www.hkbea.com
www.mckinsey.com
www.moftec.gov.cn
www.safe.gov.cn
www.shu.edu.cn

www.sinofile.com/insurance
www.site-by-site.com
www.standardchartered.com
www.statcan.ca
www.stats.gov.cn
www.wto.org

Chapter Eleven 11

www.new.usps.com
www.bakerbotts.com
www.bartleby.com
www.beijing-jeep.com
www.canadapost.com
www.chinapost.com.cn
www.cipo.gc.cn
www.cntrademark.com
www.cpo.cn.net
www.ebay.com
www.garage.com
www.gis.net/chinalaw
www.heenanblaikie.com
www.house.gov/chriscox/nettax
www.jumpstart.com
www.oed.com
www.thenrggroup.com
www.tie.org
www.ussteel.com
www.vcclawservices.com
www.vfinance.com

Chapter Twelve 12

www.canada.com
www.cari.com
www.chinaburst.com
www.chinascape.org
www.goyoyo.com
www.hotbot.com
www.jadoo.com
www.japan.infoseek.com
www.khoj.com
www.kor-seek.com
www.lycos.com
www.malaysia.com
www.maplesquare.com
www.nihao.com
www.submit.ne.jp
www.surfindia.com
www.toile.qc.ca
www.wakano.com
www.webcrawler.com
www.yahoo.com.cn

WEB SITES MENTIONED IN THIS BOOK—
ALPHABETICALLY

cyber.law.harvard.edu
www.121.com
www.163.com
www.21cn.com
www.8848.com
www.8848.net.cn

A
www.aba.com
www.abookloversshoppe.com
www.aisamix.com
www.alibaba.com
www.altavista.com
www.amazon.com
www.ariba.com
www.arizona.edu
www.asia4sale.com
www.auctionauction.com
www.auctionguide.com

B
www.babybag.com
www.babycare-direct.co.uk
www.babycenter.com
www.babyhood.com
www.babyplace.com
www.babysoon.com
www.babytrader.com
www.babyzone.com
www.bakerbotts.com
www.bank-of-china.com
www.bankrate.com
www.barnesandnoble.com
www.bartleby.com
www.bartoninc.com
www.bcg.com
www.beijing.gov.cn
www.beijing-jeep.com

www.bjbb.com
www.bupto.com

C
www.canada.com
www.canadapost.com
www.cari.com
www.ccbhk.com
www.cei.gov.cn
www.cernet.edu.cn
www.cgc21.com
www.cgibinerols.com
www.chimeb.edu.cn.org
www.china.com
www.china.org.cn
www.chinabooks.com
www.chinaburst.com
www.chinadaily.com.cn
www.chinae.com
www.china-embassy.org
www.chinainvestguide.com
www.chinalabs.com
www.chinanewsletter.com
www.chinanow.com
www.chinapost.com.cn
www.chinaren.com
www.chinascape.org
www.chinasources.com
www.chinatelecom.cninfo.net
www.chinatradeworld.com
www.chinatradeworld.com
www.chinaunicom.com
www.china-window.com
www.christies.com
www.cipo.gc.cn
www.citysearch.com
www.ckh.com.hk
www.cki.com.hk
www.cmbchina.com

www.cmgi.com
www.cnc.ac.cn
www.cnmall.com
www.cnnic.net
www.cntrademark.com
www.commerceone.com
www.community.com
www.confucius.com
www.corp.china.com
www.cpo.cn.net
www.creativity.com
www.crystalventure.com
www.csfb.com
www.csfisc.com
www.cwhkt.com
www.cwrank.com
www.cww.com

D
www.dangdang.com
www.deadradio.com
www.dell.com
www.dictionary.com
www.diglark.com
www.discovervancouver.com
www.dsl-intl.com

E
www.eachnet.com
www.east.net.cn
www.ebay.com
www.ebay.com
www.eduasian.com
www.etoy.com
www.excite.com/travel
www.expertcity.com

F
www.feer.com
www.focus.com.cn
www.forbes.com
www.franklloydwright.com
www.fudan.edu.cn

G
www.garage.com
www.gd.com.cn
www.gdcb.gd.cn
www.giftme.com
www.gis.net/chinalaw
www.goodwill.org
www.gov.cn
www.goyoyo.com
www.gztelecom.com.cn

H
www.handheld.com
www.hangseng.com
www.hastingspark.com
www.hbs.edu
www.heenanblaikie.com
www.hi2000.net
www.hkbea.com
www.hkgem.com
www.hkt.com
www.hongkong.com
www.hot100.com.cn
www.hotbot.com
www.hotmail.com
www.house.gov/chriscox/nettax

I
www.iadvantage.net
www.idgchina.com

www.idominc.com
www.igigroup.com
www.ihep.ac.cn
www.info.gov.hk
www.insurancestreet.com
www.intel.com

J
www.jadoo.com
www.japan.infoseek.com
www.jumpstart.com

K
www.kelon.com
www.kfc.com
www.khoj.com
www.kor-seek.com
www.ksg.harvard.edu

L
www.legend.com
www.lewiscarroll.org
www.lycos.com

M
www.malaysia.com
www.maplesquare.com
www.matrix.com
www.mckinsey.com
www.mckinsey.com
www.meetchina.com
www.mit.edu
www.moftec.gov.cn

N
www.nasdaq.com
www.net.cn
www.net.edu.cn
www.netalone.com
www.netcafeguide.com
www.netcel360.com
www.netcomsystems.com
www.netease.com
www.newscorp.com
www.newusps.com
www.nihao.com
www.nju.edu.cn

O
www.oed.com
www.outblaze.com

P
www.pacfusion.com
www.paulallen.com
www.pbs.org/internet/
www.pcg-group.com
www.peninsula.com
www.pez.com
www.planet-payment.com
www.portal.com
www.propertystreet.com

R
www.rdc.com.au
www.red-dots.com

S
www.safe.gov.cn
www.sh.com

www.sh.com/dish
www.shac.gov.cn
www.shanghai.chinats.com
www.shkp.com.hk
www.shu.edu.cn
www.shu.edu.cn
www.sina.com
www.sinofile.com/insurance
www.site-by-site.com
www.smprc.gov.cn
www.softbank.com
www.sohu.com
www.sothebys.com
www.sparkice.com
www.standardchartered.com
www.statcan.ca
www.stats.gov.cn
www.submit.ne.jp
www.sunevision.com
www.superhome.net
www.surfchina.com
www.surfindia.com
www.sztdb.gov.cn

T
www.taiwan.com
www.tdc.org.hk
www.tenderbuttons.com
www.thecocacolacompany.com
www.thenrggroup.com
www.tie.org
www.timewarner.com
www.toile.qc.ca
www.tom.com
www.tradex.com
www.tsinghua.edu.cn

U
www.ubuytimeshare.com
www.ucla.com
www.ups.com
www.ussteel.com

V
www.vcclawservices.com
www.vfinance.com

W
www.w3.org
www.wakano.com
www.wavdev.com
www.webcrawler.com
www.wharton.upenn.edu
www.wto.org

X
www.xinhua.org

Y
www.yahoo.com
www.yaolan.com
www.yuppy.com
www.yahoo.com.cn

Z
www.zgc.gov.cn
www.zhaodaola.com
www.zhaopin.com
www.zjcninfo.net

INDEX

N.B. Entries are located by chapter and page; thus, 1.15 indicates Chapter One, page 15.